Locating Agency

Locating Agency:
Space, Power and Popular Politics

Edited by

Fiona Williamson

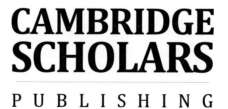

Locating Agency: Space, Power and Popular Politics,
Edited by Fiona Williamson

This book first published 2010

Cambridge Scholars Publishing

12 Back Chapman Street, Newcastle upon Tyne, NE6 2XX, UK

British Library Cataloguing in Publication Data
A catalogue record for this book is available from the British Library

Copyright © 2010 by Fiona Williamson and contributors

All rights for this book reserved. No part of this book may be reproduced, stored in a retrieval system, or transmitted, in any form or by any means, electronic, mechanical, photocopying, recording or otherwise, without the prior permission of the copyright owner.

ISBN (10): 1-4438-1448-2, ISBN (13): 978-1-4438-1448-5

TABLE OF CONTENTS

Acknowledgements vii

Introduction
Space, Popular Politics and Agency
Fiona Williamson 1

Space, Agency and Genre: Revenge Tragedy in *The Spanish Tragedy* (1587?)
George Oppitz-Trotman 19

Alehouses, Popular Politics and Plebeian Agency in Early Modern England
Mark Hailwood 51

"A fured mutton woulde contayne as much good doctrine":
Social Politics in the Seventeenth-Century Parish
Fiona Williamson 77

Neighbours and Strangers: The Locality in Later Stuart Economic Culture
Brodie Waddell 103

Custom, Memory and the Operations of Power in Seventeenth-Century Forest of Dean
Simon Sandall 133

The Pedlar of Swaffham, the Fenland Giant and the Sardinian Communist: Usable Pasts and the Politics of Folklore in England, c.1600-1830
Andy Wood. 161

Death and the Jarvises: Public Space, Private Space and the Politics of Resistance in Nineteenth-Century Norfolk (and beyond).
Rob Lee 193

Contributors 215

Index 217

Acknowledgements

I wish to thank all those who participated in the March 2008 conference at the UEA, not all of whom have been able to publish within this collection, but whose work helped make the day a success. I would also like to mention all those who helped comment on sections of this book, in particular Janka Rodziewicz, Chris Bonfield, Simon Sandall and Pearl Crossfield. I should also mention George Oppitz-Trotman, who helped refine the final title.

INTRODUCTION

SPACE, POPULAR POLITICS AND AGENCY

FIONA WILLIAMSON

In the latter half of the twentieth century, "politics" has come to mean more than simply the formal institutions and apparatus of government, run by small minority of wealthy, educated elite men. The word has been adopted by historians of different genres as synonymous with power, or agency, and the scope for "political" activity has been widened to incorporate a variety of everyday events and ordinary people. Keith Wrightson, Steve Hindle, Michael Braddick, John Walter and Mark Goldie amongst others, have all produced innovative interpretations of social politics and plebeian agency during the last three decades since Patrick Collinson's call to "put the politics back into social history".[1] Adopting a micro-historical and "bottom up" perspective, they have demonstrated how non-elite society functioned in practice, highlighting the important role of the middling-sorts in local power relations, and pointing to instances when even people of relatively low status could became minor office-holders in religious or secular positions, thus gaining a stake in the wider national polity.

Historians have challenged the way the past has traditionally been "read" in concert with interdisciplinary theory, emphasising the role played by ordinary people. James C. Scott's pioneering work on peasant communities, for example, presents strong evidence for the benefits of interdisciplinary research in exploring ideas of plebeian agency.[2] Scott argued that outright resistance to authority, such as rebellions, were exceptions to the rule which tell us little about the real workings of power in any given society.[3] Instead, he argues, we should consider the small and apparently insignificant everyday acts such as foot dragging, feigned compliance or slander, as they cumulatively acted to limit arbitrary authority in the long-term. As a result of similar research, early-modern power relationships are now considered far more complex than the traditional unidirectional flow implied by simple 'top-down' models.

Governing elites were restricted in their use of power by both common law and parliamentary restrictions on the legitimate use of their authority. Their rule was, to a point, grounded in the notion of conciliation rather than outright oppression. Explorations of this practice have led to a more nuanced and dynamic understanding of agency based on a two-way process of negotiation and reciprocity between the social ranks. Such insights offer a new way of interpreting relations of power in society, effectively suggesting that public deference did not equate to acceptance of the established order.[4] Andy Wood, for example, has drawn from this premise, proposing that outward behavioural forms of deference were often ritualized and habitual, functioning within a tradition of behavioural expectations rather than real sentiments and are, therefore, inadequate for measuring the extent to which the ruling order was accepted.[5]

This collection represents the proceedings of a conference held on these themes in March 2008 at the University of East Anglia. The symposium brought together social historians with a shared interest in recent socio-political historical perspectives and an understanding of the importance of using inter-disciplinary methodologies to explore the past. These collected essays thus explore the quotidian experience of social politics, religion, and popular culture, looking beyond conventional definitions of politics, to "re-conceptualise" the application of the term. The contributors consider, for example; the politics of the alehouse, the politics of Methodism, the interrelationship between plebeian agency, custom and memory, the politics of economics, dramatic agency and the politics of the spiritual parish. Collectively they suggest that political activity was embedded in almost every aspect of life, and that our understanding of individual agency should include a broad spectrum of social actors and interactions.

The collection as a whole expands current research on plebeian agency, and either directly or indirectly, questions Scott's conceptualisation of power which appears to set ruler and ruled in opposition, ignoring the true complexity of society.[6] It explores how far people of modest means and without a formal office could, to any degree, effect change or challenge authority within their own spheres of contact; in short, their capacity for the exercise of "agency". The notion of "agency", in this context, describes the ability (or inability) of a person or a group to influence the conditions in which they live or work, building on the premise that a large proportion of the population were active agents in the determination of local, political affairs. This is not to suggest, however, that all members of a community enjoyed the same capacity in this respect or that the exercise of such "agency" was always intentional. Instead, these essays propose that the reach of both elite and plebeian agency was often circumstantial, limited by individual events and personalities. Broadly speaking, the lower an individual or group's social status, the more limited were their opportunities to effect change. Without holding a formal office, the tools available to negotiate the terms of authority were often ineffective, or worse, may have resulted in punishment and greater social marginalisation. Indeed, the possibility of collective or individual agency for ordinary people was often only expressed through the ability to improve one aspect of their immediate situation, rather than overtly challenging the social order as a whole. For the very poor, verbal criticism of policy or physical violence against property or persons were part of a limited repertoire of resistance, but these methods were as likely to invoke harsh reprimand as they were to improve conditions in the short-term. Indeed, in the absence of a police force, or standing army, order, more often than not, relied on a populace who actively "bought into" consensus.

Although some discretion must be exercised before applying potentially incongruent or anachronistic modern anthropological or sociological theories to early modern English society, there remains, nonetheless, much value in considering different conceptual approaches. Whilst we should not look to appropriate totalising theoretical frameworks, such work, adopted selectively, can provide fresh insight. This collection, therefore, focuses not only on a broader definition of agency, but also on the "spatial turn", a term which requires further explanation.

Pierre Bourdieu, Michel De Certeau and Henri Lefebvre have all provided inspiration for social historians to consider the role of "space" as the setting for all social interactions and events. This "space" could be as simple as a room in a house, a building, a street, or an alehouse. Rather than seeing space as a "passive" backdrop, however, such theorists have conceptualised space as an active component in the shaping of individual and communal identities; a "medium through which society ... can be created and reproduced".[7] Spatial theory thus explores the significance of the environment and the connection between landscape and the people who lived within it. Buildings and landscapes developed in line with practical requirements, but also specific cultural traditions and values, the most obvious examples being segregation, or the sub-division of houses for greater privacy. Thus we can understand much about a society through its use of space. Writing extensively on the production of space as *habitus*, Bourdieu suggested that each space contains its own unique echo of the past, a "spatial identity". Conceived as such, spatial identities are traceable, not only in the style, layout and use of buildings and land, but also in how people subsequently understood that space or created new spaces around them.

The specific social, cultural or political identities spaces reflected were sometimes uniquely localised, but more often than not were constructed in terms anyone could have understood.[8] Most medieval and early modern urban dwellers, for example, would have recognised the powerful symbolism of a city's walls. They exuded civic wealth and importance, but also amplified local identity. The walls represented the embodiment of strategies of inclusion and belonging within any given community; a corporeal border beyond which people would be judged "outsiders".[9] Spatial meanings, however, were also conveyed in less tangible ways. Notorious streets or alehouses might only be known to locals by reputation, for example. These leave little trace in surviving documentation, but might occasionally be preserved in a street name, recorded in diaries or travel literature, or mentioned in a court case.

A more subjective reading of spatial identities is also possible. If, as is suggested by Bourdieu, spaces retain elements of their social and cultural origins and have a specific "spatial identity", this could in turn affect the activities and mindset of people using those spaces in a reciprocal process of interaction.[10] Historians have been keen to investigate connections between spatial and social identities, evidence of such abstract ideas being relatively abundant in extant documentation of the period. Any "illusion of transparency" quickly becomes decipherable in the record of events.[11] In practical terms this entails examining how people behaved in, used, or spoke about different places. Theoretically almost any record could be used which has some grounding in physical space, for example, the record of a crime which happened on a particular street, or the slander of an office-holder at the local market. Research has often involved the examination of court records, wills or inventories. Court cases, for instance, noted location as standard practice, facilitating comparative analysis concerning the relation of gender or social position to certain places, or whether place changed people's attitudes towards one another. As such it should be possible to consider, not only how people acted in different places, but also the extent to which this activity reflected, and was reflected in, their wider socio-cultural beliefs.

Social historians have explored the relationship between space and society by considering how contemporaries, whether consciously or not, used their environment to convey certain messages. Most obviously, how the show of civic power in the placement and design of grand buildings, ceremonial sites and prisons articulated political relationships.[12] More recently, historians also have considered how contemporary attitudes relating to questions of gender or poverty, for example, were expressed in the physical make-up of the city. Approaching sources with an awareness of how people interacted with their environment suggests that surroundings played some part in the ordering and creation of identities, and thus the subsequent performance of social relationships.[13]

It would be wise however to add a precautionary note. The spatial dominance of wealthier elites is more evident in records, especially in urban areas, as they were predominantly responsible for civic building, architecture and planning.[14] Grand building projects and civic buildings have also proved more durable than the more vernacular architecture of ordinary housing.[15] Despite the abundance of resources, uncovering popular ideas about space and its uses can be a difficult task. Socio-cultural perceptions of space were often sub-conscious or inferred, understandable only in context, or have been obscured entirely from our retrospective gaze.[16] It is thus important to recognise that our source material may present an unbalanced picture of social relations, one which privileges rich over poor and public over private space.

The nature of these problems, therefore, might help to explain why, despite the potential of spatial theories for examining past societies, only a handful of social historians have yet taken up the challenge. Paul Griffiths, for example, explored how contemporaries understood the relationship between space, crime and civic authority.[17] He investigated "penal spaces", that is the corporeal sites of punishment which symbolised and reinforced civic order, and discussed how the perception of city streets changed after dark. Robert Tittler has considered civic symbolism, showing how urban elites reinforced their position and encouraged deference by expenditure on lavish civic buildings, public ceremonies and processions.[18] Laura Gowing and Robert Shoemaker have both undertaken ambitious and comprehensive surveys of attitudes towards gender in the streets of early modern London.[19] Interested in how space influenced perceptions of gender identity; Gowing concentrated on uncovering attitudes towards women in public space using libel records and literature, concluding that women were likely to be judged more critically in public, than in private. This, she argues, was due to the prevailing attitude that women's proper place was in the home, in combination with a sexual double standard which endangered "visible" women. Shoemaker, on the other hand, explored how people moved about the city. He demonstrated that women's movements were largely unrestricted, and that middling-sort women actually enjoyed greater freedom of movement than their male counterparts. His research suggests that supposed negative perceptions of "visible" or "publically active" women may not have actually restricted what they did on a daily basis, a finding which questions the impact of those attitudes in the first place.[20] Amanda Flather undertook a geographically broader survey of space and identity in Essex. Like Shoemaker, she researched the use of space by gender with surprising results. Indeed, she argues that women enjoyed active social lives in areas traditionally thought to be male preserves, such as alehouses.[21] Pamela Graves, Christopher Marsh and Robert Tittler all considered the significance of church interior space.[22] Seating arrangements, for example, mirrored the parish hierarchy, a powerful reminder of social divisions. Church space represented a microcosmic ideal of community, symbolising order, belonging and traditional values. The expression of space in contemporary literature has also proved fruitful; Joseph Monteyne, for example, has considered the representation of urban space in printed images and the visual culture of early modern society, but also explored print and its relationship with space and social identity.[23] Finally, David Rollison and David Postles have explored landscape, space and mobility in a move away from urban led research, a theme which is picked up in this collection by Rob Lee, Simon Sandall and Andy Wood.[24] This is not a comprehensive account of all the research in this area, a survey of which would be outside the scope of this introduction, but serves to introduce the variety of ways space has been explored. The essays in this collection do not explicitly deal with space as their central theme, but aim to show how the "spatial turn" can be incorporated within an ongoing dialogue on agency or politics.

This collection also addresses change and continuity. The time frame of the essays extends through the sixteenth, seventeenth, eighteenth, and into the nineteenth centuries, so it is possible to compare and contrast society over a long period. The most striking points to arise are first, the endurance of the same social problems and second, the continuity of methods available to ordinary people to articulate their own agency in the face of these concerns, despite the passage of three hundred years. Simon Sandall's essay, for instance, explores how Elizabethan customs endured throughout the seventeenth century, forming the basis of people's inherited memories of their local customary rights. Similarly, Andy Wood explores the longevity of folklore in collective memories, which acted to legitimise and strengthen plebeian agency. Rob Lee demonstrates that the problems familiar to sixteenth-century peasants would not have been out of place in the nineteenth; the same concerns over basic rights endured or resurfaced under different guises. The contributions in this book thus collectively make a persuasive argument for expanding our sense of plebeian agency and political engagement, and the extent to which space and social interaction connected. What emerges from these is a greater awareness of contemporaries own self-motivated ability to challenge and question the world around them and the tools available to them to do so.

George Oppitz-Trotman's distinctive literary approach engages productively with interdisciplinary theory, offering a re-reading of agency and demonstrating its interconnectedness with the immediate spatial environment. In his own words, he attempts to "posit a materialist understanding of generic origin" by uncovering the close relationship between genre, violence, peripherality and plebeian protest. His argument begins with a discussion of the spatial orientation of the play's protagonist, which is often obscured or ignored, adeptly demonstrating the centrality of space as the context behind all forms of human interaction. Without this knowledge the reader is unable to fully understand the origin or meaning of violence in the sixteenth-century revenge genre. Thus he asserts that the study of revenge tragedies should be both historically and spatially located, so as not to abstract them from real-life social relationships. Based on Thomas Kyd's *Spanish Tragedy*, a play which he argues marked a turning point in English theatre, he demonstrates how concepts of space were embedded within language and then disseminated within performance literature.

Oppitz-Trotman draws a direct correlation between agency and social space, showing how space "underpins" all social relationships. The spatial disenfranchisement of *The Spanish Tragedy's* protagonist Hieronimo has a direct affect on his ability to seek justice for wrongdoing, distorting his actions into revenge. Hieronimo begins to experience a sense of spatial exclusion, not only from the formal channels of power, but from society as a whole, his character exaggeratedly mirroring the experiences of the social and economic outsiders in Waddell's discussion of exclusive communities.

Oppitz-Trotman also contemplates the revenge tragedy in its wider context; taking into account the impact of the changing legal system in later sixteenth-century society and proposing that this "crisis of legal and social participation in the commonwealth state...exists concomitantly with a fundamentally spatial crisis". He challenges the suggestion that the middling-sorts widening participation in formal offices and the law granted a larger social group access to the formal channels of power, and therefore, allowed them greater potential for agency. This change was reflected by popular protest gradually moving out of the streets and fields and into the law courts, and a concomitant decline in landowner led rebellions, such as had been popular in the mid-sixteenth century.

However, it could be argued that this effectively curtailed plebeian's potential to exert "true" agency, often without their conscious realisation, as their power to act was now directed within regulated channels.

Finally, he uses the social space of the theatre as the background to discuss popular agency and sedition. The *Spanish Tragedy's* content echoed plebeian ability to counter authority, and the fears and actions of those same authorities in response. In the same way that contemporary playwrights were exploring themes of petition, protest and royal power; real life issues were being acted out around them, as theatres were being criticised for encouraging idleness and sedition; resembling official concerns over other social spaces, such as the alehouse, which is the focus of Mark Hailwood's contribution.

With similar motives, Hailwood demonstrates how the study of alehouses can help us understand the broader social, political and cultural concerns of the later Stuart period. In particular, he argues that the history of drinking houses parallels changes in society and culture, and mirrored extant political tensions. The first part of his essay considers the problematic historiography of the alehouse, which has generated several competing frameworks of discussion. The first, popularised by Peter Clark, is probably the most well-known. Clark's formative research influenced the idea that alehouses were seen akin to "alternative societies" by Godly reformers and wealthy "chief inhabitants" who sought to suppress alehouse culture in what can only be interpreted within a cultural framework of middling polarisation. The second, borrowed from the work of anthropologist James C. Scott, speaks of alehouses as "sequestered sites" in which the disenfranchised masses acted out their "hidden transcripts" largely free from the eyes of the law. The final, far more pessimistic perspective is that promoted by James Brown and Andy Wood, who argue that alehouses were "sites of surveillance" closely monitored by governing elites as part of a wider drive to police plebeian politics. The historiography plays a crucial part in Hailwood's essay as it rests on a re-conceptualisation of these competing models. He does this by considering the alehouse as an important symbolic space, encapsulating a microcosm of society at any given time. Thus, his emphasis on the "spatial turn" allows him to conclude that it is near impossible to apply any one over-arching framework to capture all the dynamics at work in early modern alehouse culture. Indeed, he argues that the particularities of time and space undermined all the given models at different times, as regularly as the changing customers in the alehouse itself altered the dynamics of individual interactions. To support his conclusion, he uses empirical examples of seditious speech, in conjunction with alehouse licensing laws which were on the rise throughout the Stuart period. Taken together, they offer a tantalising view of both popular and official attitudes towards alehouse policing, which show that the competing desires for freedom or regulation of alehouses did not emanate from any one social group, or set of motivations.

My own chapter begins by questioning the understanding of agency as essentially political. To be true to the theme of "re-conceptualisation", I have considered the "politics" of the spiritual parish by examining the relationship between the minister and his congregation. Ministers held a position of leadership within their community, but Church court records show his authority was often challenged. These attacks were generally documented under the heading of libel, but were more often than not tied in with genuine complaints concerning his performance and behaviour, mirroring the style of speech against authority figures in the secular world. However, it would seem that distinct to attacks on secular officers, often considered seditious, libels cases dealing with ministers were treated far less seriously. I posit that this was because of the often tenuous nature of a minister's status, combined with the legitimacy of the complaints themselves. The relationship between minister and congregation, therefore, offers an exceptional insight into how early modern offices were legitimised, and reflects on how different social groups could exercise agency in the face of formal authority.

Starting from the position that early modern society was not dualistic, with rich set against poor, but inherently more complex, I argue such ideas about agency and authority should re-evaluated. If the social background of the people involved in contesting, or supporting authority are explored, they reveal a large overlap in status between those challenging, and those challenged. To this end, my essay investigates who was raising and pursuing local disputes with ministers, and it shows that the majority of people challenging the clergy were from a similar background, if not slightly higher. The importance of this simple conclusion for the study of agency, however, should not be underestimated. It challenges traditional assumptions of social conflict as a battle between rich and poor, whilst at the same time showing the difficulty of applying generalisations to early modern society. However, I also demonstrate that when poorer people did challenge their local minister, their reasons for so doing were not always to subvert the social order, but to support it.

Brodie Waddell explores community belonging and identity, and their polar opposite, social exclusion. The historiography of "inclusion" and "exclusion" is well-established, influenced first and foremost by Keith Wrightson's work on parish identities.[25] Waddell's essay deigns not simply to extend this historiography, but to explore the practical implications of social exclusivity on the local economy. As Waddell explains, much remains subjective, yet, it is undeniable that there was a real impact. His broad "holistic" approach therefore takes into account the complex factors which defined communal identity and how these identities were subsequently expressed in material and economic terms. He breaks this down into three main areas.

First, he explores cultural expressions of identity. These, he explains, were communicated and refined by popular mediums such as sermons, ballads, oaths, rituals and festivals. He suggests that cultural expressions of "localism" were ingrained into the customary uses of the immediate environment. "Beating the bounds" at Rogationtide, for example, endorsed local boundaries on the one hand, and reinforced social distinctions in the processional line-up on the other. Rogation demonstrates the importance of place, solidifying communal identities in the symbolic assertion of boundaries; the corporeal manifestation of belonging. This discussion leads into the second part of his essay, which explores the structures and institutions of community.

The next section advances his economic premise, illustrating how local identities were inseparable from traditional parish based economic provision; individual entitlement to poor relief, for example, was based around the extent the poor were perceived to "belong". Community membership legitimised requests for assistance, normally built on residence qualifications, but also made tough distinctions between the "deserving" and "undeserving poor". The poor were expected to prove their worthiness by their religiosity, morality and behaviour. Travellers and vagrants were stigmatised as "strangers" and often unwelcome. In towns and cities, vagrants suffered harsh punishments, set on hard labour or even whipped before being sent away and there was another complication: citizenship. This added a final caveat for belonging, formalising expectations which in rural areas were based on subjectivity. This restricted "un-free" city dwellers by economic sanctions, whilst protecting the privileges of the citizenry.

Finally, Waddell examines evidence that these collective identities were, on occasion, violently reinforced. He suggests communities experiencing stress resorted to their own methods of economic redress when normative systems of regulation were ineffective or insufficient. Formal community boundaries became "flashpoints" at which the collective agency of parishioners clashed with that of outsiders. In these cases it was not the poor vagrant who was the target for community angst, but official representatives of the state. The most obvious example was resisting tax officers, which showed as much about community solidarity against non-local collectors, as animosity towards state policy. However, it could also be viewed as part of a wider popular movement to protect traditional common rights against central encroachment such as had been taking place with enclosure, fen drainage or the restriction of forested areas. Waddell suggests that these communal expressions of solidarity allowed ordinary people to take the law into their own hands, arguably a form of agency asserted in self-defence.

Overall, Waddell introduces two very salient points. First, he posits a link between space, identity and agency which on the one hand reinforced social distinctions, yet on the other empowered individuals otherwise excluded from formal channels of power and authority. Second, he highlights the inadequacy of teleological community narratives which suggest their gradual decline in a changing society, offering another revisionist critique of Tönnies model. In its place, he shows the complexity of community during the late seventeenth and early eighteenth centuries, explaining why one over-arching narrative of change is inappropriate to describe early modern society.

Simon Sandall looks at the changing relationship between popular agency, local communities and custom from the sixteenth to the nineteenth centuries. His central premise is that the social practice of custom widens the range of activity which can be considered "political", allowing involvement in the negotiation of local rights and privileges by poorer men, women and children. Informed by the importance of "negotiation" as a way of understanding the operation of power in society, he looks to Antonio Gramsci's theories of hegemony. He argues that the authority of rule had to be actively supported by the populace, who legitimised or criticised power through a variety of methods, including customary rights and traditions ingrained in the collective memory of their local communities. Based on a case-study of a free mining community in the Forest of Dean, he explores the social composition, legality and authority of the local Mine Law Court which resolved conflicts between miners and other parties over customary law. Overall, he argues that the process of law was more socially inclusive than has perhaps been thought; his study demonstrating some degree of local autonomy, influence and negotiation in the formation and operation of legal practice. Laws were not always created by the elite. Many laws and legal practices had their precedent in the popular customs and rights retrieved from the memory of individuals and communities from "time out of mind". His model stresses the interplay of popular oral culture with formal written records.

Sandall's case study focuses on the gradual erosion of customary rights in the Forest and the attempts of local elites to impose their own version of customary law upon the perceived rights of the "vulgar sort". Working thus within the perimeters of oppositional politics; the local elite, in particular Sir Edward Winter, worked to polarise their position by undermining the legitimate concerns of the commons. Openly attacking his rivals in terms which cast himself as protector of the "commonweale" against the assault of disorderly, lewd and seditious criminals, Winter conveniently typecast the "commons" as one social body, avoiding any discussion of their actual social composition which ranged from the very poor to middling gentlemen. Similar to the essays by Hailwood, Lee, and myself; Sandall points out that opposition to elite policy cannot be simplified to a struggle between rich and poor, as the middling sorts played a large role in conflicts with authority. Nonetheless, popular speech incorporated stereotypes of the social orders which obscured the real dynamics of social protest and negotiation.

Sandall also considers the spatial context of customary memory, working from David Rollison's claim that landscape is "a memory palace" which harbours the collective memories of local communities.[26] In so doing, he underlines the importance of inherited knowledge of boundaries and land rights in the formation of customary and common law. The spatial context is a crucial part of the argument for plebeian agency, as "the poor" were able to exercise power in the collective spatial memories of the landscape around them, in direct conflict with the desires of the local elite.

Nonetheless, Sandall points out that by the eighteenth century, the transfer of previously oral traditions to the written record in an attempt to preserve local rights gradually took autonomy out of the hands of the commons and placed it into the keeping of the lawyers and courts. The formalisation of collective memory effectively closed the channels within which ordinary people had previously worked. Nonetheless, a strong sense of local custom and the legitimacy of common action survived well into the nineteenth century, when, like the protagonists of Rob Lee's or Andy Woods's essays, rural workers used such traditions to their own ends as part of a radicalised agenda.

Andy Wood explores connections between popular agency and folklore, opening with a story from Norfolk about the re-building of Swaffham church during the mid-fifteenth century. According to local legend, John Chapman, a poor pedlar, donated a large sum of money to re-build the north aisle. Tradition states that he had found his sudden great wealth in unusual, and magical, circumstances. Wood extrapolates from this example that to contemporaries, folklore was more than simply entertainment, but a way of understanding the world around them. In the story of John Chapman, for instance, Wood sees the broader context of a growing "non-gentry lay piety" and popular agency in the face of villainous local gentry land-owners; a direct reflection of the rising social importance and wealth of the new middling sorts, perceived as a threat by the traditional ruling classes who realised this challenge to their own place in the traditional feudal hierarchy. Stories like Chapman's provided a basis for a local "plebeian identity" which extolled Christian values and solidarity within their own ranks, rather than allegiance to an exploitative ruling elite.

In his subsequent narrative, Wood evokes several local myths from East Anglia and the north of England, from the fifteenth to the nineteenth centuries. Each stories origin was contiguous with the time and space of important local rebellions and traditions of oppressive local lordships and each endured, embedded within features of the landscape, a cross-pollination of oral and written traditions, physical space, memory, common rights, community, kinship, customary law, locality and identity. Their careful selection shows the importance of folkloristic culture to a widespread plebeian cultural assertiveness, arguably a form of agency, in the expression of a distinct culture separate and often more pervasive than that of the elite. Drawing from the inter-disciplinary theories of Maurice Halbwachs and Antonio Gramsci, he argues that folklore should not be considered valueless because of its inherent unreliability, but should instead be seen as a "basis for popular solidarity and action".

Wood shows how the coercive role of the state is at its most effective when it secures the active consent of the populace whom it governs. Therefore challenges to that state should be considered within the broader framework of a functioning cultural hegemony, which works to limit popular agency by framing authority as natural. Nonetheless, there is some suggestion that this process worked both ways, as I argue in my own contribution; plebeian challenges to authority were more successful when they adopted traditional, conservative aims, although it could be argued that this avenue of agency simply reinforces the cultural hegemony of the dominant class still further. However, Wood sees room for movement. Subaltern politics, is in itself, proof of the mitigating, shifting and competing circumstances which informed, circumscribed and enabled elite rule; traceable through the processes of everyday life, in this case, collective memory. Many traditional tales persisted into the twentieth century in rural areas, and were, in the case of the "Riding of the Black Lad" evoked time and again as symbolic of peasant/landowner relations during the working-class radical movements of the later nineteenth century. Wood's essay thus explicates the relationship between collective memory, social identity and agency, suggesting that memories and folklore were at their most powerful when embedded in physical location.

Rob Lee bases his essay on a case study of two seemingly contrasting areas, Norfolk and County Durham, arguing that they shared a tradition of political radicalism and non-conformist religion. In particular, he stresses the link between Methodism and an evolving labour politics. He concentrates on the middle decades of the nineteenth century, which he contends are often ignored in favour of the more sensational Swing Riots and Chartist movements of the 30s and 40s and trade union activism in the 70s. However, the 50s and 60s were characterised by "paternalistic neglect", deserving of study in their own right. Lee underlines the continuance of strategies of social exclusion, also highlighted by Waddell, exacerbated in this period by open and closed parish divisions. However, Lee's essay is not about continuity. Making good use of the "spatial turn", Lee shows how social relationships and power structures were reflected in the enclosed rural landscape, the Methodist Church emerging as a centre for a "new politics of resistance" instigated by the neglected poor.

From 1834, he contends that the New Poor Law had recreated the spatial landscape, privileging privatisation over public, common rights, which were gradually lost from oral history in the transference to written law. The Poor Law contributed to a volatile situation, exacerbating existing social tensions, as well as creating new ones. Although heralded as a salvation for the poor, in many cases it granted landowners greater rights to move the labouring classes, benefiting the few who were able to live within closed parishes. For the rest, like the Jarvis family of Corpusty, the benefits of closed parishes were hard to see. By the 1860s, Lee posits that paternalist provisions had almost entirely broken down. Left to their own devices, the poor sought out new ways to improve their own situation, which often meant resisting traditional support networks, such as the Church of England, which some believed had failed them. Regarded more and more as sharing the values of the landed elites and industrial giants, the Church and its representatives were shunned, despite their (largely symbolic) efforts to "include" their congregations. Instead, parishioners sought alternative political and spiritual sustenance in a telling expression of their own agency. Drawing on the tragic circumstances of one family, Lee's essay offers a unique perspective on poverty, deprivation and society, but also contributes to the wider narrative of politics and religion at this time; showing how resistance to the established church became synonymous with political allegiance.

Lee offers a final say on all the themes which this collection has raised: agency, space, custom, belonging, popular politics and religion. The Methodist movement's aims shared striking similarities with the seventeenth century non-conformists, for example, many of whom championed social and political reform. As such, Lee's contribution offers a welcome dialogue on continuity and change, illustrating the permanence of the methods of the poor in previous centuries to challenge authority, as well as showing how the clashes over land use and custom, such as in Sandall's study of the Forest of Dean, served as a precursor to Lee's tale of class conflicts in the nineteenth century. It goes to show that despite the progress of time, social progress did not follow suit: the complaints of the nineteenth-century labouring classes mirroring those of previous generations. Perhaps it would be pertinent here to mention Scott one more time. For many poor people, agency did not mean change; it only meant the ability to negotiate the terms of their own subordination.

Notes

[1] P. Collinson, *De Republica Anglorum: Or, History with the Politics Put Back* (Cambridge: Cambridge University Press, 1994). Some seminal works would include K. Wrightson, *English Society, 1580-1680* (London: Routledge, 1982); K. Wrightson, 'Estates, Degrees and Sorts: Changing Perceptions of Society in Tudor and Stuart England' in P. Corfield, ed., *Language, History, & Class* (Oxford: Oxford University Press, 1991), 30-52; P. Griffiths, A. Fox, and S. Hindle eds, *The Experience of Authority in Early Modern England* (Basingstoke: Palgrave Macmillan, 1996); M. J. Braddick, *State Formation in Early Modern England, c. 1550-1700,* (Cambridge: Cambridge University Press, 2000); T. Harris ed., *The Politics of the Excluded, c.1500-1850* (Basingstoke: Palgrave Macmillan, 2001); M. J. Braddick and J. Walter, eds, *Negotiating Power in Early Modern Society: Order, Hierarchy and Subordination in Britain and Ireland* (Cambridge: Cambridge University Press, 2001); P. Withington, *The Politics of Commonwealth* (Cambridge: Cambridge University Press, 2005) and A. Wood, "Fear, Hatred and the Hidden Injuries of Class in Early Modern England", *Journal of Social History* 39:3 (2006): 803-26. This list is by no means exhaustive.

[2] Scott's ideas were the inspiration for the important collection of essays edited by Braddick and Walter, *Negotiating Power in Early Modern Society.*

[3] Scott's ideas are best laid out in J. C. Scott, *Weapons of the Weak: Everyday Forms of Peasant Resistance* (New Haven: Yale University Press, 1985) and J. C. Scott, *Domination and the Arts of Resistance: Hidden Transcripts* (New Haven: Yale University Press, 1990).

[4] See F. D. Colburn, ed., *Everyday Forms of Peasant Resistance* (London and New York: M. E. Sharpe, 1989), ix-x.

[5] Wood suggests that deference was a known "behavioural code" which could be knowingly appropriated to achieve certain ends, see Wood, "Poore men woll speke one daye", in ed. Tim Harris, *The Politics of the Excluded*, 67-99. See also H. Newby, 'The Deferential Dialectic', *Comparative Studies in Society and History* 17:2 (1975): 139-164.

[6] Although it has proved useful, initial enthusiasm about Scott's approach has dampened in recent years, attracting a few critics. Andy Wood, for example, has criticised Scott for not taking Antonio Gramsci's writings on hegemony into account. See A. Wood, "Subordination, Solidarity and the Limits of Popular Agency in a Yorkshire Valley, c. 1596-1615", *Past and Present* 193 (2006): 41-72, especially 41-5.

[7] C. P. Graves, "Social Space in the English Medieval Parish Church", *Economy and Society* 18:3 (1989): 297. For spatial theory see P. Bourdieu, *Outline of a Theory of Practice* (Cambridge: Cambridge University Press, 1977); M. De Certeau, *The Practice of Everyday Life* (Berkeley: University of California Press, 1984); P. Bourdieu, *Language and Symbolic Power* (Cambridge: Cambridge University Press, 1991) and Henri Lefebvre, *The Production of Space* (Oxford: Oxford University Press, 1994).

[8] Bourdieu, *Outline of a Theory of Practice*, 72.

[9] The importance of "belonging" to early modern communities is explored by Brodie Waddell in his contribution to this collection. Inspired by Steve Hindle and Keith Wrightson, he sees communities as "exclusive". In part this resulted from suspicion of "outsiders" in places with established families and local traditions, but it was also economic protectionism; poor relief was only granted to those with residential rights. In rapidly growing towns and cities protectionism was motivated less by self-interest, than by practical necessity.

[10] Lefebvre discussed how social identities became inscribed in space and "in the process producing that space itself". Lefebvre, *Production of Space*, 129. See especially 68-169 for an explanation of the social production of space and place. Bourdieu claimed that spaces retain unique "signification codes" through which "through the intermediary of the divisions and hierarchies" set up "between things, persons and practices" creates a "tangible, classifying system". Bourdieu, *Outline of a Theory of Practice*, 72.

[11] Lefebvre, *The Production of Space*, 28.

[12] See, for example, R. Tittler, *Architecture and Power: the Town Hall and the English Urban Community, c. 1500-1640* (Oxford: Oxford University Press, 1991).

[13] J. Epstein, "Spatial Practices/Democratic Vistas", *Social History* 24 (1999): 294-310, 301.

[14] P. Jackson, *Maps of Meaning: An Introduction to Cultural Geography* (London: Routledge, 1989), 47-48.

[15] Robert Tittler has discussed civic symbolism in the urban environment. See in particular R. Tittler, "Seats of Honour, Seats of Power: The Symbolism of Public Seating in the English Urban Community, c. 1560-1620", *Albion* 24:2 (2002): 205-223 or R. Tittler, *Architecture and Power: the Town Hall and the English Urban Community, c. 1500-1640* (Oxford: Oxford University Press, 1991).

[16] See R. J. Johnston, *A Question of Place: Exploring the Practice of Human Geography* (Oxford: Oxford University Press, 1991) and J. Rendell, *The Pursuit of Pleasure: Gender, Space and Architecture in Regency London* (London: The Athlone Press, 2002).

[17] P. Griffiths, 'Meanings of Nightwalking in Early Modern England,' *Seventeenth-Century* 13:2 (1998): 212-38; P. Griffiths, 'Bodies and Souls in Sixteenth-and Seventeenth-Century England: Punishing Petty Crime, 1540-1700' in eds S. Devereaux and P. Griffiths, *Penal Practice and Culture, 1500-1900: Punishing the English* (London: Palgrave, 2004), 85-120; P. Griffiths, *Lost Londons: Change, Crime and Control in the Capital City, 1550-1660* (Cambridge: Cambridge University Press, 2008).

[18] Tittler, *Architecture and Power.*

[19] L. Gowing, "The Freedom of the Streets: Women and Social Space, 1560-1640" in eds P. Griffiths, and M. Jenner, *Londinopolis: Essays in the Cultural and Social History of Early Modern London* (Manchester: Manchester University Press, 2000).

[20] R. Shoemaker, "Gendered Spaces: Patterns of Mobility and Perceptions of London's geography, 1660-1750" in ed. J. F. Merritt, *Imagining Early Modern London: Perceptions and Portrayals of the City from Stow to Strype, 1598-1720* (Cambridge: Cambridge University Press, 2001).

[21] A. Flather, *Gender and Space in Early Modern England,* (Woodbridge: Boydell Press, 2007)*,* 110-120. See also Lena Cowen-Orlin's work on public and private space: L. Cowen-Orlin, *Locating Privacy in Tudor London* (Oxford: Oxford University Press, 2008).

[22] Graves, "Social Space in the English Medieval Parish Church"; C. Marsh, 'Sacred Space in England, 1560-1640: The View from the Pew', *Journal of Ecclesiastical History* 53:2 (April, 2002): 286-311; R. Tittler, 'Seats of Honour, Seats of Power: The Symbolism of Public Seating in the English Urban Community, c. 1560-1620', *Albion* 24:2 (2002): 205-223 and C. Marsh, 'Order and Place in England, 1580-1640: The View from the Pew', *Journal of British Studies* 44 (2005): 3-26.

[23] J. Montayne, *The Printed Image in Early Modern London: Urban Space, Visual Representation, and Social Exchange* (Aldershot: Ashgate, 2007).

[24] D. A. Postles, *Social Geographies in England, 1200-1640* (Washington: New Academia Publishing, 2007) and D. Rollison, "Exploding England: the Dialectics of Mobility and Settlement in Early Modern England", *Social History* 24 (1999): 1-16.

[25] Steve Hindle, *On the Parish?: The Micro-Politics of Poor Relief in Rural England, c.1550-1750* (Oxford: Oxford University Press, 2004) and Phil Withington, *The Politics of Commonwealth: Citizens and Freemen in Early Modern England* (Cambridge: Cambridge University Press, 2005).

[26] David Rollison, *The Local Origins of Modern Society: Gloucestershire, 1500-1800* (London and New York: Routledge, 1992), 70.

SPACE, AGENCY AND GENRE: REVENGE TRAGEDY IN *THE SPANISH TRAGEDY* (1587?)*

GEORGE OPPITZ-TROTMAN

Eubulus: Though kings forget to govern as they ought,
Yet Subjects must obey as they are bound.
Gorboduc (1561), V.i.50-1

King: No place indeed should murder sanctuarize;
Revenge should have no bounds.
Hamlet (1601), IV.vii.125-6

Revenge is a kind of wild justice ... For as for the first wrong, it does but offend the law; but the revenge of that wrong putteth the law out of office.
Sir Francis Bacon, "Of Revenge" (1625)[1]

The great achievements of the English theatre after the 1580s derived from the socio-economic rationalisation of theatrical activity of such an extent as to be impoverishing. The following article investigates dramatic genre's relationship to the space of theatrical performance, and to the agent of that performance, the actor, in the light of the relatively rapid reorganization and professionalization of English theatre. It argues that the imaginative power of early modern dramatic performance was reliant on the continually mediating role of the actor, whose work produced the space of the stage as much as the fictional courts, forests and houses of early modern plays. Most of the playwrights of the Shakespearean era were also actors; texts were produced with the prospect and practicalities of near performance in mind. As a result, historical analysis of such plays should not assume that they simply reflected anterior social practice from a position without; rather, history related to such plays through the mediated immediacy of performance, in which real and imaginary spaces were negotiated simultaneously and in relation to one another.

This hypothesis is tested below in a study of Thomas Kyd's *The Spanish Tragedy*, a crucial early tragedy that also crystallized the generic characteristics of what would become the immensely popular revenge tragedy form. Whilst shedding new light on the play itself by situating it in relation to early modern problems of law, domesticity and sedition, this article suggests that to use such plays for the purposes of historical exemplification, as cultural history tends to do, may actually remove the play from its space and agents, in effect constituting a dehistoricisation of the play itself and thus a distortion of its actual representation of extra-dramatic history. In other words, the model of criticism in which drama is seen to have reflected or stored an anterior social reality at the whim of its authors bypasses the changing formal conditions that enabled sixteenth century dramatic performance. As Bertolt Brecht would remark in his challenge to György Lukács during the Marxist debates concerning *avant-garde* art in the early twentieth century, literary critics are all too predisposed to ignore the problems and contingencies of production that are central to the sociality of drama, yet for the dramatist these are of primary creative concern. The aim, then, is to think about drama's relationship to history in terms of the historical construction of dramatic space: "Art is the social antithesis of society, from which it cannot be deduced immediately", wrote Theodor Adorno.[2]

This essay attempts to organize an idea of genre linked to the sociality of formal playing conditions. The problem of genre lies to some extent in its tendency to obliterate difference. Yet clearly some kind of vocabulary is needed to describe how common historical experience was abstracted into the apparently unrelated sphere of literary form. Too often one is forced to resort to the poverties of the 'thematic' or 'emblematic' to establish a common generic language, leaving untouched the greater problems of formal continuity or similarity brought about by the circumstances of English dramatic production in the late sixteenth century. The connections manifested by a play—between protagonist and court, for example—were abstracted from concrete social relationships, underpinned by space. A materialist theory of genre, to which the following article aims to contribute, would seek to expose the differences and contradictions in the generic schema that it attempts to posit; would allow the historical movement free play within the apparently fixed generic criteria; would find a way to express the work's total generic effect with reference to the work's peculiar development in performance.[3] Even in the individual work, genre has to be located spatially and historically, and the contradictions, unevenness and mutability of the history from which it is abstracted permitted to inform our understanding of the work's generic voice.

Genre is simultaneously interior and exterior to the dramatic work; at once its subject and object, it works on the play and is worked on by it: this work is of authorship, of course, but it is also that of performance.[4] Performance describes agency's relationship to space. It is from Henri Lefèbvre's conclusions that "no social relationship can exist without an underpinning", and that this underpinning is spatial, that the contemplation of early modern revenge tragedy is taken up below.[5] An emphasis on performance—a productive act in a peculiar sense—takes another cue from Lefèbvre:

> How does [...] space, which we have described as at once homogeneous and broken up, maintain itself in view of the formal irreconcilability of these two characteristics? [...] Only an act can hold—and hold together—such fragments in a homogeneous totality. Only action can prevent dispersion, like a fist clenched around sand.[6]

Returning to consider how the actor's 'action' constructed a relationship of real space to fictional or imagined spaces, the closing passages of this article will attempt to recover the actor's agency in order to propose that genre encodes lived historical experience. It will be clear that words in plays are inscribed with an expectation of where and how they be spoken and heard. Slavoj Žižek has described "[the object's] tautological gesture of positing [...] external conditions as the conditions-components of the thing and, simultaneously, of presupposing the existence of ground which holds together this multitude of conditions."[7] This technical explanation has here prompted an understanding of theatre's historical existence as comprising a special kind of relationship between language and space that cannot be redacted fully from purely textual analysis. "Theatricality" is a function of historical space and historical relationships of agency to that space (the stage). Historical spaces themselves are embedded within words as formal suppositions. This paper attempts to construe Thomas Kyd's *The Spanish Tragedy* (1586-7?), generally considered to be the foundational revenge tragedy in England, as an act of speaking and moving within historical space.

The Spanish Tragedy occupies a crucial place in the history of English theatre. Along with Christopher Marlowe's *Tamburlaine* it completely transformed the dramatic landscape in England, paving the way for a new type of theatre. "With his mad Hieronymo", Kyd is often considered "the principal developer of 'personation' besides Shakespeare", and his most famous play the first to represent human causality fully on the English stage.[8] There is no known source for the play, which is relatively unusual for the time, although the influence of Seneca is quite pronounced (ten

English versions of Senecan plays had been produced in 1581 alone). The complicated action takes place in the aftermath of a battle between Spain and Portugal. It is introduced by the ghost of Don Andrea—who was killed by the Portuguese Viceroy's son Balthazar during the fighting—and the figure of Revenge—a highly ambiguous remnant of the morality play tradition. The action is thus enframed by these two figures, who are reminiscent of a chorus. Returning victoriously to the Spanish Court, Hieronimo's son, Horatio, and the king's nephew, Lorenzo, contest the victory over Balthazar, whom they have brought back as prisoner. Horatio subsequently falls in love with Don Andrea's beloved Bel-imperia but, betrayed by their servant Pedringano, who is tasked to watch over their secret meetings, they are attacked in Hieronimo's garden by Lorenzo and Balthazar. For, in the meantime, the realms of Portugal and Spain have deemed a marriage between Balthazar and Bel-imperia diplomatically judicious (a decision that happily coincides with Balthazar's own inclinations). Stabbing and hanging Horatio, the villains take and imprison Bel-imperia. Discovering Horatio's body after hearing Bel-imperia's screams, Hieronimo, grief-stricken, investigates the crime, discovers the culprits and, after first vainly appealing to the king for justice, designs a revenge against his enemies using his trusted position at court. As the play ends, Hieronimo, Bel-imperia, Lorenzo and Balthazar lie dead in the presence of Horatio's corpse, which Hieronimo had presented during revelations to the court after his retaliatory murders.[9]

Hieronimo perceives that "justice is exiled from the earth" (III.xiii.140). Accordingly, he too occupies an exilic space as justice-seeker. This situation is revealed by *The Spanish Tragedy* in a sophisticated dialectic of stage position that also hints at the crises and vacillations of social agency that will be discussed below. In III.xii, Hieronimo considers suicide, but is interrupted by the arrival of the court:

> No, no! fie, no! pardon me, I'll none of that:
> *He flings away the dagger and halter.*
> This way I'll take, and this way comes the king;
> *He takes them up again.*
> And here I'll have a fling at him, that's flat;
> And, Balthazar, I'll be with thee to bring,
> And thee, Lorenzo! Here's the king; nay, stay,
> And here, ay here; there goes the hare away.
> (III.xii.19-24)

Having probably passed across the inner stage during this partial soliloquy,[10] the King, the Portuguese ambassador, Castile and Lorenzo enter at this point:

> King: Now show, Ambassador, what our viceroy saith:
> Hath he received the articles we sent?
> Hieronimo: Justice, O, justice to Hieronimo.
> Lorenzo: Back, see'st thou not the king is busy?
> Hieronimo: O, is he so?
> King: Who is he that interrupts our business?
> Hieronimo: Not I, Hieronimo, beware: go by, go by.
> Ambassador: Renowned king, he hath received and read
> Thy kingly proffers, and thy promised league …
> (25-33)

Hieronimo would have appeared as an irritant on the verges of official business, his strategy being to "cry aloud for justice through the court, / Wearing the flints with these my withered feet, / And either purchase justice by entreats / Or tire them all with my revenging threats." (III.vii.70-3) Here he haunts the scene's edges, shushed away by the anxious Lorenzo; the avenger is denied space in which to articulate injustice, and his later revenge emerges from, and is characterized by the successful transformation and negation of, his spatial disenfranchisement. The distinction between justice and revenge is therefore everywhere challenged and confused by the play itself and its structure at the level of spatial organization. The false opposition of the two nevertheless underlay Fredson Bower's formative work on the revenge tragedy genre, setting up a lamentable tendency to see its plays as "linked only by a delight in blood and sensationalism".[11] This critical legacy inevitably comes into play the moment one attempts to read historically contingent problems of agency and space back into such play-violence. However, to the extent that our own historically determined moral compass demands that we locate the problem of the revenge play within a certain moral zone, this distinction between revenge and justice must be addressed and revised even in the attempt to transcend it. Revenge is not justice's antithesis, but it cannot be understood without it; neither is the idea of a revenge play identical with the idea of revenge, yet it is revenge that comprises the generic essence of the revenge play. The instinct to distinguish between "revenge" and "justice" is highly fertile, therefore, but ultimately futile in this case, and is partially addressed by Žižek's observation that liberal democratic ideologies tend to obscure systemic violence by emphasizing interpersonal brutality.[12] The categories of "justice" and "revenge" must find grounds in an analysis of performance space if we are to show how genre encompasses them. It is argued here that the violence of English revenge plays cannot be understood without reference to the spatial orientation of the protagonist, the provisional focus of this article.

Walter Benjamin suggested that violence always takes up a position to law of some kind.[13] In late sixteenth century England, the relationship between violence and legal process was changing. Andy Wood has noted the complex relationship between rebellion and litigation: while enclosure rioters increasingly combined protest and violence with various forms of legal prosecution, there was nevertheless "an apparent downward trend in the scale, ferocity and frequency of organized crowd protest and riot; and a rapid increase in litigation at central equity courts."[14] The mounting willingness to settle disputes within the various and emerging structures of a centrally organized legal system gradually conditioned relationships to authority, possibly dispersing the possibilities and motivations for local confrontation. Anthony Fletcher and Diarmaid MacCulloch, in their classic work on *Tudor Rebellions*, suggest that the incorporation into developing state structures of wealthier yeoman who had earlier, like Robert Kett himself, performed roles as leaders of plebeian revolt, directly contributed to the decline in the scale, frequency and organization of plebeian commotion under late Tudor government.[15] Steve Hindle has argued that the emergence of the English state was closely tied to the development of central court usage, and in particular the Court of Star Chamber, whose combination of executive and legal power was unique and important.[16] Until recently, state formation had tended to be thought out primarily in terms of a centralizing movement initiated from the centre, precluding local agency working back towards it. In a superbly lucid and provocative statement of the historiographical problem, Derek Sayer has suggested the way in which "locally devolved, yet centrally regulated, institutions of governance", such as the equity courts, "were arguably very much better suited to the needs of a developing capitalism than either a more bureaucratized, or a more bourgeois-democratic, polity might have been." Arguing dialectically that the survival in England of apparently archaic or traditional social forms accounts both for the peculiarity and the success of capitalism there, Sayer takes Justices of the Peace as paradigms of this movement:

> [Theirs] *was* self-government, *but* at the king's command [...] The day-to-day governance of the realm was thus largely devolved to local elites acting in an unpaid, amateur capacity, and this juridical role, of course, also empowered them in their private stations as landlords.

Yet while such forms, based on the exertion of an initially royal authority, thus empowered the gentry from whom this class was largely drawn, they ultimately worked against it as much as they compromised the heterogeneity of broader customary practice at a local level, offering potential empowerment whilst demanding adaptation to a gradually homogenizing central rule:

> From the Middle Ages on, even the mightiest of subjects are increasingly impelled, by what they stand to gain as much as by what they might lose, to channel their ambitions and conflicts through the medium of state forms. But as those forms attain definition, stability, and regularity, the crown too is restrained by them, as the Stuart kings were to discover.[17]

With the historical problem of law thus sketched, the problem of administrative jurisdiction in *The Spanish Tragedy* can be more precisely interrogated. Hieronimo's peripheral, antagonistic position in relation to powerful or governmental central space does not exist in a merely ironic relationship to the fact that, as Knight Marshal of the court, he was an important part of a system of control and governance, administering the legal space generated by the proximity of the royal body. Indeed, his role as Knight Marshal not only makes him the "highest judge" in the land, as Lorna Hutson has recently noted, but in fact contributes to the play's spatial and jurisdictional problems in a considerably more concrete way.[18] Since 1301, when its power was formulated under Edward I, the Court of the Verge, or "Marshalsea court", had operated as an extraordinary and specialized jurisdiction that encompassed the "Verge", the area comprising the twelve miles around the monarch's court or residence.[19] Indeed, from 1596 it was challenged by the higher common law courts precisely concerning the definition of the "trespasses within the Verge" for which Edward had given the court remit.[20] It was dependent on the location of the monarch's body, which generated its jurisdictional space. More specifically, it related to this space as extrapolated into either court or household. The Verge "served as a focal point for the enforcement of public order in the area around the king."[21] Sometimes referred to as the King's "private liberty," in the 1580s and 1590s this archaic ambulatory court was already being challenged over its right of jurisdiction in cases not pertaining directly to royal servants, but its maintenance was an issue of royal pride and authority. For centuries the unusual speed at which the court operated had encouraged many to plead their cases there, most of them with complaints of trespass or debt, covenants or land disputes, since as it moved the Verge subsumed and superseded local forms of legality. It played a crucial role in the formation of King's Bench superiority over the

Court of Common Pleas concerning trespass, since the pretence that prisoners were detained under the jurisdiction of the Marshal enabled the King's Bench to bring, as Holdsworth puts it, "any sort of action against [the prisoner] except real actions."[22] Among other duties, it punished members of the royal household for abuse of position and its powers. In 1497 Henry VII had directed the court specifically to focus on conspiracies to assassinate the king or his ministers and to administer punishment to conspirators.[23] The Marshalsea Court became the Court of the Verge of the King's Palace in 1611, and then, with renewed doubts over its jurisdiction, the Palace Court in 1630.[24]

Clearly, the fact that Hieronimo was the administrator of such a court, so heavily defined by its space around the royal person, anticipated his capacity to organize justice in the royal household more unusually. Indeed, at the climax of Hieronimo's final revenge the corpse of his murdered son Horatio is revealed to the court like an article of evidence that also enables the disclosure of allegorical meaning. Hieronimo's responsibility is for the punishment of trespasses within the household; the murder of Horatio is as much a matter for the official as it is for the father. As Knight Marshal, and as the play opens, Hieronimo helps produce the space from which he is later excluded (I.ii.). Indeed, in the play's 'prequel', *The First Part of Ieronimo* (1605), it is the villain Lorenzo who operates from an excluded space, bemoaning

> Hard fate,
> When villaines sit not in the highest state.
> Ambitions plume, that florisht in our court
> Seuere authority has dasht with iustice;
> And policy and pride walke like two exiles,
> Giuing attendance, that were once attended.[25]

The situation now inverted, Hieronimo's individualizing—that is, characterizing—revenge entails a kind of antagonism within his administrative function. Yet the roles of court official and father prove inalienable, the later prosecution of Pedringano as wayward servant related by Hieronimo back to the blood it is now his imperative to avenge:

> Deputy: Worthy Hieronimo, your office asks
> A care to punish such as do transgress.
> Hieronimo: So is't my duty to regard [Pedringano's] death
> Who when he lived deserved my dearest blood.
> (III.vi.11-14)[26]

His discovery of his son's body, which he at first mistakes, hints at a social or official jurisdiction of responsibility ("in my bower to lay the guilt on me," II.v.11), and this does not disappear even after his recognition of his hanged and stabbed son forces him to experience the bower as an intensely personal agony.

*   *   *

Hieronimo's exit from his home in II.v. to make this discovery coincides with his entrance onto the stage and the introduction of the revenge obligation. The early modern stage was increasingly used by its plays as a place beneath or between houses. *Othello*'s opening has Iago and Roderigo shouting up at Brabantio, who appears "*at a window.*" They are below and outside his house. Brabantio, like Hieronimo, is called from his bed to receive news of a crisis of the household (the "tupping" of his daughter):

> *Brabantio appears above at a window.*
> Brabantio: What is the reason of this terrible summons?
> What is the matter there?
> Roderigo: Signior, is all your family within?
> Iago: Are your doors locked?[27]

He reprimands Roderigo: "I have charged thee not to haunt about my doors" (I.i.95). Of course, *Othello* ends in the bedroom, with the entire apparatus of state confronting the play's protagonist at the scene of his brutal personal failure, a structural move successfully contracting the home implications of Othello's jealousy with the loss of administrative power. Ironically, Cassio indeed usurps Othello's place, and in the bedroom too, being pronounced the interim ruler of Cyprus in Desdemona's bedchamber. Says Lodovico to Othello: "You must forsake this room and go with us. / Your power and command are taken off / And Cassio rules in Cyprus" (V.ii.330-2). Ahead of *Hamlet*'s closet scene, the household predominates similarly in *The Spanish Tragedy*, but largely from without: the Watch wonder why they have been asked to patrol so close to Castile's house in III.iii; Bel-imperia—a parallel avenger—drops a letter to Hieronimo from her exile there, above the stage; and Hieronimo, suspicions aroused, decides on the course of "hearkening near the Duke of Castile's house / … / To listen more" (III.ii.22-52). Hieronimo's movement outwards from the house in II.v foreshadows his abdication of official "place" shortly afterwards, whilst locating the avenger outside the house. His rhetoric is full of a sense of homeless externality:

> Yet still tormented is my tortured soul
> With broken sighs and restless passions,
> That winged mount, and hovering in the air,
> Beat at the windows of the brightest heavens,
> Soliciting for justice and revenge;
> But they are placed in those empyreal heights,
> Where, counter-mured with walls of diamond,
> I find the place impregnable; and they
> Resist my woes, and give my words no way.
>
> (III.vii.10-18)

Hieronimo seeks a place to articulate complaint: "Where shall I run to breathe abroad my woes?" (1). The play moves to associate this space with that of the (lost) home, and revenge thus takes the form of a return or homecoming, with which it was associated in its classical forms (the *Odyssey*; the *Oresteia*). As revenger, Hieronimo takes up an ambivalent position to the space of the court. The house in particular becomes a suddenly impregnable zone in which Hieronimo vainly seeks the public space required for an effective protest. His reaction is to allegorise the *domos*. This is best exemplified by his extraordinary outburst in III.xi, when two Portuguese ask the way to the Duke of Castile and his son Lorenzo:

> 2 Portingale: Pray you, which is the way to my lord the duke's?
> Hieronimo: The next way from me.
> 1 Portingale: To his house, we mean.
> Hieronimo: O, hard by, 'tis yon house that you see.
> [...]
> Where murderers have built
> A habitation for their cursed souls,
> There, in a brazen cauldron, fixed by Jove
> In his fell wrath upon a sulphur flame,
> Yourselves shall find Lorenzo bathing him
> In boiling lead and blood of innocents.
> 1 Portingale: Ha, ha, ha!
> Hieronimo: Ha, ha, ha!
> Why, ha ha ha! Farewell, good, ha, ha, ha! *Exit*
>
> (4-31)

Hieronimo's rhetorical embellishments manically contend spatial associations from a sense of his own exteriority and peripherality. The Portuguese are travelling to an authoritative hub; their journey signals the growing political affiliations of the two courts. This affiliation is predicated upon Horatio's death. His father's heckling interruption is one that refuses to accept the production of space suggested by the Portuguese journey.

The house provides the absent *locus* of this contestation. Indeed, the revenge plot terrorizes the microcosm-macrocosm relationship between household and state.[28] Early modern economic thought in the West took its cue from the ordering (*nomos*) of the household (*oikos*). That is, the idea of economy, the allocation of the totality of material goods to satisfy material requirements, inhabits first of all a domestic idiom. Government itself could not quite be extricated from the household. Such a combination was essential to the highly influential Aristotelian notion of the state and the sovereign's role in it, although even at the beginning of his *Politics* Aristotle reminds us that to say the household and the state were the same, or the householder and king, would be to misconstrue the relationships. He varies the connections between terms:

> The state is by nature clearly prior to the family and to the individual, since the whole is of necessity prior to the part.

> The state is made up of households, [so] before speaking of the state we must speak of the management of the household.[29]

The apparent contradiction—as to ontological as well as chronological precedence—leads to the suggestion that the collocation or reconciliation of these units— household, village, state—could be enabled only by the jointing figure of father/husband/master/sovereign: "The sphere of economics is a monarchy."[30] Thus an apprehension of economy gestures towards an organization of person according to the distribution of things: economics—the administration of the household and estate—is according to Xenophon "the name of a branch of knowledge", based on the appearance of "an estate [as] *identical with the total of one's property.*"[31]

Household economy was a popular and fraught topic in English elite culture of the 1580s and 1590s. Sir Thomas Smith's version (1583) read the relationship as one of expansion: an overgrown family sent out its sons and daughters, in which process "a streete or village" was created, and from there thence to "a citie or a borough" and, finally, ruled by "that one and first father of them all", the nation or kingdom was constituted.[32] Jean Bodin's influential sixteenth century political economy, described in *The Six Bookes of the Commonwealth* (1576; 1606) was much more explicit:

> The family [...] is not only the true source and origin of the commonwealth, but also its principal constituent. Xenophon and Aristotle divorced economy or household management from police or disciplinary

power, without good reason [...] the well-ordered family is the true image of the commonwealth, and domestic comparable with sovereign authority.

For Bodin, the very idea of citizenship was anchored in a patriarchal and familial paradigm. This insistent emphasis on the deep connection between family and commonwealth finds incorporation in Bodin's iteration of a private/public dichotomy:

> Nothing could properly be regarded as public if there were nothing at all to distinguish it from what was private. Nothing can be thought of as shared in common, except by contrast with what is privately owned. If all citizens were kings there would be no king.[33]

This formulation at once glorified the king, whose mere existence continued to play a structuring role, whilst determining the private citizen's sovereignty. Versions of the household economy in the late sixteenth century tended more and more to curtail the monarch's power whilst maintaining its structuring force. In 1607, when Sir Edward Coke bluntly told James I (who conceived of this as potentially seditious) that "*Quod Rex non debet esse sub homine, sed sub Deo & Lege*", he appealed also to the "artificiall reason and judgement of law" as the superior framework for "causes which concern the life, or inheritance, or goods, or fortunes of [...] Subjects."[34] Thus archaic models of domestic economy, whilst providing the theoretical grounds of nationhood, were also turned against the absolutist position they implied, asserting the ultimate supremacy of private legal agency generally employed in the defence and regulation of the private property on which such agency was tacitly dependent. Thomas Kyd had himself almost certainly written an extant translation of Torquato Tasso's *The Householder's Philosophy*. "The care of a good householder is deuided into two things," wrote Kyd:

> That is his body and hys goods. In his personne he is to exercise three offices, viz. Of a *Father*, a *Husband*, and a *Maister*. In his goods two purposes are proposed, *Conservation* and *Encrease*.

His translation went on to describe how a master should administer his household, his wife, and his servants, but closed with an expression of doubt that "gouernments or dispensations of a house are deuided into foure partes, Kingly, Lordly, Ciuill and Priuate", for

> I cannot see yet how the gouernment of a ciuill and a priuate house do differ, unlesse he call his gouernment Ciuill that is busied and employed in

office for the honours of Commonwealth, and that man's priuate that is segregat and not called to office, so that wholy hee applies him to his housholde care.[35]

The confusion of civic and domestic duties is historically symptomatic and finds violent dramatic form in *The Spanish Tragedy*. Central to the play is Hieronimo's situation as the "King's man" and private citizen. His legalistic role would seem to suggest allegiance to the king whilst offering the possibility of legal recourse beyond his power or authority, in both ephemeral and procedural senses. His vengeance, however idiosyncratic in its appeal to what Andrea advances as "Pluto's court" (I.i.55), is enacted along these lines.

The murderers' nocturnal raid of Hieronimo's garden is at once an attack on his family and its space, testing the limits of the accord between family reunion and stately spectacle apparently offered us by the victorious return to court with the Portuguese prisoners in I.ii.110-197. Even at that early point in the play, the dual presence on stage of father and king to welcome back victors as sons and citizens hinted at discord. It is the king who orders the triumphant men to "march once more about these walls" (121), creating a concentric scene of power; and it is he who disposes beneficently of the Portuguese Balthazar's ransom. Yet Hieronimo also asserts a kind of paternalistic authority (116-120; 166-172), and there is a slight sense of competition engendered despite Hieronimo's deference. If Lorenzo's villainy enacts an incursion of state into home that threatens these terms' relationship, Hieronimo's reciprocation destroys it. He obliterates the sovereign's patriarchy by establishing a superior claim to a dutiful natural fatherhood:

> Speak, Portuguese, whose loss resembles mine:
> If thou canst weep upon my Balthazar,
> 'Tis like I wailed for my Horatio.
> And you, my lord, whose reconciled son
> Marched in a net, and thought himself unseen
> [...]
> How can you brook our play's catastrophe?
> (IV.iv.114-21)

Hieronimo's remarks to the three stunned men—the Duke of Castile, the King of Spain, and the Viceroy of Portugal—are made to them in their capacities as fathers, uncles and patriarchs, and yet also to them as rulers, reprimanding their oblivion to the injustice. That the sovereigns are apparently ignorant of the act (Horatio's murder) on which the coming union of their two states is predicated may have the effect of claiming a part of our sympathy for the royal patriarchs after Hieronimo's revenge, but the form of the play's villainy evidences a tacit complicity, whilst proposing his insurrectional protest as the only means of righting injustices engendered almost automatically in the construction of their government's authority.[36] The complete destruction of Hieronimo's family finds an echo in the end of the royal line ("...whose loss resembles mine"). The Spanish king's final lament—sure to appease the patriotism and *Schadenfreude* of those watching as much as aggravate worry about the English succession—constituted a fatalistic (and perhaps even essentially tragic) reversal of Smith's "one and first father of them all": "'I am the next, the nearest, last of all" (208). The household polity dissolves into "endless tragedy" (IV.v.48).

The category of the "domestic" has featured in classic essays on revenge tragedy, as has its negation, incest.[37] Reorienting these concerns towards the *economic* in the precise way detailed above allows the genre's concern with houses and jurisdictions to be rescued from the limited arena of the thematic and restored to its relationship with the totality of objects and movements employed by the stage. Indeed, given John Kerrigan's reference to an "economy of vengeance,"[38] we can understand the historical relationship of the revenge genre to space in terms of the economic. Revenge constitutes a transaction within a structure, but it also derives from and transforms this structure itself. It pertains to materials and, further, to the extent of ownership or administrative jurisdiction. That is, it is involved in the organization of objects within space: this partly explains the generic habit of using lost, stolen or switched props to manipulate its tortuous plots. Edward Said, in his influential reading of *Mansfield Park*, noted that Sir Thomas Bertram's return from his estate in Antigua occasions a symbolic coalescence of fictional economies—his foreign estate with his English country home—that figures the co-dependence of ideologically alienated historical spaces. In Austen, this is expressed as characterization. The return of Bertram's strict and efficient administrative persona compounds his character as much as it organizes his English estate, and the novel awaits the reconciling power of its protagonist, Fanny Price, whose personal development solves formal problems that relate as much to Mansfield Park's estate as to the eponymous narrative.[39] Hieronimo's organization of revenge is as efficient as his courtly occupation promises: his official capacity for enforcing judgement is abstracted into his righteous conviction as Horatio's father. While *The Spanish Tragedy* thus represents crises of legal and social participation in the commonwealth state via a fraught kind of role-playing, this exists concomitantly with a fundamentally spatial crisis.

* * *

The image of the theatre presented by its opponents and legislators was generally that of the disorderly house.[40] This perceived disorder extended easily to the seditious. If *The Spanish Tragedy* constituted the avenger at the limits of legalistic or empowered citizenship, Hieronimo's revenge, whatever its origins, necessitates and becomes a treason or sedition, indeed an assault on the very forms of governance. The ambivalence of Shakespearean representations of popular rebellion in the history plays is well-known, as is the influence of the 1607 Midland Rising on the production of *Coriolanus*.[41] John Stow's several relevant histories (1565; 1580; 1605) and Holinshed's *Chronicles* (1577; 1587), both of which were heavily exploited by Shakespeare and other dramatists, would have reflected, either indirectly, tacitly, or with an explicit contempt, a country riven with plebeian discontent.[42] Shakespeare's use of these sources in his history plays has been the subject of sustained interest, not least for his inheritance of the way in which these chronicles collocate the major rebellions (1381; 1450; 1549) into a generalized idiom of sedition that inflected the presentation on stage of famous leaders of rebellion.[43] The Senecan overtones of English revenge tragedy, combined with its typical situation in corrupt Mediterranean courts, confronts us with a pressing problem: how to understand the way in which popular action could find itself encoded in the apparently disinterested literary abstractions of elite writers.[44] Jean Howard and Paul Strohm have suggested that although the sixteenth century witnessed the fragmentation and deterioration of the Commons as "*communitas regni*", the idea "never disappears entirely but remains available both to social actors and to playwrights in moments of social stress or radical social transition or simply as an expression of utopian or nostalgic longing. It flows, as it were, underground, forming a constituent element of what may be called a public or social 'imaginary'".[45] Certainly *The Spanish Tragedy* fully explores the scenic possibilities of petition and protest on the edges of court, used to objectify the disenfranchisement of its gentleman protagonist. From its beginnings in English drama, revenge had been brought into close association with challenge to royal power. Not only does John Pykering's *Horestes* (1567), probably performed at the court Christmas revels, posit the Vice 'Revenge' as an essentially seditious instigator, but the earlier *Gorboduc*'s (1561) main anxiety seems to be expressed by the question: "Shall subjects dare with force / To work revenge upon their prince's fact?"[46] Eubulus, the king's secretary, answers that "no cause serves, whereby the subject may / Call to account the doings of his prince, / Much less in blood by sword to work revenge." (V.i.42-4) The very pronounced critical tendency to pose the moral problem of revenge in terms relating to the moral ambivalence of taking a justice that is solely God's ("Vindicta mihi ... !") has obscured the revenge play's representation of a subject's antagonistic relationship with government.[47]

London in the 1580s and 1590s was fraught with economic tensions and the threat of disorder or riot, as Brian Manning, among others, has shown.[48] Yet while one historiographical tendency implies widespread disorder in London,[49] partly influenced by a theory of riotous speech as appealing to and thus implying a range and extent of activity hidden from historical view and thus resistant to statistical or anecdotal analysis, another emphasizes the success of emergent bourgeois city institutions, particularly the livery companies, in regulating the capital's economic and social problems. This latter view points to the highly integrated nature of the city elites, and the vigour with which economic discipline was pursued as the century drew on.[50] In contradistinction to Norwich and other, more provincial, settlements, London had been curiously resistant to the threatening rebellions of 1549 and those since, largely because of the urgent, and in some cases pre-emptive, responses of its oligarchy to such disorder as did manifest itself. The brief period of martial law declared in July 1549 saw the Knight Marshall and Sheriff process to key points in the city and its gates, warning against rebellion and incitement to it.[51] The urgency of the London response may have related to a persisting fear deriving from the remembered Evil May Day riots of 1517, in which violence against foreign merchants coincided with dissent from government economic policy. Indeed, in London, elite commentators could tend to represent the broadly seditious as a malaise of economic idleness or inactivity.[52] This provides one of the key ways in which to ground the well-known antitheatricalist strain in Protestant pamphleteering after the 1570s. Fired in 1577 by John Northbrooke, the opening salvo in a sequence of eclectic antitheatricalist pamphlets all but personified the actor as the vice of idleness, suggesting that the player's "trade [was] such an ydle loitering, a practise to all mischiefe", and extolling magistrates to use the punitive power of recent legislation against masterless actors—as "rogues", "vagabonds" and "beggars"—to put a stop to the loitering.[53] Interestingly, it is within the apparently "feudal" idiom of the body politic that this emergent bourgeois emphasis on economic efficiency takes root, in its attacks on sedition and theatre alike. Edward VI's tutor, MP and Professor of Greek at Cambridge, John Cheke, described the "rebel" in *The Hurt of Sedition* (1549, reprinted 1569 and 1641) thus: "For while theyr minde chaungeth from obedience to unrulines, and turneth itselfe from honesty to wyldnes, [...] *theyr bodies go from laboure to idlenes.*" This probably reflected the immense influence on elite views of sedition exercised by Sir Thomas Elyot's *The book named the governor* (1531), which described idleness in the following way:

> It is not onely called idlenes wherein the body or minde cesseth from labour but specially idlenes is an omission of al honest exercise: the other may be better called a vacacion from seriouse businesse.[54]

For men like Cheke and Elyot, sedition was nothing other than exorbitance itself, deriving from overeating ("gluttinge of meates") or fever ("colde in the nightes"). Cheke's description of Kett's encampment as "lyke a byle in a body" emphasized the point.[55]

For the early modern poor, it was precisely those values of limitation central to the image of an orderly Commonwealth that often predicated economic or social disadvantage or distress. The healthy global body could frequently realize itself in a multitude of emaciated or bleeding ones. Elite authoritarians like Cheke read sedition broadly, as a kind of bodily or behavioural indiscipline as much as one of thought, just as the modern social historian since Scott is wont to do. The exceeding of bounds was integral to protest because its potentially violent aspect coincided with a destruction of the objective boundaries that provoked it. Since these objective boundaries extended in perception to bodily control—the body disciplined by its labour—agency can be located in any act of idleness by design, both by the historiographical standards of the present, and in accordance with the nightmares of early modern England's antagonized elites. Seditious idleness was infectious: in 1549, as John Stow related, an Essex bailiff was executed under the legal provision for the circulation of news or rumour concerning the rebellions.[56] The complaints of London city authorities to the crown concerning the effect of theatres and plays on economic productivity frequently mentioned the stage's propensity to distract apprentices as much as they emphasized the threat its gatherings posed to plague containment. During the remembered rebellions of 1549, the Court of Aldermen had attempted in May of that year to prevent the attendance at interludes by "servants and youths".[57] Clearly, anti-seditious action went hand-in-hand with the maintenance of economic normality. Indeed, the steady legislative restriction of the theatre's space, which accompanied its professionalisation and licensing, also offered a partly economic logic. See, for example, this memo of the Privy Council in 1600:

> Especiallie yt is forbidden that anie stage plaies shalbe plaied [...] in any Common Inn for publique assemblie in or neare about the Cititie [...]

> Forasmuche as these stage plaies, by the multitude of houses and Companie of players, haue been too frequent, not serung for recreacion but inviting and Callinge the people daily from there trad and worke to misspend there time.[58]

The social space of the theatre underpinned the relationship between sedition and drama explored by *The Spanish Tragedy*. The play's thorough testing of its own space, in which eavesdropping, disguise and subtle plots are in an abundance matched only by later revenge plays, merely lent generic form to the imagined "eavell practises of incontinenyce in greate Innes, havinge chambers and secrete places adioyninge to their open stagies and gallyries," and "vtteringe of popular busye and sedycious matters." From such fears issued demands that "no person shall suffer anie plays, enterludes, Comodyes, Tragidies, or shewes to be played or shewed *in his hous, yarde, or other place whereof he then shall have rule or power*."[59] The theatre always constituted misused space; a kind of improvised idleness.

In his startlingly entitled essay "Renaissance Tool Abuse and the Legal History of the Sudden", Luke Wilson records the precipitous misuse of tools for violent reciprocation in a partly Heideggerian meditation on "use-against-design". He notes that tools are "unique in being capable of misuse, of being used in a way that disregards the purpose for which they were fashioned but takes advantage of some feature of their design." Discussing various cases of tools used for sudden murder in early modern London, Wilson goes on to reflect that "it takes a certain cunning invention to envision uses for tools that don't coincide with the purposes manufactured into them." Crucially, he then notes how this misuse in law constitutes evidence of suddenness, and thus plays a formative role in the "rise of manslaughter as a category of homicide intermediate between (felony) murder […] and exculpable forms."[60] Revenge tragedy is peculiar in that the delay of the revenger seems to encompass the play itself as much as generate the "moral" problem: suddenness would be more forgiveable, simultaneity seemingly ideal. Yet the play issues from the delay. As Lorna Hutson notes, the delay also comprises, in *Hamlet* and *The Spanish Tragedy*, "a series of processes of enquiry into the circumstances of the wrong, seeking evidence […] and corroboration."'[61] Does not the proof legitimize the act, constituting the appearance of revenge as justice? Hieronimo's vengeance veers therefore between improvised suddenness (including the misuse not only of the court masque but of himself as jurisdictional arbiter in the court) and the considered forensic suspicion outlined by Hutson. Wilson also notes how the misuse of a tool in the act of rebellion articulates a statement of social identity beyond that signalled mnemonically by the tool itself.[62] Since Edward Thompson's overhaul of the traditional "spasmodic" view of rebellion, social historians have built on anthropological theory to understand how apparently immediate or spontaneous plebeian action improvised a symbolism for itself. In one representative essay, Andy Wood has employed Victor Turner's theory of "social drama" to understand how "rituals of popular rebellion drew upon manorial, parochial, hundredal and borough forms of organization", the essential point being that rebellion took the form of misuse of existing social structures whilst exceeding them.[63] Hieronimo's revenge is an improvisation using tools and capacities already available or occurrent. This is a truth best forced into the visibility of stage action by his use of a knife, given to him, in a darkly comic misapprehension of its various applications, that he might mend his pen and thus write a confession (he having bitten off his own tongue). Taking this proffered tool, he stabs the Duke of Castile and then himself. This can be seen as the play finding a way to depict more profound structural tendencies: its protagonist launches his seditious retribution by means of his own social position as play-giver and Verge official, reasserting a clear allegorical space in which the truth of his son's murder can be made plain.

Yet this climactic phenomenon of the transparently allegorical space, making its claims upon justice in the midst of violent revenge, is predicated on an initial obscurity. Hieronimo tricks his enemies into playing parts in a tragedy of "unknown languages" (IV.i.173) and fatal consequences. Thinking the space and its action "counterfeit", they act themselves to death with real daggers. While Hieronimo thereby assumes the power over space once the preserve of his enemy Lorenzo, it is also crucial to note that at the play's climax this power is rendered as a piece of theatre, the play-within-a-play. The problems of space and authority are thus translated by Hieronimo into an opaque theatre of foreign tongues whose participants are wholly subjected to the performance. Indeed, *The Spanish Tragedy* represented power as the ability to control a given space and people's movement within it; as the administration of a spatial logic opaque to the people who live it. An important and recurrent emphasis is that of the mistaken place; that is, a place or space held for other than it is. This is hinted at by the dramatic irony of Horatio's reference to the already compromised arbour as safe, moments before it is intruded upon by agents intent on violence (II.iv.5). Pedringano, the traitorous servant, provides two interesting examples of a misconstruction of his space, both provoked by Lorenzo, his master. Having been ordered by Lorenzo to kill fellow cut-throat Serberine (III.ii.83), Pedringano arrives at "Saint Luigi's Park" and finds it fit for an ambush: "this place is free from all suspect," declares Pedringano (15). This doubles up as a reference to Pedringano's own naivety about where he is, since the audience are privy to Lorenzo's plans to eliminate both his servants in a single stroke. Serberine does idly suspect: "How fit a place, if one were so disposed, / Methinks this corner is, to close with one" (26-7). His remark ponders the gulf between subjunctive space and lived: he dies in the possibility's realisation. As for the watch, sent by Lorenzo to catch Pedringano in the act, they find their own presence strange: "But we were never wont to watch and warn / So near the duke his brother's house before" (20-1). What Lorenzo successfully pulls off, therefore, is space of which only he and the audience have full knowledge, and in which neither are present. All the characters of III.iii are used by the mechanics of a space in the construction of which they can play no part. This sense is more powerfully replicated in III.vi, the well-known scene of Pedringano's execution. Reassured by a young page holding an empty box that Lorenzo has indeed sent the promised pardon, Pedringano is confident of the space as he banters with his executioners:

> Pedringano: But sir, then you think this shall be the place
> Where we shall satisfy you for this gear?
> Deputy: Ay, Pedringano.
> Pedringano: Now I think not so.
> (III.vi.32-3)

As the scene closes with Pedringano hanging from a rope, we find a highly dramatic depiction of what Henri Lefèbvre referred to "the violence of abstraction."[64] Useful knowledge in this play equals an understanding of the stage's pliability.

Hieronimo's production of *Soliman and Perseda*, his murderous play-within-the-play, lends this violent spatial abstraction a formal language in histrionics. Hieronimo's revenge by way of misuse surely resembles the kind of improvisation within limits that was every actor's skill. Lorna Hutson has referred to the implications of Hieronimo's conversation with his two enemies over this play:

> The kings, princes and aristocrats that were so unaware, or so wilfully despising of such 'common things' as Horatio's death, Hieronimo's cause, or the love of Bel-imperia for a commoner like Andrea, are so beguiled by their faith in tragedy's aristocratic credentials [to which Hieronimo panders when he promises them *'Tragedia cothurnata*, fitting kings, / Containing matter, and not common things', IV.i.60-1] that they enact upon one another [in the play-within-the-play] the just punishment for murder that it

was Hieronimo's task, as Spain's Knight Marshal, to dispense as every citizen's legal right.

This movement is summarized by Hutson as "a fantasy of classical dramatic plotting as retribution for class injustice."[65] Hutson here recognizes Kyd's complex presentation of the play-within-the-play as a problem of social injustice abstracted to a more specifically personal revenge in the form of the classically tragic. But she does not draw the startling conclusion that, since the play-within-the-play operates analogically to the whole, at least as far as Hieronimo is concerned, this latter, the play itself, is subject to the same formal twist. "The cruell aspectes of spoyle, breach of order, treason, ill-lucke, and overthrow of States and other persons", integral to the reception of revenge in England in the 1560s onwards, do not exist as incidents within a revenge plot that survives the implications of their dramatic representation, but instead structure the plot along historical lines.[66] The struggle of the revenge protagonist is one of remembrance of an injustice that must be righted; the presentation of such a struggle in and around the royal court is one which ties the early modern revenge tragedy ineluctably to a politics of (popular) protest and rebellion. This in no way opposes or contends with the aristocratic crises and associated anxieties of middling sort citizenship that played formative generic roles in *The Spanish Tragedy* and which have been gestured to above. Rather, the revenge play in this instance, even in the apparently abstracted zones of Seneca and Spain, administers all these problems at once and in relation to one another.

*   *   *

This article has attempted to raise the closely related problems of class identity, peripherality, participation, improvisation, violence, justice, law, protest and alienation, in order to posit a materialist understanding of generic origin. So long as the *act* which makes possible the representation of these categories remains eclipsed by them, however, such a project is doomed to failure. These categories as represented on the stage ultimately find their grounds in the space of the theatre and in the act that produced it. Hieronimo's dis-placing effect on the court relates very ambivalently to his own alienation. It is his *performance*, the disguise of his true self, more explicitly undertaken by later revenge heroes such as Middleton's Vindice, that not only renders an apparent interiority but permits him to function as moving force within the drama. Thus performance is signified generically as at once alienating and participatory.[67] This permits us a way of suggesting how the complex economy of revenge in *The Spanish Tragedy* relates to an economy of the stage, or rather to an economy of performance. While the position of the early modern actor within the society and culture of late Tudor and Stuart England was heavily restricted and circumscribed at a legal level, in ideological terms the actor signified dangerous excess. London's commercial playing companies had their origins in a deep authoritarian distrust of public performance which, particularly after 1572, manifested itself in legislative and bureaucratic records. At the start of that year Henrician legislation from the fifteenth century was ratified, requiring the punishment of "unlawful retainers" and "the giving of any livery of cloths or hat by a lord to other than his menials and lawyers."[68] That summer, *An Acte for the punishment of Vacabondes and for Relief of the Poore and Impotent* specified imprisonment and branding for

> all and everye persone and persones beynge whole and mightye in Body and able to labour, havinge not Land or Maister, nor using and lawfull Marchaundize Crafte or Mysterye whereby hee or shee might get his or her Lyvinge, and can gyve no reckninge howe he or shee dothe lawfully get his or her Lyvinge; & all Fencers Bearewardes Comon Players in Enterludes & Minstrels, not belonging to any Baron of this Realme or towardes any other honourable Personage of greater Degree [...] shalbee taken adjudged and deemed Rogues Vacaboundes and Sturdy Beggars.[69]

This document specified playing as pertaining to the scope of service to a nobleman, and this alone. It was ratified by a Jacobean act of 1604 which made similar corporal provision for "idle persons [...] usinge any subtile Crafte or unlawfull Games or Playes", but which in a parenthesis excluded those "Players of Enterludes belonginge to any Baron of this Realme [...] authorized to play under the Hande and Seale of Armes of such Baron".[70] Legislatively, playing was not a lawful occupation in itself. In the royal patent the shareholder-players were still decisively referred to as "our Servauntes", and one of the Marprelate tracts in 1589 wryly described players as "plaine rogues (saue onely for their liueries)".[71] An early letter from the Privy Council to the Lord Mayor of London, presumably in response to that administration's fundamental antitheatricalism, specified that the companies of Warwicke, Leicester, Essex and the Children of Paul's be allowed to put on performances "by reason that the companies aforenamed are appointed to playe this tyme of Christmas before her Majestie."[72] Therefore, the legislative and monarchical support for playing in London existed in a specific sense. The actor was a servant, and playing an extension of the great household. A large proportion of extant actors' wills from the time occlude their professional status; Richard Tarleton, the famous Vice of the Queen's Men, described himself not as an actor but as "one of the Groomes of the Queenes maiesties chamber".[73] Since the regular changing of liveries comprised the very occupation of actor, it is clear that the theatre's fraught relationship with economic regulation and law had origins both in an incomprehension born of socio-economic change and the "inherent" qualities of theatre itself. The latter permitted the theatre to exert a social incongruity during performance, but were themselves fashioned socially.

In the late 1580s, when *The Spanish Tragedy* was probably written, and first staged to a rapture that would develop into long-lasting popularity, some of the later restrictions on space governing the performance of late sixteenth and seventeenth century plays had not yet been implemented. Playing in inns was still permitted, for example. The shareholder enterprises of the later acting companies were, at the time of Kyd's writing and the early performances of *The Spanish Tragedy*, still in their infancy. Yet the paradoxical work of the players can be perceived even in the early days of the public theatres. These were men whose social place was guaranteed only by positions of patronised service to a noble lord and performance at court, yet whose ability to live was in great part governed by the commercial enterprise of the theatre, the appeal of their plays, and touring performances away from London out of season or at times of plague. While Andrew Gurr cannot find evidence of what prompted the creation of a consistent Jacobean patronage in 1603, therefore, the origins of this preference can be found in earlier attitudes manifested in theatre legislation, and "Christmas revels" frequently played an important part in determining which companies would receive such favour.[74] If the Vagrancy Act spelled out the law tautologically for those "persons [...] *misordering themselves* contrary to the purport of this present Acte of Parliament", a crucial worry underpinning much later antitheatricalism was that plays encouraged the *mis-spending* of time.[75] Acting was not an occupation that addressed itself to any economic rationale, and in some senses constituted an abandonment of the servile status which enabled it legally. One of the problems was that the legislation of playing confronted the end to all legislation, addressing the space of performance in which the legalistic power of language was dissolved.

"The players of playes [...] are a very superfluous sort of men, and of such facultie as the lawes haue disalowed" wrote Lord Mayor Woodroffe in 1580.[76] We can take the term "superfluity" to mean here both the seeming that characterized the actor's work and the non-productive relation of this work to an increasingly rationalized and centralized legal and material economy. Let us reconsider the word "jurisdiction" given Hieronimo's role as Knight Marshal and avenger. Its etymology implies an area in which law is spoken and functions performatively. Theatrical language resists the functional; by the standards of the time it was beyond the law in an almost constitutive sense. The false antithetical relationship between the plain sight and speech of law and the opaque practices and language of the theatre was even implied by George Puttenham in his book *The Arte of Englishe Poesie* (1589), written almost exactly contemporaneously to *The Spanish Tragedy*: "As figures [of speech] be the instruments of ornament [...] so be they also in a sorte abuses or rather trespasses in speech, because they passe the ordinary limits of common vtterance [...] drawing [the mind] from plainnesse and simplicitie to a certaine doublenesse." Puttenham reflected on the Areopagite judges, who forbade "all manner of figuratiue speaches [...,] saying that to allow such manner of forraine & coulored talke [were] to make the iudges affectioned [...] [for] the straite and vpright mind of a Iudge is the very rule of justice till it be peruerted by affection." [77] (Here he echoed Elyot, who insisted that "in vertue may be nothing [...] counterfayte [but] onely the image of veritie called simplicitie."[78]) The revenge of the affected judge Hieronimo—a fundamentally figurative set of actions as *The Spanish Tragedy* presents it—is *sub judice* but not quite *ex lege*. It takes place within a certain legal space, but its arbiter is very much outside both the law and the space that he may nevertheless organize. The abstraction of the actor's social superfluity into the quasi-individualist assertions of the avenger should also condition our understanding of the "interiority" so famously associated with early modern avengers, beginning with Hieronimo's affectedness. Interiority was here dependent on a superfluity that at the time corresponded to an economic idleness or excess, and which was dissolved in the violence the preparation of which gave it form.

If it was the monarch's body that sustained the image of a healthy commonwealth, it was the actor's body that guaranteed dramatic representation at this level. All thematic or narrative problems cannot be fully understood from a historical perspective without understanding the status of the bodies that lent them form in performance. The protagonist of Bertolt Brecht's *Der gute Mensch von Sezuan*, Shen The, faced with the irresolvable problem posed to her altruism by economic necessity, creates a ruthless double (her 'cousin') who plays the role of troubleshooting capitalist entrepreneur. Brecht embodies the social contradiction via the simple trick of a double-disguise, mercilessly lampooning the Janus-headed morals demanded by capitalism by exploiting the moral duplicity implied by dramatic representation. In attempting to recuperate the actor's agency from the text of the revenge play, we are faced with a comparable but distinct problematic of embodiment. Hieronimo vacillates between the sense of self lent him by grief and the social antagonism to which it provokes him. In III.xiii, Hieronimo is confronted by another grieving father, Don Bazulto, amongst the gaggle of petitioners he receives almost customarily as a former magistrate, the position he held "before [his] marshalship" (57). Tearing up the petitions of the other plaintiffs, he runs manically off- and onstage, chased comically by the citizen petitioners, who cede the dramatic space of Commons protest in which they were introduced. Moving from a determination to "bear a face of gravity" to this hysteria, Hieronimo proclaims to Bazulto that "thou art the lively image of my grief: / Within thy face my sorrows I may see." (162-3) For a moment Bazulto is proposed as an actor of Hieronimo, his person merely mimetic: "The lively portrait of my dying self" (85). The "face of gravity" with which Hieronimo equated official duty morphs into the mimetic façade of Bazulto's stoic grief. At the same moment that Hieronimo abandons his official duties for his semi-hysterical surge in and out of "the place", his double constructed the melancholic avenger on the stage in silence. This doubling of Hieronimo, at the moment when his riotous grief confronts the solemn duties of state and the decorum of the grieving stoic, is the juncture at which the problems of participation and individuality central to revenge tragedy should be situated. As has been suggested, Hieronimo's revenge is provoked by an intrusion of central diplomatic motives on locally devolved governance: "The devastatingly heedless destruction of good local governance by global political ambition is painfully and effectively expressed in Kyd's skilful juxtaposition of Hieronimo's wild destruction of his plaintiff's evidences with the smug unawareness of a court rapt in the thought of the imperial consequences of diplomatic triumph", writes Hutson acutely.[79] Hieronimo's participation and alienation are indivisible yet irreconcilable, each empowering yet disowning the other. The former's madness seems to demand and find rest in the restraint of quiet grief. His solitude and introspection create senses of impotence and indignity that demand violent action. The melancholic avenger is not at variance with his bloodthirsty counterpart. He is his apologist. Thus the actor performed vacillation.

Yet we might also describe a vacillation of and in performance. The abstraction of one to the other is permitted by the competition of formal gestural rhetoric and the riot of superfluity and excess attaching to the person, as social object within the scope of an impossible occupation, that enacted its techniques. Genre encodes lived historical experience: later revenge plays would more fully exploit the homologous relationship implied between the avenger's rhythm of hesitation and action and the actor's rhythm of rehearsal and performance. The revenge tragedy's so-called *meta-theatre* did not suggest the theatricality of all social life so much as construct the actor's segregation from it via an emphasis on the techniques of his occupation. The conceit of *Theatrum mundi* in fact proposed its negation as the actual. As Sarah Beckwith writes:

> The localization and professionalization of theatre under forms of profit, patronage, and privatization represent a drastic reduction of actors in sheer numerical numbers and [...] a drastic reduction in the dissemination of role-playing, festivity, and ceremony in the structures of everyday life [...] [P]laying tends to shift indoors.[80]

The avenger's search for a space of representation coincided with his actor's. For this reason, the trespass and dissolution of bounds central to revenge in early modern revenge plays took forms at once of dangerous sedition and histrionic self-expression. The agency of the early modern actor ultimately entailed a kind of self-negation: the applause was received by another. Witness the early modern avenger's suicidal deference to his own theatrical achievement:

> And princes, now behold Hieronimo,
> Author and actor in this tragedy,
> Bearing his latest fortune in his fist:
> And will as resolute conclude his part
> As any of the actors gone before.
> And, gentles, thus I end my play:
> Urge no more words: I have no more to say.
> *He runs to hang himself.*
> (IV.iv.146-52)

If "a work is only real in the form of a genre", then the converse is equally true: the revenge tragedy no longer exists.[81]

Notes

[*] I would like to thank John Kerrigan and Andy Wood for reading and commenting in detail on earlier drafts of this article.
[1] Francis Bacon, "Of Revenge", in *The Essays or Counsels, Civill and Morall*, ed. Michael Kiernan (Oxford: Clarendon, 1985, repr. 2000), 16.
[2] The Brecht-Lukács exchange concerning the social position of art has been presented in the collection *Aesthetics and Politics* (London: NLB, 1977); Theodor W. Adorno, *Ästhetische Theorie*, in *Gesammelte Schriften*, eds. Gretel Adorno and Rolf Tiedemann, 19 vols. (Frankfurt A.M.: Suhrkamp, 1973), 7: 19.

[3] Henri Lefèbvre, *L'idéologie structuraliste* (Paris: Seuil, 1975), 174-5, where he addresses the dialectical emphasis on movement within structure. This fundamental interest can be found iterated elsewhere in Lefèbvre's thought. See, for example, Henri Lefèbvre, *Rhythmanalysis: Space, Time and Everyday Life*, trans. Stuart Elden and Gerald Moore (London: Continuum, 2004), 31: "Overlooking the garden, the differences between habitual [...] rhythms blur; they seem to disappear into a sculptural immobility [...] To your eyes, they situate themselves in a permanence, in a spatial simultaneity, in a coexistence. But look harder and longer. This simultaneity, up to a point, is only apparent: a surface, a spectacle"; Henri Lefèbvre, *The Production of Space*, trans. Donald Nicholson-Smith (Oxford: Blackwell, 2000), 391: "The more carefully one considers space [...] the more clearly one becomes aware of conflicts at work within it." Herein lies the interpretively strategic, mediating role that the idea of genre is capable of fulfilling, as Fredric Jameson notes. Fredric Jameson, *The Political Unconscious: Narrative as a Socially Symbolic Act* (London: Routledge, 1983, repr. 2008), 92.
[4] M. M. Bakhtin and P. N. Medvedev, *The Formal Method in Literary Scholarship*, trans. Albert J. Wehrle (Cambridge, Mass.: Harvard University Press, 1985), 29: "Every literary phenomenon [...] is simultaneously determined from without [...] and from within. From within it is determined by literature itself, and from without by other spheres of social life."
[5] Lefèbvre, *Production of Space*, 401; 404.
[6] Ibid., 320.
[7] Slavoj Žižek, "Hegel's 'Logic of Essence' as a Theory of Ideology", in *The Žižek Reader*, eds. Elizabeth Wright and Edmund Wright (Oxford: Blackwell, 1999), 233.
[8] Andrew Gurr, *Playgoing in Shakespeare's London* (Cambridge: Cambridge University Press, 1987), 139; see Lukas Erne, *Beyond the Spanish Tragedy: A Study of the Works of Thomas Kyd* (Manchester: Manchester University Press, 2001) on causality, and for a good introduction to Kyd and his work.
[9] Thomas Kyd, *The Spanish Tragedy*, ed. J. R. Mulryne (London: A&C Black, 1989, repr. 2003). All reference is to this edition.
[10] Robert Weimann argued that the inner stage could be differentiated from the downstage area (where Hieronimo may have stood), in order to create effects of fluctuating representative authority, with the inner stage the site of what medieval producers referred to as the *locus*. See Robert Weimann, *Shakespeare and the Popular Tradition in the Theater: Studies in the Social Dimension of Dramatic Form and Function* (Baltimore: Johns Hopkins University Press, 1978), 208-15. Compare the opening scene of Thomas Middleton's *The Revenger's Tragedy* (1607).
[11] Fredson Thayer Bowers, *Elizabethan Revenge Tragedy 1587-1642* (Gloucester, Mass.: Peter Smith, 1959), 62.
[12] Slavoj Žižek, *Violence* (London: Profile, 2008), 9; and *passim*.
[13] Walter Benjamin, "Zur Kritik der Gewalt", in *Gesammelte Schriften*, eds. Rolf Tiedemann and Hermann Schweppenhäuser, 7 vols. (Frankfurt a. M.: Suhrkamp, 1977), 2/i:179-203; 190: "All violence as a means either determines law or is itself

determined by it. If it abrogates either of these predicates, it itself disposes with every legitimacy [*Geltung*]."

[14] Andy Wood, *Riot, Rebellion, and Popular Politics in early modern England* (Basingstoke: Palgrave, 2002), 24-38; 46. Lawrence Stone noted that the success of the expanding Tudor government in this respect also contributed to the sharp rise in the litigiousness of the nobility. Lawrence Stone, *The Crisis of the Aristocracy, 1558-1661* (Oxford: Clarendon, 1965), 240-70; esp. 241: "All the pride, obstinacy and passion [of the English nobility] that hitherto had found expression in direct physical action was now transferred to the dusty processes of law."

[15] Anthony Fletcher and Diarmaid MacCulloch, *Tudor Rebellions* (5th ed. Harlow: Pearson and Longman, 2004), 123-38. Cf. Andy Wood, *The 1549 Rebellions and the Making of Early Modern England* (Cambridge: Cambridge University Press, 1997), Ch. 5.

[16] Steve Hindle, *The State and Social Change in Early Modern England, c.1550-1640* (Basingstoke: Macmillan, 2000), Ch. 3.

[17] Derek Sayer, "A Notable Administration: English State Formation and the Rise of Capitalism", *The American Journal of Sociology* 97: 5 (March, 1992): 1382-1415, at 1406-7.

[18] See n.61.

[19] This is also the approximate area from which Shakespeare's Henry V banishes Falstaff at the end of *2 Henry IV*. William Shakespeare, *King Henry IV, Part 2*, ed. A. R. Humphreys, *The Arden Shakespeare Complete Works*, ed. Richard Proudfoot, Anne Thompson and David Scott Kastan (London: Arden, 2005), v.v.63-5. I owe thanks to Doug Eskew for allowing me to read his forthcoming essay on Shakespeare's *King Lear*, which reflects on later developments in the judicial life of the Marshalsea Court and comparable problems of sovereignty and exclusion within early modern drama.

[20] Douglas G. Greene, "The Court of the Marshalsea in Late Tudor and Stuart England," *The American Journal of Legal History* 20:4 (Oct., 1976): 267-81, 268. My description makes heavy use of this and the following important articles: Marjorie M. McIntosh, "Immediate Royal Justice: The Marshalsea Court in Havering, 1358," *Speculum* 54:4 (Oct. 1979): 727-733; W. R. Jones, "The Court of the Verge: The Jurisdiction of the Steward and Marshal of the Household in Later Medieval England," *Journal of British Studies* 10:1 (Nov. 1970): 1-29. My thanks to Janka Rodziewicz, who directed me to a further source that both summarizes the court's earlier function and also provides some examples: J. H. Johnson, "The King's Wardrobe and Household", in *The English Government at Work: 1327-1336*, ed. James F. Willard and William A. Morris, 3 vols. (Cambridge, Mass.: Medieval Academy of America, 1940), 1: 243-5.

[21] McIntosh, "Immediate Royal Justice", 727ff.

[22] William Holdsworth, *A History of English Law*, ed. A. L. Goodhart and H. G. Hanbury, 16 vols. (London: Methuen, 1936-72), 1: 219. See n.51 for an anecdotal example of the Knight Marshall's symbolic centrality.

[23] Jones, "The Court of the Verge," 29.

[24] Unfortunately, the records for the relevant years of the Marshalsea Court are not extant: *Records of the Exchequer*, E37. Some examples from 1316 to 1359 exist, for which see Johnson, "The King's Wardrobe", and four rolls from the Court of the Verge from 1611. For a defence of the court's jurisdiction over trespass outside that defined strictly as the royal household, deriving from the early seventeenth century, see "Reasons that the Court of Marshalsy may be fittly enabled in certain Cases to hold plea of all Manner of Trespasses, as well upon the Case as others, albeit, neither Party be of the King's Household", ed. Thomas Hearne, *A Collection of Curious Discourses written by Eminent Antiquaries upon Several Heads in our English Antiquities*, 2 vols. (London, 1771), 2: 146: "This court is more necessary for the publick weale of this state than any inferiour court, for herein the resiants within the verge have a most speedy triall for their causes in foure court days."

[25] Anon. (Thomas Kyd?), *The First Part of Ieronimo*, in *The Works of Thomas Kyd*, ed. Frederick S. Boas (Oxford: Clarendon, 1955), I.i.99-104.

[26] *Deserved* refers, ironically, to Pedringano's "service" to Horatio.

[27] William Shakespeare, ed. E. A. J. Honigmann, *Othello*, Arden Shakespeare Complete Works, I.i.81-4.

[28] For a concise summary of the household's importance throughout early modern society, both in theory and practice, see Garthine Walker, *Crime, Gender and Social Order in Early Modern England* (Cambridge: Cambridge University Press, 2003), 9-13.

[29] Aristotle, *Politics*, in *The Complete Works of Aristotle*, ed. and trans. Jonathan Barnes, 2 vols. (London: Princeton University Press, 1984), 2: Book I, 1986-8.

[30] Aristotle, *Economics*, Ibid., 2: Book I, 2130. Regarding his conclusions as to this embodied role, cf. *Politics*, Book I, §12-13, 1998-9, for example: "Of household management we have seen that there are three parts – one is the rule of a master over slaves [...] another of father, and the third of husband."

[31] Xenophon, *Oeconomicus*, in *Xenophon*, ed. and trans. E. C. Marchant, 7 vols. (London: William Heinemann, 1968), 4: VI, 409, my emphases.

[32] Thomas Smith, *De Republica Anglorum*, ed. Mary Dewar (Cambridge: Cambridge University Press, 1982), Book I, xii., 59.

[33] Jean Bodin, *The Six Books of the Commonwealth*, ed. and trans. M. J. Tooley (Oxford: Basil Blackwell, 1967), 6; 8. Cf. Karl Marx and Friedrich Engels, *Das Kapital: Kritik der politischen Ökonomie: Band I*, in *Werke*, 44 vols (Berlin: Dietz Verlag, 1962) 23: 98, n.21, for this idea within historical materialism.

[34] Edward Coke, *The Twelfth Part of the Reports of Sir Edward Coke*, in *The Struggle for Sovereignty: Seventeenth Century English Political Tracts*, ed. Joyce Lee Malcolm (Indianapolis: Liberty Fund, 1999), 18.

[35] Torquato Tasso, trans. Thomas Kyd?, *The Housholders Philosophie*, in *Works of Thomas Kyd*, ed. Boas, 261; 283-4.

[36] Lefèbvre notes that violence is always implicit in the state's production of space. *Production of Space*, 280: "Every state is born of violence, and [...] state power endures only by virtue of violence directed towards a space".

[37] In particular, see Leo Salingar's essay, "*The Changeling* and the Drama of Domestic Life", in *Dramatic Form in Shakespeare and the Jacobeans: Essays* (Cambridge: Cambridge University Press, 1986), 222-235.
[38] John Kerrigan, *Revenge Tragedy: Aeschylus to Armageddon* (Oxford: Clarendon, 1996), 7.
[39] Edward Said, *Culture and Imperialism* (London: Vintage, 1993), 102-14.
[40] See, for example, the letter of early 1592 from the Lord Mayor to the Archbishop of Canterbury, which referred to "the daily and disorderlie exercise of a number of players & playeng houses erected within this Citie." Chambers, *ES*, 4: 307. For further evidence and discussion of the connections between the theatre and delinquency and riot see, for example, Charles Whitney, "Usually in the Werking Daies": Playgoing Journeymen, Apprentices, and Servants in Guild Records, 1582-92", *Shakespeare Quarterly* 50:4 (Winter, 1999), 433-458.
[41] See Richard Helgerson, *Forms of Nationhood: The Elizabethan Writing of England* (Chicago: University of Chicago Press, 1992), 195-245, in which *2 Henry VI* is interpreted as the last history play in which a politically organized Commons is to be found. On *Coriolanus*, see Steve Hindle, "Imagining Insurrection in Seventeenth-Century England: Representations of the Midland Rising of 1607", *History Workshop Journal* 66:1 (2008): 21-61. Possibly the single best source on such subjects is Annabel Patterson, *Shakespeare and the Popular Voice* (Oxford: Basil Blackwell, 1989).
[42] See, for example, Barrett L. Beer, "John Stow and Tudor Rebellions, 1549-1569", *Journal of British Studies*, 27:4 (Oct., 1988): 352-374.
[43] See Patterson, *Popular Voice*, 38-9.
[44] Andy Wood discusses the interdependence of theories or proclamations of Commonwealth stability and the pervasive fear of sedition. *Riot, Rebellion*, 24-32.
[45] Jean E. Howard and Paul Strohm, "The Imaginary 'Commons'", *Journal of Medieval and Early Modern Studies* 37:3 (Autumn, 2007): 549-577, at 551.
[46] Thomas Norton and Thomas Sackville, *Gorboduc*, in *Minor Elizabethan Tragedies*, ed. T. W. Craik (London: J. M. Dent, 1974), V.i.17-8. All further reference is to this edition. *Gorboduc* may have a claim over *Horestes* to being the first English play of blood.
[47] The modern scholarly tendency becomes pronounced after Lily B. Campbell's seminal essay, "Theories of Revenge in Renaissance England," *MP* 28 (1931): 281-86.
[48] Brian Manning, *Village Revolts: Social Protest and Popular Disturbances in England, 1509-1640* (Oxford: Clarendon, 1988), 207-8.
[49] See James C. Scott, *Domination and the Arts of Resistance: Hidden Transcripts* (London: Yale University Press, 1990), which is the seminal example.
[50] Ian W. Archer, *The Pursuit of Stability: Social Relations in Elizabethan London* (Cambridge: Cambridge University Press 1991), esp. 33-57; 100-140; 257-60.
[51] Charles Wriothesley, *A Chronicle of England during the Reigns of the Tudors, from AD 1485 to 1559*, ed. William Douglas Hamilton, 2 vols. (New York: Johnson Reprint, 1965), 2: 15-16. Note that the implementation of martial law in resistance to the possibility of rebellion at this time in effect expanded the

authority of the Marshal's court, subsuming other jurisdictions in an assertion of absolute royal dominion. See Barrett L. Beer, *Rebellion and Riot: Popular Disorder in England during the Reign of Edward VI* (Kent State University Press, 1982), 164-181, on the response of London to the disturbances of 1549.
[52] Beer, *Rebellion and Riot*, 164-5.
[53] John Northbrooke, *A Treatise against Dicing, Dancing, Plays, and Interludes, with other idle pastimes* (London: Shakespeare Society, 1843), 98. On the timidity of the magistrates, see 12-13.
[54] Thomas Elyot, *The Book named the Governor* (Menston: Scolar Press, 1970), fol. 95.
[55] John Cheke, *The Hurt of Sedition* (Menston: Scolar, 1971, facsimile), fol. E.i, my emphasis; fol. B.ii.
[56] John Stow, *A Survey of London, reprinted from the text of 1603*, ed. Charles Lethbridge Kingsford, 2 vols. (Oxford: Clarendon, 1908 repr. 1971), 1: 144.
[57] CLRO, Rep. 12 (1), fol. 91v., cited in Beer, *Rebellion and Riot*, 168.
[58] *Acts of the Privy Council of England*, xxx. 395; repr. *Malone Society: Collections* (Oxford: Oxford University Press for the Malone Society, 1907-Present), 1: 80-3, hereafter "*MSC*"; E. K. Chambers, *The Elizabethan Stage* 4 vols. (Oxford: Clarendon, 1923), 4: 329-31, hereafter "*ES*".
[59] 1574, Dec. 6. Act of Common Council of London, repr. *MSC*, 1: 175; Chambers, *ES*, 4: 273-6. My emphasis. See Chambers, *ES*, 3: 90-8, for a discussion of stage usage.
[60] Luke Wilson, "Renaissance Tool Abuse and the Legal History of the Sudden", in *Literature, Politics and Law in Renaissance* England, ed. Erica Sheen and Lorna Hutson (Basingstoke: Palgrave Macmillan, 2005), 121-45; 122; 125.
[61] Lorna Hutson, *The Invention of Suspicion: Law and Mimesis in Shakespeare and Renaissance Drama* (Oxford: Oxford University Press, 2007), 269.
[62] Wilson, 133.
[63] Andy Wood, "Collective Violence, Social Drama and Rituals of Rebellion in Late Medieval and Early Modern England", in Stuart Carroll, ed., *Cultures of Violence: Interpersonal Violence in Historical Perspective* (Basingstoke: Palgrave Macmillan, 2007), 99-116.
[64] Lefèbvre, *Production of Space*, 281.
[65] Hutson, *Invention of Suspicion*, 285-6.
[66] William Painter, *The Palace of Pleasure; Elizabethan Versions of Italian and French novels from Boccaccio, Bandello, Cinthio, Straparola, Queen Margaret of Navarre, and others*, ed. Joseph Jacobs, 3 vols. (London: D. Nutt, 1890), 1: 5.
[67] See György Lukács, *Die Theorie des Romans: Ein geschichtsphilosophischer Versuch über die Formen der großen Epik* (Berlin: Paul Cassirer, 1920), 29: "Loneliness is […] dramatically paradoxical: it is the actual essence of the tragic, since, having realized itself in fate, the soul may have brothers among the stars, but no earthly companion. Yet the dramatic mode of expression–the dialogue– presupposes, in order to remain many-voiced, truly dialogical, and dramatic, a high degree of communality between these lonely ones."
[68] Chambers, *ES*, 4: 268.

[69] Ibid., 270.

[70] 1604, July 7 *An Acte for the Continuance and Explanation of the Statute made in the 39 yeere of the Raigne of our late Queene Elizabeth, intituled An Acte for Punishmente of Rogues, Vagabondes and Sturdie Beggars* (*I Jac. I.* c. 7), repr. Chambers, *ES*, 4: 336-7.

[71] *P. R. I Jac. I, pars 2, membr. 4*, *MSC*, 1: 264; Chambers, *ES*, 4: 208; *Theses Martinianae, or Martin Junior*, sig. D. ij (Martinist), repr. Chambers, *ES*, 4: 230.

[72] Chambers, *ES*, 4: 278.

[73] E. A. J. Honigmann and Susan Brock, ed., *Playhouse Wills 1558-1642: An Edition of Wills by Shakespeare and his Contemporaries in the London Theatre* (Manchester: Manchester University Press, 1993), "1588 Sept. 3 Richard Tarlton", 57.

[74] Andrew Gurr, *The Shakespearian Playing Companies* (Oxford: Clarendon, 1996), 111.

[75] Chambers, *ES*, 4: 269.

[76] 1580, April 12. Sir Nicholas Woodroffe, Lord Mayor, to Sir Thomas Bromley, Lord Chancellor, repr. *MSC*, 1: 46; Chambers, *ES*, 4: 279.

[77] George Puttenham, *The Arte of Englishe Poesie*, ed. Gladys Doidge Willcock and Alice Walker (Cambridge: Cambridge University Press, 1936), 154-5. (The Areopagus was the hill where the Athenian Court of Appeal functioned; it is where Orestes was tried.) Annabel Patterson also finds Puttenham's lexicon highly receptive to anxiety concerning seditious transgression: *Popular Voice*, 39-40. See Puttenham's discussion of Cade, Kett and Straw in the context of the "ambiguous", *Englishe Poesie*, 260-1.

[78] Elyot, *The Governor*, fol. 182.

[79] Hutson, *Invention*, 285.

[80] Sarah Beckwith, *Signifying God: Social Relation and Symbolic Act in the York Corpus Christi Plays* (Chicago: University of Chicago Press, 2001), 132-3. Compare James Simpson's recent work, which sees a correlation between the homogenisation of legal and administrative forms and the narrowing of literary practice. James Simpson, *Reform and Cultural Revolution (The Oxford English Literary History, Volume 2. 1350-1547)* (Oxford: Oxford University Press, 2002).

[81] Bakhtin and Medvedev, *Formal Method*, 129. Cf. Mikhail Bakhtin, "Response to a Question from *Novy Mir*", in *Speech Genres and Other Late Essays*, trans. Vern W. McGee (Austin, TX: University of Texas Press 1986), 4: "The work cannot live in future centuries without having somehow absorbed past centuries as well."

ALEHOUSES, POPULAR POLITICS AND PLEBEIAN AGENCY IN EARLY MODERN ENGLAND

MARK HAILWOOD

> There is a greate complaint of Bastardies, sheep-stealers, hedgbreakers, quarrellers and the like. Would you be eased of these diseases? Believe it, they gather in Alehouses as humers doe into ye stomack. Doe you but drive them thence with som strong Physick, and you heale our towne and Villages of infinite distempers.
> — *John Newman, Minister of Upavon, Wiltshire, to the Justices of the Peace* (1648)[1]

To seventeenth-century Englishmen there was no doubt that alehouses were intimately connected to the broader problems that confronted their towns and villages; linked, even, to malignancy in the body politic itself. It is perhaps unsurprising then that historians of the period have come to see drinking houses as a valuable focus of study, perceiving their potential to "mirror nearly all the tensions of their time".[2] The pioneer of research into the English alehouse, Peter Clark, believed that a history of the alehouse could "illuminate at least some of the complex economic, social and political changes affecting pre-modern England".[3] Similarly, Keith Wrightson argued that "by focusing upon the controversy which raged over the role of the alehouse in late-Elizabethan and early-Stuart England, one may discern the shifts in attitudes and social relationships which accompanied the making of the rural society of the later seventeenth and eighteenth centuries".[4] More recently, the merit of paying scholarly attention to drinking houses as a means of shedding light on wider issues has been reinforced by a "spatial turn" in the humanities. As *physical* sites where "interactions of heterogeneous guests in confined spaces created dynamic and volatile situations", it has been suggested that drinking houses "may well provide the single most rewarding access points for the studies of local communities". They have also been conceived of as important *symbolic* spaces, at the centre of contested political, social and cultural "meta-discourses". This focus on drinking houses as "space" has increased confidence in the view that they can be "interpreted as microcosms of early modern society, allowing the scrutiny of human relations and institutional cultures within suitably condensed physical settings".[5]

These historiographical developments have established the early modern English alehouse as a particularly appealing "space" to study for historians interested in aspects of social relations. The problem, however, is that this consensus that peering through the alehouse window affords us insight into the socio-political constitution of early modern society stands in contrast to the diversity of views that historians have glimpsed through it. This is especially true with regard to the conclusions drawn about popular politics and plebeian agency. The alehouse has been seen by some as the stronghold of a subversive "alternative society" or the location of a "hidden transcript" of subordinates. Others have argued that it served the opposite function, playing a key role in the establishment of the "cultural hegemony of the parochial elite" or acting as a "site of surveillance" in the service of civic governors. Another perspective has associated the alehouse with a less conflictual political culture, identifying it as a potential facilitator of an emerging "public sphere". Considered individually, these claims reflect convincing research. Yet, when taken together, the result is a contradictory and seemingly incompatible historiography. This essay proposes, therefore, that the relationship between the alehouse, popular politics and plebeian agency is in particular need of reconceptualisation.

This task will be undertaken in four sections: an opening section will review existing characterisations of popular politics and plebeian agency that have emerged from a focus on alehouses. The second and third sections will draw on archival research to present two case studies that will look to probe the relative strengths and weaknesses of the interpretations laid out in section one: section two will focus on seditious speech in later-Stuart alehouses; and section three on alehouse licensing in Jacobean Somerset. Subsequently, the concluding section will suggest a more appropriate mode of conceptualising the relationship between alehouses, popular politics and plebeian agency in early modern England. In particular it will argue for the importance of locating the relationship between alehouses and plebeian agency both in time and in geographical space, and for greater sensitivity towards less dramatic forms of political activity and agency.

I: The Historiographical Landscape

An account of the historiography of the alehouse in early modern England can sensibly begin in only one place: with the work of Peter Clark. Although Clark's interest in the institution reached far beyond its relationship to popular politics, the most enduring legacy of his research was the association of the alehouse with an "alternative society".[6] Clark emphasized the elite perception of the alehouse as "the command post of men who sought to turn the traditional world upside down and create their own alternative society", and described it as a space which "came to serve as a focus for traditional values, which were often in conflict with those Puritan concerns and social attitudes now steadily gaining ground among the middling and upper orders of local society". Clark suggested that this perceived conflict of values led to a concerted campaign against alehouses that was not only limited to those committed godly men such as the minister of Upavon, but "undoubtedly attracted a broader spectrum of support, embracing many moderate Protestants, county landowners, yeoman farmers and prosperous merchants".[7] What Clark offered, then, was a dramatic interpretation of the alehouse as a central battlefield in a major historical conflict between popular culture and emerging "middling sort" sensibilities. This struck a chord with other research of the time that emphasized a growing social and cultural polarisation between "the poor" and "the middling sort" in early modern society.[8] The continuing popularity of this meta-narrative of social relations has ensured that the connection between the alehouse and a subversive "alternative society" has endured, though it is questionable whether this was ever Clark's intention. Clark was actually rather sceptical of the radical credentials of the alehouse, and he looked to question, rather than to argue for the validity of, the connection contemporaries made between the alehouse and a vibrant popular politics. He was unconvinced that the alehouse was "the general headquarters of revolution as some [of its] opponents claimed", and argued that "popular protest in alehouses was mostly confined to the desperate seditious outbursts of individual labourers, outbursts which seem almost invariably to have fallen on deaf ears". This ineffectiveness was, he argued, unsurprising, considering that "the political awareness of these marginal people was minimal."[9] The explanation for this lack of political consciousness was the same reason that had caused alehouses to proliferate in the century before 1640: poverty. Clark argued that the increased economic and social dislocations of that century led to the poor taking refuge in the alehouse, which offered an opportunity for "the desperate pursuit of drunken oblivion" that could serve as "an anaesthetic against a harsh, oppressive world and their own route march of misery".[10] For Clark, alehouse-haunters were seeking narcotic escapism from a poverty that militated against the development of political consciousness: they were "too concerned to keep themselves together body and soul to become radical activists".[11] The debilitating poverty of its patrons explained why the alehouse rarely "exercised a positive independent function in popular society rather than simply responding to large-scale economic and other change".[12] Clark therefore envisioned a relationship between alehouses, popular politics and plebeian agency in which the corrosive effects of poverty meant that these institutions and their patrons were passive victims of, rather than active agents in, broader political and socio-economic processes.

After Clark, the most influential early work on the alehouse was produced by Keith Wrightson. Wrightson looked to highlight the ways in which the history of the institution might shed light not only on broader processes of socio-economic change, but also and especially *cultural* change. The proliferation of alehouses in the seventeenth century was, for Wrightson, caused not so much by a growing desire for drugged relief from poverty as by their growing importance as a centre of communal relations: "their role in the provision of recreations for the poor was becoming increasingly central as the century between the Reformation and the Book of Sports of 1633 saw a steady erosion of alternative facilities, a decline in particular of the vigorous communal festivities and sports of the early sixteenth century".[13] As alehouse space became an increasingly important focus for communal activities and popular culture, the hostile attention it received from specific sections of the community intensified. The resulting local conflicts over alehouse regulation were, Wrightson argued, elements of a "broader concern with order and reformation", in which "the village notables who mediated between obscure rural communities and the institutions of Church and State learned to share the growing hostility of magistrate and minister to the alehouse".[14] Wrightson subsequently saw this campaign to exert control over the alehouse as fundamental to the establishment of what Edward Thompson (following Antonio Gramsci) has called the "cultural hegemony" of the parochial elite, which consolidated its position in the course of the seventeenth century. In this account, popular culture was penned into the alehouse, after which it was an easier target for evisceration by hostile parish elites: "it was the establishment of that hegemony which ultimately transformed the truncated remains of a once vital popular culture into a culture of poverty and petty disorder".[15] Wrightson's history of the alehouse portrays an institution and a culture "forced on the defensive in the sixteenth and seventeenth centuries" and powerless to resist the onslaught of the emerging "middling sort".[16] Again, as in the work of Clark, the alehouse and its patrons were depicted as victims of larger historical processes.

The first challenge to some of the key shared features of the alehouse histories offered by Clark and by Wrightson came from Anthony Fletcher.[17] In his consideration of alehouse regulation Fletcher agreed that historians needed to take account of the important role played by "village notables in some places who were moved by the hostility to the alehouse which appears most stridently in puritan propaganda", and also that regulatory campaigns could attract a broad alliance of parish worthies: "we should not assume that every petitioner and grand juryman who was active in pursuing this matter was a militant puritan."[18] Yet Fletcher was not convinced that the battle over the alehouse represented a war against popular culture, arguing that "it is too simple to regard alehouses as popular institutions which can be identified with one side only of a cultural divide". Instead, Fletcher found evidence of a "strong sense that the alehouse was an essential village institution" that was "often promoted by substantial parishioners and was usually accepted by JPs". In part, the more ambivalent attitudes of parish worthies and those officials responsible for alehouse regulation were a result of "the pressure upon them from below ... villagers wanted the chance to drink".[19] Fletcher documents a situation, in which both anti-alehouse and pro-alehouse factions of villagers were involved in a process of petitioning local authorities, and as such "the magistracy found itself in a pivotal position; it stood between the government and the people on one hand and between antagonistic groups who held sharply contrasted views on the other".[20]

What Fletcher offered then was a history of alehouse regulation in which ordinary villagers were able to exert influence and agency through collective petitioning. This more prominent place for popular politics and plebeian agency in the history of the alehouse also led Fletcher to draw a very different conclusion to Wrightson about the situation by the end of the seventeenth century. Wrightson concluded that the growing willingness of both parish notables and governors "to participate in the closer control of village behaviour" meant that by the eighteenth-century parochial elites had "a control over the labouring population which would have been the envy of their innovating predecessors, who had battled against unlicensed and disorderly alehouses."[21] In contrast, Fletcher argued that:

> justices had by and large come to terms with the limitations on the control they could exercise and had abandoned the attempt to execute sections of the alehouse legislation ... that the community most firmly resisted. The

alehouse had taken its place as a necessary institution in the fabric of English society. It had survived both the onslaughts of puritans and the campaigns of magistrates.[22]

For Fletcher, the history of the alehouse did not reflect a severely limited form of popular politics and plebeian agency resulting from poverty or a successful, hostile campaign against popular culture. Instead, it reflected a more complex set of political processes and social allegiances in which ordinary people were significant actors.

Despite offering a convincing reappraisal of what the alehouse might reveal to historians about early modern society, Fletcher's contribution curiously failed to make an impact on the scale of Clark's "alternative society" paradigm or Wrightson emphasis on the "reformation of manners". An alternative model of the relationship between space, popular politics and agency that did have a significant impact on thinking about the alehouse was, however, provided by James C. Scott. In his theorisation of power relations, Scott argued that subordinates in societies with a profoundly unequal distribution of power rarely risk an open challenge to elite hegemony, instead reserving their criticisms for expression in situations that were free from the usual constraints of power—criticisms he collectively labelled the "hidden transcript" of power relations. Particularly important to the development of the "hidden transcript" in Scott's formulation are "sequestered social sites", those "locations in which the unspoken riposte, stifled anger, and bitten tongues created by relations of domination find a vehement, full-throated expression". For early modern England, Scott identified the alehouse as such a space: "a privileged site for the transmission of popular culture ... that was usually at odds with official culture".[23] Scott's conceptualisation was enthusiastically received by scholars of early modern England. Andy Wood suggested that Scott was correct to identify seditious mutterings against social superiors with the alehouse, as he had found evidence that labourers "sitting in their alehouses spoke of how 'rich men' starved the poor and imagined bloody day-dreams of 'knocking down' the 'rich churls'".[24] Adam Fox was similarly inspired by Scott in arguing that "denied the right openly to question those in authority"; people were only able to vent grievances freely "away from their watchful eyes". As such, he argued that the alehouse "offered a sanctuary for relative freedom of speech, for cathartic release."[25] John Walter also followed Scott in seeing the alehouse as a relatively "unregulated" and "sequestered" space.[26] Further evidence supporting Scott's theorisation can be identified in the sensibilities of early modern contemporaries—such as the seventeenth-century radical Roger Crab, who wrote in 1657:

> When the all-seeing eye looks into every alehouse of this nation, and seeth of which sort are most there ... they will appear to be labouring poor men ... [who] in times of scarcity pine and murmure for want of bread, Cursing the Rich behind his Back; and before his Face, Cap and Knee and [assume] a whining countenance.[27]

The appeal of Scott's understanding of an alehouse-based "hidden transcript" may have been as much a product of its conceptual as its evidential foundations. Scott still located the alehouse, as had become historiographically orthodox, at the centre of a conflict between elite and popular culture. At the same time, however, he was able to offer a much more positive account of the political consciousness and resistance capabilities of alehouse patrons than those offered either by Clark or by Wrightson.

Despite this initial enthusiastic response, Scott's stock has more recently been in decline amongst historians of early modern England. Scott argued that a key condition required for the hidden transcript to emerge is that it can find a sequestered social site "where the control, surveillance, and repression of the dominant are least able to reach".[28] Andy Wood has suggested that we cannot assume this condition for the early modern English alehouse, because in a society without a formal policing mechanism "every case of seditious words lodged within the archives of the criminal courts ... speaks not only of some plebeians' capacity to formulate a social critique, but also of the willingness of others to inform against them".[29] Indeed, in light of the fact that seditious words uttered in the alehouse could often be betrayed to authorities, Wood has more recently argued that "distinctions between a secretly articulated "hidden transcript" of plebeian dissidents and a "public transcript" of apparent acquiescence begin to break down. In its place, we find labouring people constantly monitoring one another's reactions to political gossip and hiding behind pretences of innocence."[30] These findings have led Wood to offer a much bleaker analysis of popular politics and plebeian agency: "There is an agency at work here, but only of the most limited and self-protective kind. Where the Tudor state could rely upon popular denunciation, plebeian dissidents perhaps felt that popular political culture had been 'poisoned... with mistrust'."[31] This could be seen as part of a broader trend in Wood's recent work in which he has sought to qualify the "emphasis upon the agency of labouring people" and tell a "darker, more pessimistic" story.[32]

James Brown has followed Wood in expressing scepticism about Scott's theorisation as an accurate depiction of the relationship between alehouses, popular politics and agency in early modern England. In work on drinking houses in early modern Southampton, Brown has found that "far from being inaccessible or unregulated, drinking houses were in fact ventilated and shot through by modes of looking and listening and thus could perform stabilising political work as facilitators of surveillance within the civic community". He agreed that a more pessimistic story could potentially be told, "a story in which alehouse remarks were dangerous, not empowering, and where publicans informed on paying customers, patrons on jovial hosts and drinking companies on each other not out of deference or respect for authority but because of 'repression, fear [and] anxiety'".[33] Consequently, Brown concluded that "for all the insistence on the negotiated character of authority within recent work, the co-option of drinking houses by Southampton's governors arguably reveals more about the reach and adaptability of early modern ruling structures than their susceptibility to forms of contestation".[34] The most recent work on alehouses has, then, left us with a rather bleak conclusion on the relationship between the alehouse, popular politics and plebeian agency that in some respects echoes Keith Wrightson's earlier emphasis on cultural hegemony. It has sketched a relationship in which mistrust, fear, betrayal and surveillance served to reinforce the cultural hegemony of ruling elites by poisoning popular political culture and suffocating plebeian agency.[35]

And yet, Andy Wood's pessimism comes with a crucial caveat: that a focus on the limits to plebeian agency should make us appreciate those moments when "labouring people could unite and defeat their rulers".[36] Whilst his recent research on late-sixteenth century Norfolk and on the Yorkshire valley of Nidderdale has demonstrated the very serious limits that could operate on plebeian agency in early modern society, he does suggest that such a configuration of relations of domination was not a-historically fixed. For example, Wood suggests that "the evidence of the wide geography and co-ordinated outbreak of the 1549 rebellions, like that of 1536, provides stark evidence that at certain moments popular politics could remain closed and opaque to rulers."[37] So, the alehouses found in the regions from which rebellion sprung in those years may well have played a key role in popular political organisation—perhaps even fostering a "hidden transcript"—even if those in Southampton and the valley of Nidderdale were less favourable environments for insubordination to flourish in.[38] The crucial implication to draw from Wood's caveat, then, is that our understanding of popular politics and plebeian agency needs to be historicized and localised. The study of alehouse space may well provide a privileged vantage point for surveying such historical and regional specificities of plebeian agency in the period.

As it stands, then, the historiographical landscape is inhabited by a diverse range of partly overlapping, partly conflicting interpretations of the relationship between alehouses, popular politics and plebeian agency. Most recently, this landscape has fallen under a cloud of pessimism with regard to popular politics and plebeian agency. Yet, it is a cloud whose shadow should not be assumed to fall on the entire terrain of early modern England. If a more complete conceptualisation of the relationship between alehouses, popular politics and plebeian agency is to be reached, then we should heed Wood's reminder that there may be times and places for which a more positive story may be appropriate. With this in mind, this essay will proceed with two case studies of the relationship between alehouses, popular politics and plebeian agency that will, within limited historical parameters, test existing historiographical interpretations, before a final section will integrate these findings into a more complete conceptualisation of that relationship.

II: Seditious Speech in Later-Stuart Alehouses

When considering the relationship between sites of sociability and political forms in late-seventeenth-century England it is not the alehouse-focused debates about an "alternative society" or a "reformation of manners" that bear most heavily on recent scholarship. Rather, the historiography of later Stuart politics has become "preoccupied with the formation of a "public sphere" defined by legal, open political debate" that has been most strongly associated with the coffee house.[39] We might reasonably ask whether the alehouse has been unduly neglected as a potential locus of such a "public sphere". Indeed, Peter Clark suggested that after the Restoration the alehouse was "clearly becoming more respectable", "starting to attract visitors from higher social groups" and emerging as "the focus of a bustling array of social and leisure activities". This "growth of respectability" was concomitant with a shifting political culture in which the alehouse transformed from "the enemy of the political establishment" to a "weapon of political influence": canvassing and electioneering had come to replace "the blood-curdling prophecies of the downfall of the King and the rich churls which resounded in tippling houses before the Civil War".[40] Similarly, Beat Kümin has suggested that "informed public reasoning" could be associated with early modern drinking houses, and that such an association could be made even before the supposed rise of the "public sphere". Kümin has argued that "bourgeois flagships" such as the coffee house were "built on foundations laid by 'traditional' drinking establishments".[41] The association between political debate and the alehouse in this period has also been highlighted by Buchanan Sharp, who remarked that "the events of 1640-60 marked an important turning point in the political education of large segments of the English population", and that after the Restoration "high politics were routinely the stuff of alehouse conversations."[42]

A note of caution is necessary though before characterising political discourse in the alehouse as a component of an emerging "public sphere". Indeed, it is difficult to see these alehouse conversations as contributions to "legal, open political debate" when we consider Sharp's point that "the large number of post-Restoration indictments for seditious words also reflects a heightened governmental anxiety about possible threats to political and social stability".[43] Further, Andy Wood has suggested that Charles II's advisors believed that the downfall of the early-Stuart state had in part been a product of a groundswell of popular politics, and they had therefore resolved that "the restored monarchy would build itself upon the closure of public politics".[44] A raft of legislation relating to treason, petitioning, conventicles and the swearing of oaths of loyalty created a climate of intelligence and espionage in which informing was reformulated as "a legitimate, necessary expression of citizenship".[45] It may then be the case that the "surveillance" model is more applicable than the "public sphere" in relation to later-Stuart alehouses.[46]

Evidence of the surveillance of political speech can certainly be identified in later-Stuart drinking houses. At "the Signe of the Angel" in Warminster in 1683, for example, a gentleman and excise officer, Thomas Morris, had been drinking with John Kerlye, a tailor, Richard Horler, a cloth worker, and Nicolas Bolton, a butcher. Morris proposed that the company should drink a health to the King, but another cloth worker, William Seare, rejected the proposal and said "what had he to doe with the King or the King with him he did not care a turd for the King repeating the same words over two or three times but he would drinke a health to the honest Duke of Monmouth". Morris was moved to report Seare's insubordination to a local Justice of the Peace, as was the proprietor of the Angel, John Hawkins. They may have been encouraged to do so by the fact that Seare's was not just an isolated outburst: others in the drinking company were also "desirous to drinke the Duke of Monmouth's health saying it would come in fashion in a short time".[47] The Angel was clearly not then a site of open political debate, but rather a place where the expression of certain opinions was likely to result in a serious confrontation with authority. However, Seare's mistake may not have been to misjudge the appropriateness of a drinking house as a site at which to express rebellious sentiment, and clearly some patrons were in sympathy with him. Rather, his error may have been to do so within earshot of two men who were potential agents of surveillance: Morris was in the service of the King as "one of his majesties officers of the Exize"; and Hawkins, as a publican, was expected to monitor any subversive speech and activity under the conditions of his license.[48]

Information about seditious words was not, however, only provided to authorities by these formal agents. In 1691, Thomas Hibbert of Bath had gone along to a revel in Box, Wiltshire, and ended up drinking in the house of John Cottle. There, "Hibbert taking a glass of beer severall times in his hands began and drank severall Healths to the late King James", and "spoke severall approbious words against the present King and Queen and their government". This information was relayed to a local JP not by an "agent of authority", but by William West, a baker who had also been present drinking in Cottle's house. Cottle himself, who would have been the man formally responsible for surveillance of this drinking site, proved far less effective at this than the baker: when examined by the JP he declared that "he was sometimes in one room and some times in another and that he never heard any person whatsoever speak concerning the King and Queen or their government". It may be the case that Thomas Hibbert had prudently avoided voicing his preference for "the King over the water" in the presence of Cottle, and yet this had not prevented him from being ensnared by the less formal mechanism of plebeian informing. That the expression of political opinion at sites of communal drinking was therefore fraught with danger was implied in Cottle's remark to the JP that "he usually advises those he keepeth company withall not to talke of the gouvernment".[49]

The policing of seditious words could then have a marked degree of social depth, as the Wiltshire miller William Dawkins discovered in 1665. He had been conversing with two labourers and brothers, Andrew and Thomas Waters, "concerning magistrates and justices of the peace". Andrew Waters had said to the miller "that wee had a king now and that he must live under a government now", to which he replied "don't tell me of a King, I care not a fart for a King, nor for never a Magistrate in England". At first the labourer did not take any action, but later the same day he encountered the miller again at an alehouse in Great Durnford, where he confronted Dawkins over his remarks, and told him "that he should answer for the words that he had spoken" to which the miller replied "that he should doe his worst". Waters duly reported the seditious words to a JP. Perhaps Dawkins had underestimated the reach of surveillance, and assumed that expressing a lack of respect for authority in the company of an illiterate labourer (Waters signed his deposition with a cross), over a pot of ale, was a relatively innocuous activity.

If an illiterate labourer may have seemed an unlikely agent of authority to Dawkins, then the Covent Garden mercer Edward Rigby may have been equally surprised when he was indicted in 1690 for intending to incite sedition against William and Mary on the information of a woman, Mary Cox. Rigby had publicly drunk a health to William, but in a subsequent conversation about "the election of Knights of the Shire for the County of Essex to serve in Parliament", Rigby told Cox that the King "will not doe as wee would have him, we will make a King that shall doe as we would have him". Mary Cox objected, answering, "O dear Sir these things wee must leave to God". Cox later stood as a witness against Rigby and assured his indictment.[50] These examples of relatively humble informants seem to provide support for James Brown's claim that the functioning of drinking sites as "vectors of surveillance" should not "be imagined as top-down or wholly oppressive. They framed not the monitoring of the many by the few so much as the monitoring of the few by the many".[51]

What are the implications of this for an understanding of popular politics and plebeian agency in later-Stuart England? A study of drinking sites does seem to reveal a quite sophisticated political consciousness with noteworthy social depth: illiterate labourers having conversations "concerning magistrates and justices of the peace", or women involved in discussions regarding "the election of Knights of the Shire for the County of Essex". This suggests the political awareness of these alehouse patrons was far from "minimal". And yet, alehouses and other drinking sites do not appear to have been unregulated spaces fostering a "hidden transcript", nor sites of "legal, open political debate": a climate of surveillance appears to have restricted the development of both of these forms of popular political culture. There is, perhaps, a bigger question mark over the issue of agency. Should we necessarily assume that Andrew Waters or Mary Cox informed on their drinking companions out of fear and anxiety, emotions produced by a climate of repression and subordination in which plebeians felt powerless, and thus refused to risk defying their legal obligation to report sedition? In both of these cases the informants were reporting on social superiors, and it is possible to read their actions as attempts to lay claim to a role in governance—and to wield a power—that their status officially denied them. Waters, a humble labourer, may have felt empowered by the experience of confronting a miller—a man who, if popular culture is to be taken as a guide, may not have been a popular figure in the local community and therefore all the more satisfying to report.[52] Likewise, Mary Cox may have revelled in the opportunity to turn gender relations of domination and subordination on their head by playing the central role in bringing the traitorous Rigby to justice.[53] Evidence of plebeians informing on seditious speech need not necessarily be read as an indictment of *individual* plebeian agency: taking such action might in certain instances be seen as empowering those without a formal stake in early modern "grids of power".[54]

Another instance of the reportage of seditious speech in this period raises further questions about the relationship between plebeian agency and the politics of surveillance. In North Bradley, Wiltshire, in 1685, William Jennings, a tinker, and John Moore, a labourer, were drinking together in a victualling house. Jennings proposed and drank a health to the new King, but his companion refused, stating that "he would drink noe health to any popish Rogue" before taking up a stick and striking Jennings on the head with it, "so that he lost much blood by it", leaving Jennings "afraid that hee will some tyme or other kill him or doe him some bodily harme".[55] Jennings decision to inform on Moore is likely to have been motivated as much by fear for his safety as by fear of the consequences of association with Moore's seditious opinion. What motivated Moore's attack though? There may have been some pre-history of hostility between the two—although they were on good enough terms to be drinking together—or Moore's temper may have flared up simply because he was drunk. Yet, there is another possibility that should not be overlooked: perhaps Moore's angry reaction was a product of deeply held convictions, such as a strongly felt Protestantism which James II's accession seriously offended. Moral or religious convictions may also have influenced Mary Cox's decision to inform on Edward Rigby: she had after all objected to his plotting to remove King William by stating that "these things wee must leave to God". A desire to prevent interference with divine providence may have guided Mary's choice to expose Rigby.[56] Again, in the case of Andrew Waters, genuine loyalty and a sense of duty may have encouraged him to remind the seditious Dawkins "that wee had a king now and that he must live under a government now". Rachel Weil has suggested that informing in this period had been fashioned as "a legitimate, necessary expression of citizenship", and that plebeian informants may have perceived of themselves as active agents in defence of monarchy and the *collective* national interest. Similarly, in early modern Southampton ordinary citizens may have "voluntarily informed... against a variety of perceived threats to the peace of the port" out of a sense of *collective* civic pride and responsibility.[57] It should not then be assumed that evidence of a strong climate of surveillance in later-Stuart alehouses necessarily indicates an absence of either individual or collective expressions of agency on the part of ordinary people—though these expressions may look rather different to those proposed by conceptual models of a "hidden transcript" or "public sphere".[58]

Existing conceptualisations of the relationship between alehouses, popular politics and plebeian agency have in large part overlooked these alternative forms of agency, tending instead towards extremes of more dramatic forms of collective agency on the one hand or stressing the serious limits on agency on the other. One way of conceptualising these alternative forms of agency that might prove useful in redressing this situation can actually be found in the earlier work of James Scott. Before developing the concept of the "hidden transcript", Scott had been less interested in the dramatic exclamations of popular opposition to elite hegemony and had directed his attention at much more subtle forms of plebeian political activity and agency: "the constant, grinding conflict over work, food, autonomy, ritual—at everyday forms of resistance".[59] John Walter, in particular, has seen great potential in these forms of resistance, collectively termed by Scott the "weapons of the weak", to point to "the agency subordinates could exercise and extend the range of activities by which they might do so." Walter also felt that there was scope for applying Scott's thinking to early modern England: "It is certainly possible to recover something of the quotidian and largely unremarked exchanges by which individuals attempted to blunt the exercise of power in the micro-politics of manor and parish."[60] Influenced as much by Joan Scott as James Scott, Keith Wrightson has also urged historians of early modern England to expand the range of activities that we consider "political" beyond those relating to "the conduct and management of affairs of state". In particular, Wrightson suggested that we might consider "the manner in which relationships of power and authority, dominance and subordination are established and maintained, refused and modified", and like Walter argued that "one of the best ways to appreciate this is to survey parts of the field from a parochial perspective: to consider the rich variety of political processes which can be observed in the local community", processes that Wrightson termed "the politics of the parish".[61]

Previous interpretations of the relationship between alehouses, popular politics and plebeian agency have been primarily concerned with the ways in which alehouses facilitated, or served to stifle, any serious popular threats to the entire political order of early modern England. However, Scott's conceptualisation of "weapons of the weak" and Wrightson's notion of the "politics of the parish", invite us to look for forms of popular politics and plebeian agency that were somewhat less sensational, though no less significant to those involved in these everyday power struggles. A study of alehouse licensing may, from this perspective, disclose a great deal about these "everyday forms of resistance".

III: Alehouse Licensing in Jacobean Somerset

The regulative campaign waged against the alehouse in post-Reformation England is perhaps the best known assault on drinking houses in early modern Europe.[62] For Peter Clark, a critical turning point in the process of "mounting official control over the alehouse" came with the accession of James I. Clark argued that "government efforts to spur the justices to more vigorous action were at best spasmodic before 1600", but that "James I's accession brought a resurgence of Crown activity", including a number of bills "calling for more stringent controls over the popular drink trade".[63] The hostility towards the alehouse was clear in the 1606-7 Acts intended for "the better repressing of alehouses, whereof the multitudes and abuses have and are found intolerable", and for "repressing the odious and loathsome sin of drunkenness".[64] This renewed campaign had apparently enjoyed tangible effects by the 1620s.[65] The reign of James I was clearly then a crucial period in the history of the early modern English alehouse.

These hardened attitudes at the centre certainly seem to have been shared by the magistrates of Somerset. At the General Sessions held in Wells in 1607, for example, an order was issued in response to examinations which had revealed that "divers notorious misdemeanors and abuses have been committed by such as without or by or under pretence of licenses have kept Tippling or Alehouses upon the hill of Mendipp". The county bench accordingly decided to throw the book at the tipplers of the Mendips, ordering that "no person or persons whatsoever at or in any place upon the said hill shall be licensed, permitted, or suffered to keep any Alehouse or Tippling house". Further, in building the case to ban any tipplers on the Mendips, the order revealed another aspect of the attitudes of authority: alehouses in the region were condemned for "standing remote from the eye and view of such officers as have the charge of government". The politics of surveillance were also clearly at work in Jacobean Somerset.[66]

The strong arm of authority in dealing with alehouses may also be glimpsed in an order suppressing the alehouse of William Cleye, of Langport Westover, in 1623. Cleye had been accused of permitting adultery "as well as many other misdemeanours" in his tippling house. Cleye strongly denied the truth of these claims, but the Court nonetheless decided to suppress his alehouse, a decision which led Cleye to challenge openly the integrity of the authorities in a declaration that "whatsoever he should say [to disprove the accusation], the Clerk of the Peace and some other should swear to it to be true". Whilst bold, this direct verbal challenge to the licensing authorities was hardly an effective form of everyday resistance: Cleye was subsequently charged with "insolent behaviour in Court".[67]

Whether through the blanket banning of them in whole areas, keeping a close watch on them, or turning a deaf ear to appeals in court, those responsible for licensing alehouses in Jacobean Somerset were clearly prepared to take a hard line approach to alehouses and alehouse keepers. And yet, their authority did not always go unopposed. James Hayball, for instance, kept an alehouse at Green Oar in the Mendips. Reports that it was a centre of drunkenness and blasphemy; was "scandalous and offensive to all well disposed Christians"; and that Hayball harboured criminals and thieves there, had all formed part of the evidence that had led to the decision to suppress all the alehouses on the hill in 1607.[68] Twelve years on, however, Hayball surfaces in the quarter sessions records again, still running his alehouse at Green Oar despite having being suppressed at previous quarter sessions and contrary to numerous orders issued by magistrates. Further orders in 1619 and 1620 tried again to suppress the house, but it turned out that Hayball had been letting the house out to tenants to run as a tippling house, in an attempt to dodge the problem that he had personally been forbidden from selling ale.[69] Indeed, the inhabitants of nearby Emborough petitioned the quarter sessions to complain about his tactics: "noe sooner one is suppress but another stranger shortlye after farmes [i.e. rents] the said housse and tiples being not lycensed in the said housse into which at this instant there is another tenant come into and tiples before the old [tenant] is gon forth".[70] The authorities had taken a strong stance against alehouses in the Mendips, but it appears that James Hayball had exercised an impressive degree of resistance in deliberately and tactically evading licensing laws to keep a technically illegal alehouse running for over a decade in the face of official hostility.

This was not an isolated case of defiance. In 1609, the magistrates of Somerset were becoming increasingly agitated with an alehouse keeper named Walter Withers, a resident of Pilton. A letter was presented to the quarter sessions explaining that Withers had been presented at a petty session for tippling without a license, and describing him as "a man verie malapert, sawcie and obstinate". Despite having been "often suppressed and warned from his unlawful tipling", the authorities could "find noe conformitie in him". Indeed, Thomas Hughes, author of the letter and a JP of the county, alleged that Withers "hath confessed his offence before me, and that he hath no licence but would justify himself by quillets and evasions".[71] It seems that Withers, like Hayball, thought it was possible to resist the strong arm of authority.

There were others who looked not only to evade but to challenge the licensing authorities. Lewis Lyninge of Mark was presented at the quarter sessions in 1615 for keeping a common tippling house without a license, but he appealed to the JPs not to suppress his house on the grounds that it was "an ancient inn". This met with some success, and the Court issued an order sending for "the ancient men of Marck" to attempt to verify the truth of the claim.[72] Similarly, in 1616, Richard Gellicombe faced indictment for unlicensed tippling and made recourse to the same defence, claiming "his house at Croscombe to be an ancient inn". Gellicombe's proofs were not sufficient to convince the Court, so an order was made for two officials to "call before them some parishioners of Croscombe to examine whether the house be an ancient inn or not".[73] We might interpret these challenges to licensing decisions within a broader "politics of custom".[74] E.P. Thompson described custom as "the interface between law and common practice", and it certainly seems that these alehouse keepers were invoking the latter to challenge the former.[75] This evidence also bears heavily on our consideration of popular politics and plebeian agency. Keith Wrightson has suggested that defence of custom "could mobilise whole communities, or sections of them, with a conviction of their rectitude in disputing power".[76] If the "ancient men" of Mark or the parishioners of Croscombe united in support of these appeals to "ancient inn" status then these communities would potentially have been able to overturn the legal decisions of magistrates through an appeal to customary practice. Indeed, in 1616, Edward Joanes of Burton was able to draw on the collective memory of the community to do just that. Joanes had his license taken away after information was given against him about disorders that had occurred in his alehouse. In response, he petitioned the quarter sessions to reissue his license on the grounds that his alehouse had been licensed for "tyme out of mynde whereof mens memory is not to the contrary". The plea was successful and it was ordered that "he shall again be licensed". What this example demonstrates then is that an appeal to custom, when backed by at least a section of the community (and we should assume that Joanes' claim was verified by the "ancient men" or inhabitants of Burton), could provide a form of collective and effective resistance to power, authority and the law at a local level. That defence of custom could provide a powerful way to "blunt the exercise of power in the micro-politics of manor and parish" is also hinted at in the language of the order re-issuing Joanes' license: it stated that the license was for "as long as he shall keep himself and his house in good order, *and no longer*" (my emphasis).[77] Clearly the authorities were anxious to downplay the force of custom by reminding Joanes that it was his conduct, rather than custom, that his claim to a license was based upon. Considering that Joanes had just used a claim to custom to regain a license that had been taken away from him for keeping a disorderly alehouse, this may have sounded like an empty threat.

A case study of alehouse licensing in Jacobean Somerset can reveal, then, that early modern plebeians were involved in forms of "everyday" resistance to authority: whilst authorities were involved in a hard line campaign to crack down on alehouses, this was at times frustrated by recalcitrant individuals and communities. Yet, there is further evidence that suggests that the "politics of the parish" revolving around the alehouse was not always a straightforward contest that pitted authority against plebeians, or "better sort" office holders against "the poor". Indeed, in 1609 the inhabitants of Wanstrow sent a certificate to the quarter sessions in support of a license extension for a man who had been tippling lawfully for three years. It was signed by several key local authority figures: the constable, a tithingman and two churchwardens. Further, it deemed the alehouse appropriate on the grounds that it was in accordance with a statute made for "allowing a typler in every parish needful for the poor of the same parish and other passengers travelling through".[78] If opposition to the alehouse could, in Peter Clark's phrase, attract a "broader spectrum of support" than just the godly, it seems that a similarly broad alliance of local power holders and the "poor of the parish" could in some cases have shared interests in defending the institution.[79]

On the other hand, the burgesses of Yeovil petitioned the JPs of the county in 1618 calling for the suppression of alehouses, passing on what they claimed was a "complaint of the commons". They explained that "in our towne in former tyme" poor men of "small meanes" were able to rent houses in which to practice their trades, "wherby they mayntayned themselves" and their families "very well". In more recent times, however, houses which had formerly been available to rent "for Fourtye shillings or three poundes at the most" by such poor men were "now lett for eight or tenne poundes to be used for typplinge howses to the greate hurte of the Inhabitants of our towne".[80] In this instance it appears as though a broad alliance of burgesses and poor men had a shared interest in suppressing alehouses in Yeovil, a conclusion that also raises a question about the widely held assumption that these institutions were "run by the poor for the poor".[81] Clearly in some instances the poor could also take their place alongside the ranks of those that campaigned against the alehouse. This evidence brings to mind Anthony Fletcher's regrettably neglected conclusion that "it is too simple to regard alehouses as popular institutions which can be identified with one side only of a cultural divide".[82]

It may also, however, be useful to revisit Keith Wrightson's thinking about the "politics of the parish". In his earlier work on alehouses, Wrightson argued that "village notables ... learned to share the growing hostility of magistrate and minister to the alehouse".[83] More recently, whilst suggesting that hypotheses which associate certain sets of attitudes with particular social, economic and political groups in early modern England contain a "kernel of truth", Wrightson has also warned that they "run the risk of acquiring a predictive rigidity, of assuming that particular patterns of social relations were coincident with given economic structures or positions within them". It may be sensible to heed Wrightson's suggestion that: "If more refined models can be developed, they must be ones which leave more room for the contingent element in social processes, for the peculiar configurations of structure, circumstance and individual agency which could prove vitally important in the experience of particular places."[84] Adapting this conclusion to the context of this case study, we might argue that, for Jacobean Somerset at least, the socio-economic or political status of certain groups or individuals – whether burgesses, village constables, or officially powerless poor men – did not predetermine their attitudes towards alehouse licensing.[85]

IV: Conclusion

The preceding sections of this essay have attempted first to delineate, then to test, scholarly attempts to conceptualize the relationship between alehouses, popular politics and plebeian agency in early modern England. What conclusions can be drawn? The notion that the alehouse was the stronghold of an "alternative society", perhaps erroneously associated with Peter Clark, is clearly problematic, and evidence from Jacobean Somerset suggests that we should we wary of assuming that the alehouse was situated at the centre of a war between popular and elite culture, an interpretation associated also with Keith Wrightson's early work. Whilst James Scott's concept of a "hidden transcript" of popular politics located at "sequestered sites" is both appealing and convincing for those societies on which his research is primarily based, it seems less suitable when applied to the early-modern English alehouse. Admittedly, it is impossible for historians to know whether for each seditious conversation that was reported there were not numerous others which did indeed remain hidden, but this seems unlikely in light of the evidence from later-Stuart England that there was a significant social depth to plebeian informing. The fact that political opinions were closely policed also undermines the idea that any significant form of the "public sphere" can be associated with alehouses in that period. The evidence does, however, tend to support the arguments of Andy Wood and James Brown that drinking spaces could be "sites of surveillance" in which subversive political opinions were likely to be betrayed to the authorities. And yet, evidence from both later-Stuart England and Jacobean Somerset suggests that we should not necessarily accept their pessimism with regard to the susceptibility of ruling structures to forms of contestation in these particular contexts.

Considered in isolation, then, none of these frameworks sufficiently captures the full range and dynamics of the relationship between alehouses, popular politics and plebeian agency. The intention here is not, however, to suggest a one-size-fits-all conceptualisation to remedy this situation. Instead, one of the central arguments here has been to argue for the importance of locating the relationship between alehouse space and plebeian agency both in time and in geographical space. Whilst parochial elites may have established control over the alehouse in, for example, early modern Terling without encountering significant resistance, this was clearly not the case in Jacobean Somerset; and although something akin to a "hidden transcript" may have formed in early-sixteenth-century Norfolk, it seems less likely that anything similar could have developed in the drinking houses of Southampton or later-Stuart Wiltshire. Future attempts to conceptualize the relationship between alehouses and agency might also benefit from developing these arguments about the particularities of time and space even further. It may be helpful to think not only in the sense of variations across and within counties or decades, but also on a smaller scale in terms of how the political culture of an alehouse might have varied from day to day, or perhaps even depended on where people were sitting. A seditious opinion expressed in an alehouse on one evening may have received approval from those around the ale-bench and thus remained unreported, and could therefore be considered as part of a "hidden transcript". The same words repeated on another evening within earshot of the publican may have been passed on to the authorities, transforming that same alehouse into a "site of surveillance". Or these hypothetical conversations might have taken place at different tables – one within earshot of the publican, the other tucked away in a back room. Considered in this way, the seemingly incompatible and contradictory accounts of the relationship between alehouses, popular politics and plebeian agency explored in this essay can be reconciled. Whilst the exact balance between the extent of surveillance, elite hegemony, social polarisation, communal cohesion and the force of custom might vary from parish to parish, from county to county and from year to year, these various interpretations of the political culture of the alehouse could be considered not so much as in competition with each other but as each capturing different *aspects* of a complex social reality. Any attempt to conceptualize the relationship between alehouses, popular politics and plebeian agency should therefore bear in mind Beat Kümin's point that "the physical framework of a drinking establishment was not inherently 'good' or 'bad'", and as such the relationship between these spaces and the political culture that could be formed in them in different contexts might present "an almost infinite range of scenarios".[86]

That said, and despite the difficulties of drawing on case studies such as those offered here to make representative generalisations, some broader conclusions emerge from this essay which might usefully inform future, contextual studies of the relationship between alehouses, popular politics and plebeian agency. First, whilst straightforward binary models which situate the alehouse at the heart of divisions between elite and popular culture—or authority and subordinates—may often contain a "kernel of truth", allowing them to dominate our analysis of alehouses obscures the full range of complex socio-political allegiances, conflicts and processes upon which the study of drinking houses may be able to shed valuable light. Second, polarized conclusions on the extent of plebeian agency in the period may be equally obstructive. Conceptualisations of plebeian agency which are either overly pessimistic or dismissive on the one hand, or overly optimistic—perhaps even idealistic—on the other, can distract us from the diverse range of political forms and resistance that lie somewhere in between: struggles which, to those involved, might have seemed every bit "as dramatic and important as the struggle against arbitrary … power within the national body politic".[87] Reconstruction of the popular political culture of alehouses may well provide a point of access to the analysis of the "politics of the parish" and the "weapons of the weak", and thus help to drive away some of the darker clouds that loom over the history of early modern plebeians.

Notes

* I am grateful to Steve Hindle, Beat Kümin, Brodie Waddell and Fiona Williamson for their comments on earlier versions of this essay.
[1] E.B.H. Cunnington, ed., *Records of the County of Wilts: Being Extracts from the Quarter Sessions Great Rolls of the Seventeenth Century* (Devizes, 1932), 204-5.
[2] Beat Kümin and Ann Tlusty, eds, *The World of the Tavern: Public Houses in Early Modern Europe* (Aldershot: Ashgate, 2002), 11.
[3] Peter Clark, *The English Alehouse: A Social History, 1200-1830* (London: Longman, 1983), x.
[4] Keith Wrightson, "Alehouses, Order and Reformation in Rural England, 1590-1660", in *Popular Culture and Class Conflict, 1590-1914: Explorations in the History of Labour and Leisure*, ed. Eileen Yeo and Stephen Yeo (Brighton: Harvester, 1981), 1-2.
[5] Beat Kümin, *Drinking Matters: Public Houses and Social Exchange in Early Modern Central Europe* (Basingstoke: Palgrave, 2007), 131, 147-171, 3. For a "spatial" approach focusing on the physical and material properties of drinking spaces see James Brown, "The Landscape of Drink: Inns, Taverns and Alehouses in Early Modern Southampton" (PhD diss., University of Warwick, 2008). For an approach focusing on the symbolic importance of drinking spaces in literature and discourse see Steven Earnshaw, *The Pub in Literature: England's Altered State* (Manchester: Manchester University Press, 2000).
[6] Clark, *The English Alehouse*; Peter Clark, "The Alehouse and the Alternative Society", in *Puritans and Revolutionaries: Essays in Seventeenth-Century History presented to Christopher Hill,* ed. Donald Pennington and Keith Thomas (Oxford: Clarendon Press, 1978), 47-72.
[7] Clark, "The Alehouse and the Alternative Society", 48, 60; Clark, *The English Alehouse,* 167.
[8] Keith Wrightson and Davis Levine, *Poverty and Piety in an English Village: Terling, 1525-1700* (London: Academic Press, 1979); Keith Wrightson, *English Society, 1580-1680* (London: Hutchinson, 1982), esp. 230-6.
[9] Clark, "The Alehouse and the Alternative Society", 64, 66, 68.
[10] Clark, *The English Alehouse*, 215, 111.
[11] Ibid., 160.
[12] Clark, "The Alehouse and the Alternative Society", 67.
[13] Keith Wrightson, "Alehouses, Order and Reformation", 9.
[14] Ibid., 20, 18.
[15] Ibid., 21; E.P. Thompson, "Patrician Society, Plebeian Culture", *Journal of Social History* 7 (1974): 387-8.
[16] Wrightson, "Alehouses, Order and Reformation", 20.
[17] Anthony Fletcher, *Reform in the Provinces: The Government of Stuart England* (London: Yale University Press, 1986), esp. 229-52.
[18] Ibid., 239.
[19] Ibid., 252, 234, 233.
[20] Ibid., 241.

[21] Wrightson, "Alehouses, Order and Reformation", 16, 21.
[22] Fletcher, *Reform in the Provinces,* 252.
[23] James C. Scott, *Domination and the Arts of Resistance: Hidden Transcripts* (London: Yale University Press, c.1990), esp. 120-1.
[24] Andy Wood, "'Poore men woll speke one daye': Plebeian Languages of Deference and Defiance in England, c.1520-1640", in *The Politics of the Excluded, c.1500-1850,* ed. Tim Harris (Basingstoke: Palgrave, 2001), 91.
[25] Adam Fox, "Ballads, Libels and Popular Ridicule in Jacobean England", *Past and Present* 145 (1994): 72.
[26] John Walter, "Public Transcripts, Popular Agency and the Politics of Subsistence in Early Modern England", in *Negotiating Power in Early Modern Society: Order, Hierarchy and Subordination in Britain and Ireland,* ed. Michael J. Braddick and John Walter (Cambridge: Cambridge University Press, 2001), 128, 139-40.
[27] As quoted in Steve Hindle, "Exhortation and Entitlement: Negotiating Inequality in English Rural Communities, 1550-1650", in *Negotiating Power,* ed. Braddick and Walter, 116-7.
[28] Scott, *Domination and the Arts of Resistance,* 120.
[29] Wood, "Poore men woll speke one daye", 81.
[30] Andy Wood, *The 1549 Rebellions and the Making of Early Modern England* (Cambridge: Cambridge University Press, 2007), 140-1.
[31] Ibid., 141.
[32] Andy Wood, "Subordination, Solidarity and the Limits of Popular Agency in a Yorkshire Valley, c.1596-1615", *Past and Present* 193 (2006):70-2; a pessimism also shared by Alexandra Shepard in her recent, "Poverty, Labour and the Language of Social Description in Early Modern England", *Past and Present* 201 (2008): 95.
[33] James Brown, "Drinking Houses and the Politics of Surveillance in Pre-Industrial Southampton" in *Political Space in Pre-Industrial Europe,* ed. Beat Kümin (Farnham: Ashgate, forthcoming; 2009), here quoting Wood, "Subordination, Solidarity and the Limits of Popular Agency", 70-1. I am grateful to Dr Brown for allowing me to see this essay prior to publication.
[34] Ibid.
[35] For more on the roles played by fear and the participation of "honest men" in the surveillance of seditious speech, and the implications for the applicability of Scott's model to early modern England, see Andy Wood, "'A lyttull worde ys tresson': Loyalty, Denunciation and Popular Politics in Tudor England", *Journal of British Studies* (forthcoming; 2009). I am grateful to Professor Wood for allowing me to see this paper prior to publication.
[36] Wood, "Subordination, Solidarity and the Limits of Popular Agency": 72.
[37] Wood, *The 1549 Rebellions,* 142.
[38] There is evidence that in the Walsingham conspiracy of 1537 it was not just alehouses but also fairs and archery matches that were used as cover for rebel organisation—though the identification of a "hidden transcript" here is complicated by the fact that the conspiracy was ultimately betrayed: C.E. Moreton, "The

Walsingham Conspiracy of 1537", *Historical Research* 63 (1990): 29-43. Similarly, Heather Falvey has recently found evidence that football matches could provide cover for the organisation of riots: "Custom, Resistance and Politics: Local Experiences of Improvement in Early Modern England" (PhD diss., University of Warwick, 2007), 356-63. This evidence suggests that the alehouse may not be the only, nor perhaps even most fruitful, place to look for a "hidden transcript" in early modern England.

[39] Andy Wood, *Riot, Rebellion and Popular Politics in Early Modern England* (Basingstoke: Palgrave, 2002), 172; Jurgen Habermas, *The Structural Transformation of the Public Sphere: an Inquiry into a Category of Bourgeois Society,* trans. Thomas Burger with the assistance of Frederick Lawrence (Cambridge: Polity, 1989); Steve Pincus, "Coffee politicians does create': Coffee Houses and Restoration Political Culture", *Journal of Modern History* 67 (1995): 807-34.

[40] Clark, *The English Alehouse*, 225, 232, 237.

[41] Kümin, *Drinking Matters*, 188, 195-6.

[42] Buchanan Sharp, "Popular Political Opinion in England, 1660-85", *History of European Ideas* 10:1 (1989): 13-14.

[43] Ibid.

[44] Wood, *Riot, Rebellion and Popular Politics*, 174.

[45] Ibid; Rachel Weil, "Matthew Smith versus the 'Great Men': Plot Talk, the Public Sphere and the Problem of Credibility in the 1690s", in *The Politics of the Public Sphere in early modern England,* ed. Peter Lake and Steve Pincus (Manchester: Manchester University Press, 2007), 233; see also Alan Marshall, *Intelligence and Espionage in the Reign of Charles II, 1660-1685* (Cambridge: Cambridge University Press, 1994).

[46] Of course, coffee houses were also the target of official concern over sedition, such as the one suppressed at Warminster in 1681: Cunnington, ed., *Records of the County of Wilts*, 266. This did not, however, stop Habermas according them a key role in the formation of the "public sphere", and it could thus be argued that "surveillance" and "public sphere" models need not be seen as mutually exclusive. Nonetheless, the argument here is that although the two may not be mutually exclusive, any notion of a "public sphere" that could be comfortably associated with alehouses or taverns in the late-seventeenth century would have to be a very limited one when the extent of the surveillance of political opinion is considered.

[47] Wiltshire and Swindon Record Office (hereafter WSRO), QSR/1683/T/115-6.

[48] For the notion of publicans as "authorities' agents" see Michael Frank, "Satan's Servants or Authorities' Agents? Publicans in Eighteenth-Century Germany", in *The World of the Tavern,* ed. Kümin and Tlusty, 12-43. For an example of an English ale-selling license that required of a publican that in the event that any patron was guilty of disorder, felony or suspicious behaviour "you shall imediately declare to the constable or other officer as neere as you can the names apparrell and dwellinge places of all such psons" see Somerset Record Office (hereafter SRO), Q/SR/28/95.

[49] Cunnington, ed., *Records of the County of Wilts*, 276.
[50] Essex Record Office, Q/SR/464/4, 65.
[51] Brown, "Drinking Houses and the Politics of Surveillance".
[52] For the notoriety of millers as both commercially and sexually avaricious see E.P. Thompson, *Customs in Common. Studies in Traditional Popular Culture* (London: Merlin, c.1991), 218-21.
[53] Indeed, James Scott has suggested that the psychological effects of reversing the normal relations of domination and subordination can play a key role in social relations: Scott, *Domination and the Arts of Resistance*, esp. 206-10.
[54] For the term "grids of power" see Michael J. Braddick and John Walter, "Introduction. Grids of Power: Order, Hierarchy and Subordination in Early Modern Society" in *Negotiating Power*, ed. Braddick and Walter, 1-43.
[55] Cunnington, ed., *Records of the County of Wilts*, 271.
[56] For the importance of providence in early modern systems of belief see Alexandra Walsham, *Providence in Early Modern England* (Oxford: Oxford University Press, 1999).
[57] Weil, "Matthew Smith versus the 'Great Men'", 233. Weil also identifies the motivations of one particular informer in the late-seventeenth century who sold information about plots to government officials, which appear to be a mixture of commercial opportunism and patriotism: "I was pleased with the hopes of making my fortune, when at the same time I was endeavouring to save my King and country", 245; Brown, "Drinking Houses and the Politics of Surveillance".
[58] For more on the debate over whether fear or genuine loyalty to the social order motivated the denunciation of seditious speech see Wood, "A lyttull worde ys tresson"; and Ethan Shagan, "Rumours and Popular Politics in the Reign of Henry VIII", in *The Politics of the Excluded, c.1500-1850*, ed. Tim Harris (Basingstoke: Palgrave, 2001), 30-66.
[59] James C. Scott, *Weapons of the Weak: Everyday Forms of Peasant Resistance* (New Haven: Yale University Press, c.1985).
[60] Walter, "Public Transcripts, Popular Agency and the Politics of Subsistence", 124.
[61] Keith Wrightson, "The Politics of the Parish in Early Modern England", in *The Experience of Authority in Early Modern England*, ed. Paul Griffiths, Adam Fox and Steve Hindle (Basingstoke: Macmillan, 1996), 10-11; See also Joan W. Scott, *Gender and the Politics of History* (New York: Columbia University Press, 1988).
[62] Kümin, *Drinking Matters*, 140.
[63] Clark, "The Alehouse and the Alternative Society", 69-70; Clark, *The English Alehouse*, 172.
[64] 4 Jac. I, c.4; and 4 Jac. I, c.5.
[65] Kümin, *Drinking Matters*, 140.
[66] SRO/Q/SR/2/125. They may also have been at work in the labelling of a Westbury alehouse as unfit in 1612 because it was located "oute of the towne in the fild, out of the most usuall way": SRO/Q/SR/16/79.
[67] E.H. Bates, ed., *Quarter Sessions Records for the County of Somerset. Vol.1, James I, 1607-1625* (Frome: Somerset Record Society, 1907), 326.

[68] SRO/Q/SR/2/46.
[69] Bates, ed., *Quarter Sessions Records for the County of Somerset,* 257, 274.
[70] SRO/Q/SR/35/108.
[71] SRO/Q/SR/6/5; see also Q/SR/6/48.
[72] Bates, ed., *Quarter Sessions Records for the County of Somerset,* 120-1.
[73] Ibid., 157-8.
[74] Wrightson, "The Politics of the Parish", 22-5; see also Andy Wood, "The Place of Custom in Plebeian Political Culture: England, 1550-1800", *Social History* 22 (1997): 46-60.
[75] Thompson, *Customs in Common,* 101-2.
[76] Wrightson, "The Politics of the Parish", 24.
[77] Walter, "Public Transcripts, Popular Agency and the Politics of Subsistence", 124; SRO/Q/SR/25/79 [Note - the Somerset Quarter Sessions Rolls contain two sets of numbering, the second added when the rolls were transferred to micro-film. In all other cases I have provided the second, most recent number. In this case, due to an error, the "79" refers to the older numbers.] See also: Bates, ed., *Quarter Sessions Records for the County of Somerset,* 180.
[78] SRO/Q/SR/6/15.
[79] Clark, "The Alehouse and the Alternative Society", 60. A similar ambiguity in the attitudes of the Somerset authorities towards institutions associated with "popular culture" may be seen in the fact that it's JPs "had mixed feelings about the propriety of revels". See Thomas G. Barnes, "County Politics and a Puritan Cause Celebre: Somerset Churchales, 1633", *Transactions of the Royal Historical Society* 9 (1959): 108.
[80] SRO/Q/SR/30/73.
[81] For its origins see Clark, *The English Alehouse,* 53.
[82] Fletcher, *Reform in the Provinces,* 252.
[83] Wrightson, "Alehouses, Order and Reformation", 18.
[84] Wrightson, "The Politics of the Parish", 30.
[85] For a similar conclusion that stresses "the shifting configurations of interest within the social order" in relation to enclosure disputes see Steve Hindle, "Persuasion and Protest in the Caddington Common Enclosure Dispute 1635-1639", *Past and Present* 158 (1998): 75-6.
[86] Kümin, *Drinking Matters,* 140.
[87] Andy Wood, "Industrial Development, Social Change and Popular Politics in the Mining Area of North-West Derbyshire, c.1600-1700" (PhD diss., University of Cambridge, 1994), 155.

"A FURED MUTTON WOULDE CONTAYNE AS MUCH GOOD DOCTRINE": SOCIAL POLITICS IN THE SEVENTEENTH-CENTURY PARISH

FIONA WILLIAMSON

I

Over the last few decades many social historians have shown that ordinary people were informed about the political world around them. In particular, it has been argued that the middling-sorts played an active, participatory role in city and parish governance.[1] Freemen could vote in local elections or become a councilman, and even the less affluent could hold a minor civic office, like constable. Further down the social scale, people might contribute to parish or vestry meetings and raise petitions, or less formally, voice their opinion by gossiping, spreading rumours and even slandering officials. Although these latter avenues had limitations, the ability to question, challenge or agree with political policy, events and personalities is considered a core part of popular agency.

In this context then, "agency" means the *potential* to act as an agent for change. Of course, this ability was circumscribed by current events, individual socio-economic circumstances, local traditions and values.[2] The efficacy of popular scrutiny of authority was also, in part, determined by the extent to which the challenged authority was considered legitimate; which could involve any combination of factors such as whether that body or person adhered to common law, established social expectations or paternalistic values. In practice, this was the foundation that meant early-modern rule, at whatever level, never became absolute or tyrannical. The twin ideals of order and patriarchal responsibility - although often unrealised in practice - offered a baseline against which judge political and moral conduct. At the parochial level, legitimacy was just as important and far easier to scrutinise, as local office holders were not always protected by the ancient standing and tradition of nobility, which might excuse, if not condone, some of the top official's transgressions. Local officials had a duty to at the very least, maintain appearances. Officers, often drawn from the middling sorts, therefore found that their own personal attributes, conduct and reputation were tantamount to qualifying their authority in circumstances where many of the people they governed were of their own social rank. If their conduct was judged inappropriate, it would seriously undermine their right to hold an office, as a formal title bestowed only limited protection from confrontation.

Yet the exercise of agency was not always about conflict, challenge and change. Opposition to authority did not necessarily reflect a subversive agenda, or a radicalised subaltern class set in direct opposition to their social superiors. Disputes were more likely to arise because ordinary people were concerned to maintain continuity with the past. Popular agency was, indeed, at its most effective within the perimeters of *legitimate* complaint, demonstrating an essential conservatism of purpose and intent; that is maintaining order and the continuity of established practice. In these circumstances, ordinary people were more likely to effectively achieve their goals, suggesting agency was a key part of a legitimising process which worked from both the bottom upwards and the top down.

To explore both why and how ordinary people engaged with such practices, this essay draws upon defamation records from Norwich's seventeenth-century Diocesan Court, the work of recent historians who have investigated disputes between clergy and their congregations, and the historiography of popular agency laid out in the introduction.[3] The Norwich diocese was large, encompassing Norfolk and much of Suffolk, including Thetford, Bury St Edmunds, Ipswich, King's Lynn and Great Yarmouth. With the exception of fourteen years between 1647 and 1661 when the sessions were discontinued by parliament, its records are rich and well-preserved.[4] Following the Restoration, the court enjoyed a twenty year high during which business equalled, if not exceeded, the pre-war era before gradually declining in use by the end of the century. The court had several functions, including the record keeping and administrative side of parish business. However, it also took on "office" and "instance" causes, which more closely resembled civil or criminal court proceedings, including defamation. "Instance" procedures were initiated by parties who felt they had been wronged and sought redress, whereas "office" procedures were mainly disciplinary, most often in the case of moral transgressions.[5] In reality the two causes frequently overlapped. Defamation cases were instigated after an initial complaint and comprised a rather drawn out process of written articles, interrogatories and responses alongside the statements of witnesses and compurgators about the parties and events in question.[6] For the historian, the benefit of this practice is the resulting detailed accounts, which include personal information about the deponents, such as residence, occupation, age and marital status (for women).

The clergy themselves were not immune to prosecution. The Church Court's role as a disciplinary body for the regulation of clerical behaviour makes it possible to trace cases of clerical non-conformism, pluralism, laziness, drunkenness and dishonesty, alongside personal disputes with their parishioners.[7] Thus, defamation depositions reveal tantalising glimpses of everyday parish life; local rivalries, popular engagement in parish governance, moral ideals and expectations of the clergy. Their value also lies in the recording of witnesses' social backgrounds and their "original" speech. The articulation of grievances via the medium of defamation was one of the few means of expression open to all levels of society, and a crucial part of plebeian agency. The depositions thus contain invaluable records of the words and thoughts of ordinary people (that is people below the level of the titled gentry) which might otherwise have been lost. The only exception to this was the very poor who may have been less likely to have been called upon as a court witness, or to have raised a suit themselves, except in exceptional circumstances.

Many historians have used defamation cases to explore agency in the secular world, but this essay explores the politics of the spiritual parish; expressly the relationship between the parish minister and his congregation.[8] In the same way that ordinary people exerted agency by verbally attacking political figures, so to they questioned their religious superiors and the quality of spiritual provision. Thus the dynamics of agency in politics and religion can and should, at this micro-level, be considered closely related.[9] It is for all the reasons outlined above that I have chosen to draw upon defamation cases to consider the following questions: what was the relationship between ordinary people and their local clergyman and, in what circumstances did they challenge his authority?

Before commencing however, it is worth highlighting a few points. First, there was some disparity between criticism of secular officials and that of clergy. In secular life, open criticism of a social superior or office holder could end in serious punishment. In cases where a mayor, an alderman, or a constable was defamed, for example, those convicted faced prison, hard labour or a fine. People who defamed their local minister however, were not necessarily punished or, if they were, this action fell under the remit of the Church, rather than the stricter, lay courts. In the Church Courts, the offending party could either be prosecuted by the court itself, or sued by the minister in question for defamation. In the case of the latter, conviction would depend on the minister winning his suit. Either way, punishment was relatively light, if humiliating. This generally involved some form of public confession, often in front of the whole congregation whilst dressed in a white sheet or carrying a rod to symbolise penitence. Alternatively, penitents could petition to have their punishment commuted to a fine which would go into the parish coffers and be given to the poor.[10] In instances where groups of parishioners banded together to present a poorly performing minister, their united front and legitimate grievance circumvented potential punishment, in fact such complaints were viewed as, if not always welcome, certainly far from slanderous.

Second, a minister was far more constrained by behavioural expectations than was a secular officer. Ministers were expected to set a moral benchmark for their congregation, leading by example. Transgressing from this strict standard eroded a minister's authority and could, in turn, legitimise the grievances of his parishioners. Not only this, but he had to act in accordance with reform movements and trends within the Church. During the early part of the seventeenth century, the Church's internal reform programme emphasised the importance of clerical behaviour and education. "Godly" belief in individual participation in church life and moral reform encouraged some parishioners to more closely monitor the behaviour of their minister. Dan Beaver correctly notes that a reformed clergy were deemed a "necessary prelude to a reformed laity" which ties in with the wider moral reform programme of the lay parish.[11] However, popular involvement in moral regulation of the preaching ministry was not a new phenomenon. The medieval Church had stressed the duty of self-regulation to all its members; that is all Christians theoretically. By the seventeenth century, this formal duty had fallen to a limited number of Church officials, but nonetheless, the long standing tradition of popular regulation had never entirely disappeared, having re-surfaced with a vengeance during the Reformation to form a core element of Protestant values.[12]

Third, a few ministers started their careers disadvantaged by a combination of relative economic hardship in their family background, a low clerical income and insufficient formal education. Financial and educational impoverishment thus undermined one fundamental constituent of ministerial power and influence; wealth, honour, status and reputation, placing many clergymen on a financial par with the ordinary parishioners; those husbandmen and artisans over whom they were expected to exert spiritual authority.[13] Judith Maltby has suggested that parishioners saw the relationship with their minister in terms of a "contract", expecting sufficient services in return for their tithes.[14] This effectively downgraded the minister's position to that of a paid "employee" which could result in serious problems if this reciprocal relationship broke down.[15] In the absence of wealth, education and status, it would be down to an individual minister to build on his personal qualities, such as piety and benevolent acts, to achieve the deference and respect nominally established by money or title. Respect was a formidable precursor of legitimacy in any position of authority, but this was especially true in the Church.

Finally, seventeenth-century religion and society were punctuated with peaks of conflict. As the century progressed, traditional social relationships underwent dramatic stress and religion became intrinsically enmeshed with politics and radicalism. Personal conscience became public property as formal methods of censorship broke down and political and religious debate undoubtedly influenced ordinary lives, leading people to question governance closer to home.[16] Although this point should not be overstated, it is no surprise that peaks of religious and political tension, such as during the 1620s and 1630s, coincided with peaks of complaints against the clergy in the Church Courts.[17] Yet, many of these cases expressed concern for conformity, rather than revolution, possibly reflecting a desire for stability at a time of social, political and religious anxiety.[18] Despite the sweeping political changes of the mid-century, continuity of belief, order and morality remained the benchmark for much of the century, especially outside the major towns and cities.

This essay is in three parts. The first explores ministerial relationships with the chief inhabitants of the parish.[19] Church Court proceedings were dominated by those people described as "the smaller part ... of the gentry ... and the greatest part of the tradesmen, and freeholders, and the middle sort of men; especially in those corporations and counties which depend on clothing and such manufactures".[20] Their prominence is perhaps not surprising given their central role in many tight-knit parishes as community leaders.[21] However, it is worth remembering that the middling sorts were not a homogenous 'third' group sitting squarely between the elite and the poor; their range of incomes and interests traversed social boundaries and cultural stereotypes.[22]

The second section of this essay investigates the role of personal conduct in justifying ministerial authority and legitimising popular complaint against transgressors. The importance of reputation to contemporaries should not be underestimated. Ordinary people would go to great lengths to defend their "good name" and "fame" as good character was a vital precursor of belonging to a community and its loss undermined individual credit and worth.[23] Finally, I consider ministers who failed to adequately perform their duties. This may have been a result of commitments to other parishes, or because their religious views were at odds with those of their congregation. During the discussion of each individual case, the physical location of disputes should be noted. Perhaps not unsurprisingly, many conflicts were played out within sacred spaces, in the church or church yard for example. However, this element should not be taken for granted; setting was an important dynamic in clergy-parishioner power relationships.

Lastly, it is worth mentioning that Church Court proceedings by necessity paint a very negative picture of parochial relationships, as clergymen only appear if they are prosecuting, being prosecuted or acting as a witness in a dispute. This glosses over the majority of parishes where clergy and parishioners enjoyed bearable, if not positive associations, or where ministers and local elites were united in their support for one another. It is thus wise to display a sense of caution before making sweeping generalisations.

II

Ministers had no formal political authority, but nonetheless, many had an important role and responsibility as a member of the parish vestry which in many isolated rural areas commanded some influence.[24] Remarkably though, in such a supposedly deferential society, a minister's position on the vestry and prerogative over spiritual matters was no guarantee that his parishioners would automatically respect his wishes. This required some effort on his part, especially if he was new to the parish. Several factors influenced this. The starting point would have been his family background and social contacts which influenced both which benefice he would be allocated and on arrival, the possibility of carving a place for himself amongst the "chief inhabitants" of the new parish.[25] It is very unlikely that a poor clergyman would have been accepted into gentlemanly ranks simply because of his position, although he may have found himself somewhat elevated in society, his title displacing conventional social stereotyping.

Money also constituted an important part of a minister's relationship with his congregation. Again, this was largely determined by his family connections, but importantly regional differences in stipends and wages. Wealth was an important determinant of status and therefore authority. For ministers, incomes ranged so widely that generalisations about where he fell on the social scale are problematic; suffice to say a Norfolk minister would have fallen anywhere between lower middling and chief inhabitant status.[26] Poorer ministers found they could not live on their modest stipends and had to supplement their incomes by farming land or selling produce, but this antagonised parishioners who had struggled to pay their tithes, and others who felt their minister, however poor, should not be working like a "commoner". Thus some clergymen found themselves unable to please anyone. In 1669, for example, the small parish of Geyton, Norfolk, was up in arms about their vicar, Mr Brookebank, who had decided to farm his vicarage lands. He had been driven to this necessity by a lack of money, but his congregation still reported him to the Diocesan authorities, saying he did "pitch the earthe and rake after the carte" and "sow barly as an ordinary husbandman".[27] The snub was obvious.

Strict social conventions meant that many ministers were targeted perhaps unfairly by "chief inhabitants" (and others) who could be quick to bring down a man they felt was not acting in accordance to his proper place in the local social hierarchy. Understandably, clergymen may have felt themselves to be equal to the "better sorts" in rank and education, yet, those people paying his "wages" may not have agreed. Occasionally, this tussle between pride and position ended in court. During 1633, for example, Mr William Butte, a gentleman of Brockford in Suffolk raised a suit against his minister, William Withers. Butte had five supporters: all middle-aged yeoman and gentlemen.[28] One of these men, Richard Jessop, told the court he had overheard Withers and Butte arguing in the church after service. Withers haughtily asked Butte "doe you knowe to whom you speake[?]", to which Butte defiantly answered "yes very well". At this point Withers grew angry retorting, "you shall answeare it as proude as you are".[29] As a leading figure in the community with moral and spiritual responsibility for his parishioners, Withers clearly felt equal to William Butte. Butte, however, was adamant Withers should know his place, so much so that he was prepared to pursue the point at his own expense in court.[30]

This was not the only occasion when a local gentleman had cause to rebuke a presumptuous minister. In 1628, John Parlett witnessed a heated exchange between Stradsett's incumbent, Mr Hodgeson, and local gentleman, Mr Francis Piggott. The two men had started arguing after Sunday service in St Mary's parish church, Parlett reporting that Hodgeson, "not being p[ro]voked" rushed to confront Piggott who was still in the church. In "great anger" he had shouted "I am as good a man as you and an honester man than you and ... you have cozened me of Tenne pounds".[31] The long-standing dispute was not only about money, but status. Hodgeson thought himself equal to men like Piggott, but Piggott and his wealthy compurgators saw their minister in a very different light.[32] In theory, Hodgeson had a point. A well educated man with two degrees, he must have come from a wealthy or well-connected family, but he underestimated the local influence and reputation of the Piggott family. Piggott had been baptised and lived in Stradsett all his life. He had been married in St Mary's church and all his ten children had been baptised there. Hodgeson on the other hand had only moved to Stradsett in 1603 in order to take up the vacant ministerial post.[33] At court, Piggott choose his compurgators and witnesses with care, picking well-to-do yeoman with established local families, including John Parlett, whose brother, Francis, had first introduced Hodgeson to Stradsett's benefice. Faced with such united local opposition, Hodgeson was unlikely to find himself in a strong position arguing his case at court.

Like Piggott, Mr James Seaman believed that Richard Anguish, the rector of Sturston in Norfolk had pretensions above his station. In 1637, Seaman complained that Anguish "was a devil & no man ... and did look after thee fleece but for his flocke they might goe starve". He further "swore by god he cared not for any Clergy man in England" and that "if the parish or men of the towne would be by him, he would make ... Mr Anguish eate barley bread".[34] Seaman's comments involved the use of metaphor, directly attacking Anguish's sense of self-importance, the reference to cheap barley bread an early modern equivalent of "eating humble pie". Seaman also made it known that he would have the support of the Sturston's chief inhabitants in prosecuting Anguish. Unlike Hodgeson, Anguish's clerical income would have put him on a lower social level than his opponent, so the accusation that he prioritized his own well-being over that of his congregation may not have been far off the mark.[35] There was also some suggestion that Anguish owed money at this stage of his career. Ten years later, Sturston rectory was sequestrated for arrears of over eighteen pounds, debts which may well have begun accumulating many years before.[36] However, despite his poor reputation and debts, Anguish remained at Sturston for some time to come; Seaman's threats seemingly hollow. Anguish was finally ejected, but not until 1655.[37]

Across the course of the whole century, it was the "chief inhabitants" who pursued the majority of accusations against ministers, whether status was the crux of the disagreement or not. During the 1660s, the wealthy inhabitants of Crostwick presented their minister Thomas Ramsey at the Church Court. Ramsey stood accused of defaming Sir William Paston and

Thomas Le Gros, both very important men, locally and nationally. Their witnesses were all were literate middle-aged men with established, affluent backgrounds, from a geographical spread of twenty-five miles around North Walsham and the east coast of Norfolk, where the Paston family owned land and property.[38] William Hardyman, a blacksmith of fifty, stated that Ramsey was "a man much given to rayling against and abusing p[er]sons of qualitie" and further "that he hath published severall abusive letters or libels tending to dishonour of Sir Wm Paston Baronett, Thomas Le Gros esq and others."[39] Forty-two year old Stephen Greene recalled that "in the time of divine service" Ramsey had "publiquely read a libel abusing the Auncesters of Thomas LeGros Esq".[40] On the surface at least it seems that the chief inhabitants were justified in using their combined power to prosecute Ramsey for defamation. However, it was not this simple. Ramsey had already confessed to defaming Paston and Le Gros two years previously and had been punished for it.[41] This strongly suggests the men had other motives in bringing the case back into the public eye. There is some evidence that they were trying to push Ramsey out of his benefice because of a more recent disagreement over money. Richard Gase of nearby Ridlington told the court that there had been an "agreement made betwixt ... Mr Ramsie and Mr Henrie Midleton" concerning Ramsey's financial entitlements for an additional cure: Ridlington. Mr Hardyman, likely the same Hardyman mentioned earlier, had helped set up the agreement, but according to Ramsey had later tried to change the original terms. Hardyman claimed Ramsey would only be entitled to "halfe a crowne a daie for having of Ridlington Cure" but Ramsey disagreed, telling him "he was a lying knave ... the agreement was for five shillings a day". Thomas Lewin also gave his support to Hardyman saying he "was much abused by the said Mr Ramsie" and further added that he had seen the "veire abusive" letter Ramsey had previously written to Paston. He also confirmed he had heard Ramsey publically read out libellous letters in which he "abused" other clergymen in the surrounding area, some of whom subsequently provided witness statements against him.[42]

Ramsey had a history of contentious behaviour which made it easier for the chief inhabitants to present a very convincing prosecution. He had lost his previous benefice of Repps with Bastwick during the 1640s and been imprisoned for loyalty to the Royalists during the civil wars. Referring back to what he had called "impetuous and violent" times, he wrote a "long and erudite" letter to John Utting, then Mayor of Norwich, a known Royalist who had been involved in events leading to the Great Blow of 1648.[43] Ramsey's letter read "that yeare I lost Repps, some lost theyre witts, others lost theyre honestie, and ... the City of Norwich lost the Mayor ... I shall not fear death in a just cause".[44] Repps was situated only a few miles from Crostwick and the other villages involved in the 1663 defamation case. Paston's witnesses were all old enough to have lived through the civil wars and may well have known Ramsey, indeed, Ramsey, Paston and Le Gros had all fought for the Royalist cause. Ramsey's experiences during the civil wars most likely proved a key turning point in his life, reflected in his attitude and general behaviour afterwards. By 1663, William Cooke of Winterton had reported that Ramsey was much given to "excessive drinking" and "uncivill and rude behaviour" and John Duck, constable of Martham, recalled a night when he had been called from his bed on report of "a man [Ramsey] in a pittifull condicion in a ditch".[45] Thomas Ramsey "was in such a distemper with excessive drinking ... that he was not able to help himself", so Duck and a companion had dutifully carried him home. Worse still, Edmund Chatham, minister of Felmingham, told the court Ramsey was "a notorious rayler and abuser", slandering one "Mr Plumstead a minister Mr John Fisher and his wife". Ramsey had written "scandalous letters" about all three people, including one which had accused Fisher of "detaining some tithes from him". Ramsey seems to have been at odds with many people, but rather than seeing him as a disreputable figure, it is tempting instead to picture him as a lonely individual, scarred by his war-time experiences and isolated by those people he had fought alongside, who now used his failing reputation against him.

Ramsey's case highlights a recurrent criticism of ministers in general: their unsatisfactory personal conduct and behaviour. In 1635, for example, Thomas Berie had accused the minister of Earsham, Mr Sherwood, of leading a "base and dishonest life", stating he would do well "to learne good manners of him" and "desired god that he would redd the towne of him ... or else that the devil might".[46] Similarly, in 1640, the clerk and sexton of Wymondham, Thomas King, insulted Mr Locke the minister of nearby Bunwell. Their argument had started during a visit to Mr and Mrs Clarke, whom Locke and King were supposed to be helping with a "difference between them". However, the meeting descended into chaos; King shouting that Locke's "soule will hange in hell for neglecting his parishioners" and Locke's wife trying to drag her husband away whilst he cried "he would not leave a knave in the howse for fear he should give ... Clarke ill counsel". King then revealed his intentions to remove Locke from his benefice for good, retaliating "that the towne of Windham was troubled w[i]th a knave ... but he hoped thay should shortly be redd of him".[47] There is no evidence that King succeeded, but his allegations did result in being sued for defamation by Locke.[48]

Failings such as excessive drinking were also considered unbecoming to a minister, fundamentally undermining his authority. In 1663, John Parker reported Alexander Kirby incumbent of Benacre. Parker found plenty of support amongst Kirby's congregation who had endured his drunken behaviour for long enough. Mary Myles, for example, had often been bothered by Kirby at her family's alehouse where he was regularly found "from Tenn a clock in the morning till about eleven or twelve a clock of the next night drinkinge and tipling and would not bee persuaded to goe home … until … the beere … [she] had brewed to entertaine her friends and neighbours w[e]re all drunke".[49] Myles also reported that Kirby was a gambler. He had invited her and her husband, Peter, to his house to play cards on several occasions; a claim which John Chickering also confirmed saying Kirby was a "frequent gamester". Peter and Mary Myles were not the only inn-keepers to have cause to complain about Kirby's drinking. John Griffin of Southwold told the court that after over-indulging at his alehouse, Kirby was "seen to reele to and fro and tumble downe in the streete".[50] Drinking was not the only problem. Kirby also had a reputation for falling out with his neighbours and then suing them at the Church Court, sowing discord within their small community and was likely a more serious issue in the long-term than the odd drunken night out. However, Kirby's drinking habits provided a rather more spectacular and shocking set of events to use against him at court.

In 1635, there was a particularly notorious case of drinking and immorality presented at the Yarmouth visitation and finally at the Norwich Diocesan Court. Rector John Utting's scandalous reputation had spread at least twenty miles around east Norfolk and he was known in places like Yarmouth, Blundeston, Martham, Lound, Reedham, Gorleston and Fritton for behaviour that challenged the core values of decency and morality, let alone the standards of a clergyman. There was a "common fame" that John Ward's wife was pregnant with Utting's child, although nobody could prove the allegations. However, many people believed the truth of the rumour by the weight of evidence against him. William Ward of Gorleston swore he had seen Utting kissing Joanne Underwood and later "saw him have the use of her body". On questioning, Underwood said she had tried to resist Utting's advances "telling him she wondered a man of the cloth should offer to commit such a sinne" but had eventually succumbed after he told her "he was a man of god and could take away the sinne of a woman and that w[hi]ch he persuaded her unto was no sinne but a sweete pleasure".[51] Underwood's naivety led her to allow Utting to have the "carnal use of her body" at least three times when her husband had been away on business.[52] Utting had also attempted to seduce his maidservant Martha Langlie, but Langlie was rather shrewder than Underwood. She threatened to tell Sir John Westworth, a local landowner. Utting's response was to dismiss her in disgust, but his actions only succeeded in proving his guilt. As if his reputation with women were not enough, Utting was also known to be an incorrigible drunk. He was a regular at several different alehouses where he managed to upset the owners with his excessive consumption and abusive language, swearing, blaspheming, throwing pots of beer, vomiting and, on occasion, passing out.[53]

As the two above cases highlight; complaints about behaviour tended to be used as a final "nail in the coffin" when other aspects of the minister-congregation relationship had already broken down. Utting's situation however also raises another important problem: pluralism. Utting held two cures, one at Weston and the other at neighbouring Reddisham, three miles away. Given the attractions of additional income, it is not unsurprising that Utting would find an additional cure appealing.[54] The problems presented by pluralism for the congregation, however, arose time and again as parishioners complained that incumbents were spreading themselves too thinly. Utting's bad behaviour may simply have been another in a long list of general complaints that he was neglectful of his duties, adding to the reasons to request his replacement.[55]

Pluralism was a regular bone of contention and complaints about it were often embellished with ones about behaviour, probably to emphasise the general unsuitability of the incumbent overall. The case of Naunton versus Long is one such example. Sir Robert Naunton, one time Secretary of State and Master of the Court of Wards for James I, presented Robert Long for neglect during the 1630s; the result of an ongoing disagreement between the two men.[56] It is likely, although not entirely clear, that Naunton had some influence over the appointment of the parish clergyman, possibly through the right of advowson. Long was a pluralist, holding the cure of Letheringham as well as receiving a stipend of six pounds for the impropriated parish of Charfield. More commonly however, problems arose because of pluralism as ministers had to divide their time between two or more parishes, resulting in the poor provision of pastoral care and occasional abandonment of key services. This was certainly the case with Long. Naunton had warned him about neglect on several occasions, and had asked if he would give up his additional cure, but Long stubbornly refused. However, when Long's personal behaviour deteriorated, Naunton had the perfect excuse to increase the pressure. Together with several other respectable and sufficient local inhabitants, they compiled a long list of complaints against Long to present to the Church Court. Henry Appleton, for example, recounted an incident which had happened over two years earlier, saying he had seen Long "soe disguised and distempred w[i]th excessive drinkinge of wyne and beere as he staggered and reeled up and downe" and "could not keepe his way but ... fell into a deeke". The day after he said Long was seen in the village with "his face much battered & bruised & in an ould suite of clothes w[hi]ch he had not lately worne": Long's experience had clearly taken its toll.[57] Appleton also revealed some of Long's history with Naunton. Some years earlier, he had been employed to conduct Naunton's private services, but Naunton had been forced to dismiss him because he was a drunk. On several occasions Long was so inebriated he was unable to read the service properly. Naunton eventually persuaded Long to give up Charfield, but only by offering a financial incentive. On the same day that he agreed to resign his cure, Long spent some of his newly acquired money on a drinking binge.

Regardless of who was right or wrong in this case, the incident as a whole raises some interesting points about parochial relationships. Despite his wealth and position, Naunton seemed unable to remove Long from the extra cure without considerable trouble. He had to gather influential friends and peers to help him bring together a personally costly prosecution, which did not rely on the strength of their position or Long's pluralism alone, but recounted a catalogue of incidents over a period of years. Ministers had to beware that although minor behavioural lapses could be overlooked, they served as a useful weapon to legitimise complaints about more serious issues. Finally, it seemed Naunton had to resort to bribery to get his way. Considering he was one of the "chief inhabitants" and had held a national position at court, his personal agency was surprisingly constrained by the legal system.

Occasionally, rather than circumvent problems like Naunton; parishioners took direct action. During the 1660s, the Puritanically inclined congregation of Needham worked outside the legal system to exclude their pluralist minister, Robert Gilbert. Gilbert also held the cure of Flixton seven miles away, resulting in prolonged absences from each parish. One morning, when Gilbert and his friend John Soanes arrived at Needham church to conduct a service, they found "gathered togeather in the church yard a greate number of people". Among them was the wealthy and respected Mr Lodge, who took the part of ringleader and spokesperson for the angry villagers.[58] He told Mr Gilbert "in a very scornfull disgracefull and base deriding manner" that "neither the Bishopps nor Chancell should have nothing to doe there". Then "together with the rest of the Route then there did expulse force and drive away the said Mr Gilbert" even threatening to have him "sett in the stockes" if he returned.[59] Henry Tubby, also a wealthy local man and friend of Lodge, added "that he cared not for their authority ... and that hee ... would have them beaten out of towne ... he would spend a thousand pounds before the said Mr Gilbert should have anything to doe there".[60] In the face of united opposition, Gilbert was powerless and made a hasty retreat. Gilbert was an "outsider" and a pluralist, disadvantaged by both in a culture which placed value on "belonging", responsibility, and in this case, conformism.[61]

Differences in conscience and doctrine were a serious problem for ministers. Parishioners could demonstrate non-conformism by not attending church services with little repercussion, but if it were the minister himself who did not toe the line, parishioners were not shy about voicing their opinions, safe in the knowledge that they had the law on their side. Thomas Chapman, for instance, attacked Samuel Hooke the minister of Stibbard in 1614 saying "a fured mutton woulde holde or contayne as much good doctrine" and that "he would be ashamed to lye as he Mr Hooke had donne and ... hee would prove Mr Hooke a lier".[62] Criticism was not restricted by gender either. Mary Love of Reedham in Suffolk slandered the incumbent Mr Welham saying "if she were a minister as he was she would [not] speak or preach lyes in the pulpit".[63] In Hevingham, several conforming parishioners reported their minister John Brooke for neglecting to read divine service or prayers on key feast days between 1616 and 1618. He also refused to baptise at least two babies who had been brought to him on a weekday for that very service to be performed.[64] Brooke had only been a minister in the parish since 1615, and the parishioners were finding it hard to become reconciled to what, in their opinion, were his decidedly Puritanical leanings.

An extreme break down in parochial social relations occurred during the late 1620s in King's Lynn resulting in several parishioners petitioning the Lord Bishop of Norwich about their minister John Stalham. Stalham's outspoken views had touched on political, as well as religious issues. He had slandered Charles I, saying that since he had come to the throne "there is pollucon in the court, pollucon in the church & comon wealth". He believed Charles' reign heralded the return of Catholicism and told his congregation in no uncertain terms, preaching "o lord ... canst thou behould us w[i]th eyes of mercie seeinge pop[er]y & supersticon ... secretly sett upp in the chiefest places" and put the blame squarely on Charles "for the sinnes of this kingdome". Further, he warned that "great miseries and calamities would fall and our wifes and children shall see them & that God would judge this Kingdom for the sinnes of it w[i]thin twelve month".[65] His proselytising did not go down well with his parishioners who labelled him an extremist. He was ejected from his post shortly after.

Nonetheless, it is clear that not everyone shared the same opinion and Stalham's ejection showed he was a victim of local rivalries as much as his outspokenness. Thomas Rivett, the town clerk, had thought him a "foole" and had played a role in the faction demanding his removal.[66] Several of the deponents in the case were presented for giving false evidence and two men, Cuthbert Champney and Samuel Thacker, gave a statement in Stalham's defence, stating that he was "a man of honest sober life and conversac[i]on & hath worne the surplice when he hath administered the Lords Prayer" in accordance with the law. Interestingly, they also noted that one of the men who had accused Stalham of false doctrine had confessed to embellishing Stalham's actual words.[67] Stalham, a pious Puritan, finally found refuge in Terling, Essex, attracted to his new like-minded congregation by "that inviting report which was given of you that you were a fasting and praying people: which I found true, among the best of you, who gave me a call hither".[68]

III

Finally, and somewhat briefly, it is worth drawing attention to a unique aspect of the cases above, and many more besides. Not unsurprisingly, arguments with, or the slander of clergymen often took place within the church or churchyard. It would be obvious to point out that this would be where congregants would have had most contact with their minister, but it could also be argued that challenging religious authority within sacred space had a special significance of its own. The church and its yard were sacrosanct; set apart from ordinary buildings and greens. In theory, people were expected to behave in a manner befitting the place, in line with all that it represented.

On another level, church interiors acted to emulate and strengthen the principles of order which were the lynchpin of society. Churchwardens allocated seats to people according to their position in the community, for example.[69] The importance of pew placement to contemporaries should not be underestimated. People went to court if they felt that they, or others around them, had been misallocated, or had tried to usurp a seat which was too high in the church for their actual status. Seats were also connected to family heritage, handed down from one generation to the next, so an attempt to appropriate or reallocate a seat could easily be taken as a personal slight. The importance of pews was so great that individuals even resorted to violence to assert their right to a seat, or to remove somebody else from theirs. So, in 1635 for example, the Witherells of Framlingham Piggott presented Martha Harris of Framlingham for taking a seat which had been in their family for fifty years. Harris had "intruded and thruste herself into the ... seate ... without the consent or good likeing of ... James Witherell or his wife ... and having ben asked to forbeare setting in the seate aforesaid did notwithstanding presse to the said seate ... in a violent manner". Further, in her "violent humour" she threw a piece of matting from the pew wherefrom "duste ... fell upp[o]n the hatt" of Mrs Witherell "to the greate disturbance of the whole congregation".[70] In 1638, Robert Theoderick sued John Bude when Bude sat in Theoderick's seat in Swaffham parish church. When Theoderick arrived to find Bude in his seat, Bude "leaned himselfe over ... soe as that ... Theoderick could nott well get in" and violently thrust ... Theoderick w[i]th his elbowe and shoulder on purpose to keep him out of his said seate".[71] However, it seems that Bude was not entirely in the wrong. Although Theoderick had been using the same seat for some time, Robert King, the parish's minister, testified that he had not agreed to give Theoderick the seat and "that Theoderick is an Oatemeale maker & that the seate in w[hi]ch Theoderick doth usually sett in is a seate more convenient for the best men in the parish to sett in".[72] Bude's place in the church directly related to his wider reputation in the community, so it is no wonder that he saw an "oatemeale maker" sitting in front of him as an affront. Similarly, in 1679, Richard Gilbert fought John Shuckford in the church over his right to a pew reserved for the twenty-four men of Eye council. It was no coincidence that the day of the fight was also the day when new bailiffs were sworn into office. Shuckford had held office the previous year, but had not been re-elected, therefore was expected to relinquish his seat to the new council members. However, when he did not, Gilbert punched Shuckford on the chest and forced him to take a seat elsewhere.[73]

Church space, therefore, was the ultimate illustration of *habitus* in practice. It contained in microcosm the local hierarchies and social values, and was an important component in the reproduction of culture and power in the community.[74] Words spoken within sacred space had the proclivity to become more sensational, by appropriating the authority and formality of the setting, for example, a minister's authority was heightened by delivering his speeches from the pulpit, rather than the street, and a parishioner could gain more attention by attacking the minister within his own space, the fundamental source of his authority. To question church authority within its own "home" had serious legal and moral consequences for both challenger and challenged, violating the peace and sanctity of the church and upsetting the congregation as a whole.

IV

This chapter has explored popular agency and concepts of legitimacy. Personality, behaviour and personal circumstances played crucial roles in both areas, but it is possible to draw some general observations. For both minister and layman background, education and wealth were tantamount to power. For a minister, the size and wealth of his benefice, but more importantly, his personal conduct, would signify whether he would play a leadership role in his community. Indeed, ministers drew much of their authority from the dynamics of reciprocal respect, co-operation and the fulfilment of certain obligations, buttressing their legitimate right to office in line with social ideals. Thus, if a minister did not conform to such norms, parishioners from all social ranks could justifiably complain, bolstered by their sense of moral righteousness and the inherent legality of their grievances.

The majority of the cases discussed above were initiated by the "chief inhabitants". This was probably for two reasons: the financial ability to raise a Church Court suit and the weight behind their collective voice. However, many of their supporters and witnesses were from a broad cross-section of middling society, including yeomen and husbandmen, men and women, the educated and the illiterate.[75] That poorer men and women could criticize the behaviour of clergymen alongside their richer neighbours conveys some sense of the circumstances which could empower ordinary people. Perhaps most elementally, they were able to contest the authority of their minister using the spoken word. A poorer person's words might have carried less weight than those of a richer neighbour in a court of law, but it was at least possible, if not always acceptable, for many within the community to criticize their minister with good reason. Indeed, status did not always empower: in the case of Sir Robert Naunton, for example, it seems his wealth enabled him to do little more than offer a bribe.

Society therefore functioned within vertical and horizontal perimeters of power, whereby certain circumstances constrained or facilitated the agency of different groups. In contrast with the parochial political forum, in the religious world it was possible for "commoners" to articulate their concerns as a fundamental part of their Christian conscience. This was highly efficacious when used within the traditional and conservative context of correcting a deficient social order, rather than attacking it.

Furthermore, for some, it was a way of exercising personal power in a society which ranked both morality and religiosity as a merit.[76] Thus it was not simply the upper-middling sorts or minor gentry who were able to exercise power within their parish and neither were claims to "belonging" and "inclusivity" simply the prerogative of the rich.

Notes

[1] See C. Muldrew, *The Economy of Obligation: The Culture of Credit and Social Relations in Early Modern England* (London: Macmillan, 1998); M. J. Braddick, *State Formation in Early Modern England, c. 1550-1700* (Cambridge: Cambridge University Press, 2000); Steve Hindle, *The State and Social Change in Early Modern England, c.1550–1640* (London and New York: Macmillan 2000) or Mark Goldie, "The Unacknowledged Republic: Office-holding in Early Modern England", in ed. Tim Harris, *The Politics of the Excluded, c. 1500-1850* (Basingstoke: Palgrave, 2001), 153-194.

[2] See for example A. Leftwich, *Redefining Politics: People, Resources and Power* (London: Taylor and Francis, 1983).

[3] For clergy/congregation disputes, see in particular, J. Addy, *Sin and Society in the Seventeenth Century* (London and New York: Routledge, 1989); D. Beaver, *Parish Communities and Religious Conflict in the Vale of Gloucester, 1590-1690* (Massachusetts and London: Harvard University Press, 1998; C. Haigh, "Dr. Temple's Pew: Sex and Clerical Status in the 1630s", *Huntington Library Quarterly* 68:3 (2005): 497-518; J. Maltby, *Prayer Book and People in Elizabethan and Early Stuart England* (Cambridge: Cambridge University Press, 1998) and D. Spaeth, *The Church in an Age of Danger: Parsons and Parishioners, 1660-1740* (Cambridge: Cambridge University Press, 2000).

[4] A good overview of Church Court procedure is to be found in R.B. Outhwaite, *The Rise and Fall of the English Ecclesiastical Courts, 1500-1860* (Cambridge: Cambridge University Press, 2006), esp. Ch. 1 and 2. The courts were officially disbanded in 1646, but in Norwich, new cases were recorded throughout the following year.

[5] M. Ingram, *Church Courts, Sex and Marriage in England, 1570-1640* (Cambridge: Cambridge University Press, 1987), 43.

[6] Outhwaite, *English Ecclesiastical Courts*, 9.

[7] These disputes were widespread. See Haigh, "Dr. Temple's Pew" and Spaeth, *The Church in an Age of Danger*, 59-82 in particular.

[8] See for example, Ingram, *Church Courts* or L. Gowing, *Domestic Dangers: Women, Words and Sex in Early Modern London* (Oxford: Oxford University Press, 1998).

[9] For work on plebeian challenges to political authority see, for example, A. Wood, *Riot, Rebellion and Popular Politics in Early Modern England* (Basingstoke: Palgrave, 2002) or A. Wood, 'Subordination, Solidarity and the Limits of Popular Agency in a Yorkshire Valley, c. 1596-1615', *Past and Present* 193 (2006): 41-72.

[10] The most severe punishment the Church Court could order was excommunication. Alternatively, it had the power to hand serious cases to the secular authorities. For more on this refer to R. Houlbrooke, *Church Courts and the People during the English Reformation, 1520-1570* (Oxford: Oxford University Press, 1979).
[11] Beaver, *Parish Communities,* 132.
[12] Addy, *Sin and Society,* 15.
[13] It is not my intention to discuss the economic role of the parish clergyman, suffice to say that his part in poor law administration was often a bone of contention, as was dependence on his parishioner's tithes. For an in-depth and useful discussion of the tensions caused by tithe payments, see C. Hill, *Economic Problems of the Church from Archbishop Whitgift to the Long Parliament* (Oxford: Oxford University Press, 1956); E.J. Evans, "Some Reasons for the Growth of English Rural Anti-Clericalism c.1750-1830", *Past and Present* 66 (1975): 84-109; E.J. Evans *The Contentious Tithe: The Tithe Problem and English Agriculture, 1750-1850* (London: Routledge, 1976) or Spaeth, *The Church in an Age of Danger,* 133-155.
[14] Maltby, *Prayer Book and People,* 37, 65.
[15] Spaeth has covered this topic in some detail, so further discussion should be referred to his text, especially 34-40. He bases some of his assumptions on the work of Gregory King, reproduced in the later article by G.S. Holmes, 'Gregory King and the Social Structure of Pre-Industrial England', *Transactions of the Royal Historical Society,* 5th ser. 27 (1977): 41-68. Spaeth discusses the problems with King's figures in addition to highlighting the wide gap between clerical incomes, some falling well below the poverty line, whilst others reaped the benefits of pluralism and wealthy parishes. This, he suggests, contributed to growing criticism of the church during the later seventeenth and early eighteenth centuries.
[16] See Beaver, *Parish Communities,* Ch. 4. Beaver suggests that conflicts between religious non-conformism and obedience to secular authorities had an enormous impact on everyday life, many people feeling a profound "sense of participation" in the religious debate.
[17] Between 1600 and 1640 there were forty-four separate cases against members of the clergy brought to the attention of the Church by laypeople in Norfolk. Peaks are in 1617 and 1633, the latter at a time of increasing paranoia about Catholicism, Arminianism and the rising ascendancy of Laud. Between the restoration of the Church Court in 1661 and the Glorious Revolution there are twenty cases, peaking in the 1680s before a drastic downturn post-1688. The decrease may merely mimic the declining use of the courts in general terms, rather than reflect any changes in circumstances between parishioners and ministers. After the 1680s the majority of court business concerned wills, general church upkeep and administration, rather than defamation. It is also possible that by the end of the seventeenth century the growth of non-conformist churches may have had an impact, non-conformist ministers or parishioners choosing to attend an alternative Church rather than complaining about their own parish provision.
[18] A preliminary survey of presentments for non-conformity in the Norwich Diocese compiled from the Compton Census of 1676, suggests that the parishes

which recorded problems with their minister were predominantly those with very low or non-existent levels of non-conformity, suggesting there may be some correlation between religious conservatism and criticism of ministers. For the figures see A. Whiteman, ed., *The Compton Census of 1676: A Critical Edition* (Oxford: Oxford University Press, 1986).

[19] For a thorough discussion of the middling sorts see H. French, *The Middle Sort of People in Provincial England, 1600-1750* (Oxford: Oxford University Press, 2007).

[20] Richard Baxter quoted in B. Manning, *Aristocrats, Plebeians and Revolution in England, 1640-1660* (London: Pluto Press, 1992), 67-8. In the Norwich Diocese defamation cases were brought to court predominantly by and between the middling sorts. This includes all types of defamation, not only that of a minister. To some extent this is not surprising as it cost money to take a case to court, but it does not explain the absence of the poorer sorts as defendants. It is possible that their voices were considered less important, or that the contentious poor ended up prosecuted in the civic courts instead, for "crimes" such as vagrancy, abusive speech or misrule, rather than being sued for defamation. It must also be remembered that in many of these cases the backgrounds of the participants are obscure, which creates problems compiling accurate figures. Interestingly, at the other end of the scale, there were very few cases between "gentlemen" or above, except as compurgators. Very wealthy or titled nobles may have used central courts, such as the Court of Chivalry between 1634 and 1640, the Court of Arches or the Court of Admiralty for defamation settlements. However, these were for serious cases and predominantly used by men, so this does not sufficiently explain the absence of wealthier people in the Diocese Court. Barbara Hanawalt also notes the predominance of the middling sort in court records during the medieval period for all types of prosecutions. However, she is similarly unable to offer any definitive conclusions as to why. See B. Hanawalt, "Community Conflict and Social Control: Crime and Justice in the Ramsey Abbey Villages", *Journal of Medieval Studies* 39 (1977): 402-423.

[21] This role extended to the moral welfare of the community. Daniel Beaver argues that wealthier families played a central role in presenting their poorer neighbours at the Church Courts as part of the wider moral reformation of the late sixteenth and early seventeenth centuries. See: Beaver, *Parish Communities,* 120.

[22] Interestingly, the middling sorts also feature heavily in criminal court records from the same area defaming secular office holders. These findings tie in with recent research which highlights the central role of the middling sorts in urban and rural micro-politics, rather than seeing early-modern society as essentially dualistic, at odds between rich and poor which has been a criticism of work by James C. Scott, for example. See J.C. Scott, *Weapons of the Weak: Everyday Forms of Peasant Resistance* (New Haven: Yale University Press, 1985) or J.C. Scott, *Domination and the Arts of Resistance: Hidden Transcripts* (New Haven: Yale University Press, 1990). Even critics of Scott fall into the same trap. Andy Wood's research into seditious speech, for example, tends to discuss rich and poor in oppositional terminology, as this is often how they choose to present

themselves. See A. Wood, "Poore men woll speke one daye: Plebeian Languages of Deference and Defiance in England, c. 1520-1640" in ed. Harris, *The Politics of the Excluded*, 67-99. His article neglects to consider the social backgrounds of those on either "side", whilst highlighting how people of all social levels deliberately adopted adversarial speech in order to appropriate a universally recognised language of social conflict.

[23] This usually involved suing for defamation in the Church Court, see F. Williamson, "Aspects of Social relations in the Seventeenth-Century Diocese of Norwich: Space, Agency and Identity" (PhD Diss., UEA, 2008), Ch. 2.

[24] A useful analysis of vestry powers is to be found in S. Hindle, "Hierarchy and Community in the Elizabethan Parish: The Swallowfield Articles of 1596", *The Historical Journal* 42:3 (1999): 835-851. See also Rosemary O'Day, *The Professions in Early Modern England, 1450-1800: Servants of the Commonweal* (Harlow: Pearson Education Ltd): 91-107.

[25] Donald Spaeth discusses ministerial backgrounds in some depth. See Spaeth, *The Church in an Age of Danger*, 30-58. Steve Hindle discusses social exclusivity in the parish and the "chief inhabitants" in Hindle, "Hierarchy and Community" or S. Hindle, "The Political Culture of the Middling Sort, c. 1550-1700" in ed. Harris, *The Politics of the Excluded*, 125-52.

[26] Whilst there would have been considerable regional and personal variations, it has been estimated that an average clerical wage would have fallen between fifty and eighty pounds per annum. See Spaeth, *The Church in an Age of Danger*, 35. The exceptional number of parishes in Norfolk suggests this might have been especially true here.

[27] Norfolk Record Office (hereafter NRO), DN/DEP/48/52, fol. 151r, 11 March 1669. Gibbs v. Brookebank. Brookebank was vicar incumbent between 1662 and 1694, so this incident did not affect his long-term career in this parish. He had initially been presented to his benefice by a widow, Anne Beck, once part of a family of some importance in Geyton. See Francis Blomefield, *An Essay Towards a Topographical History of the County of Norfolk*, Vol. 3, (London, 1808). Vicars were entitled to less money in tithes than rectors, which corroborates Brookebank's "hard-luck" story.

[28] I have included these facts in this discussion because it seems that not only did people of a certain rank present ministers, but of a certain gender and age, namely middle-aged men. Alex Shepard suggested that age was an important contributing factor in respectability. Between the exuberance and irrationality of youth and the frailties of old-age, the middle years were regarded as the pinnacle in masculine achievement in combination with wealth, marriage, children and a household. See A. Shepard, *Meanings of Manhood* (Oxford: Oxford University Press, 2003), 54-5.

[29] NRO, DN/DEP/41/46, fol. 486r, October 1633. William Butte v. William Withers.

[30] Christopher Haigh's case of Dr Temple and Bray Ayleworth is very similar. Like the case of Butte v. Withers; their argument centred around which had the superior status, eventually ruining the reputation of one man. See Haigh, "Dr. Temple's Pew": 497-500.

[31] NRO, DN/DEP/38/43, fol. 105r, 7 July 1629. Piggott v. Hodgson.
[32] Stradsett vicarage's yearly value was £25, based on the figure for yearly tenths, which in 1534 was £3 6s 8d. John Ecton, *Liber valorum et decimarum* (London, 1711), p.251. I am grateful to Donald Spaeth for this reference.
[33] John Peile, *Biographical Register of Christ's College, 1505-1905 and Earlier Foundation: God's House, 1448-1505* (Cambridge: Cambridge University Press, 1910), 198. Hodgeson remained in Stradsett until his death in 1651.
[34] NRO, DN/DEP/45/48b, fol. 58r, 21 July 1640. Richard Anguish v. James Seaman.
[35] The only evidence of the stipend attached to this benefice was recorded eighteen years later 1655. Although inflation would have to be taken into account; this information offers some idea of the benefice's worth, which by 1655 was sixty-five pounds. See *National Church Institutions Database of Manuscripts and Archives*, COMM XIIb/3, Survey 3, 1655-1657.
[36] NRO, MC 134/8, Receipt of Richard Anguish to John Wythe and others, sequestrators of Starston rectory, for £18 19s. 7d. arrears of the profits of the rectory paid to Anguish by order of the Standing Committee for Norfolk, 1647. It is possible however that the sequestration was linked to the civil war.
[37] *National Church Institutions Database of Manuscripts and Archives*, COMM XIIb/3, Survey 3, 1655-1657.
[38] Both Le Gros and Paston were from wealthy Norfolk families. Thomas Le Gros is less well known to us today than the famous Paston family. Le Gros was the son of Sir Charles Le Gros of Crostwick, Norfolk, the nephew of Thomas Knyvett, another well-known Norfolk pedigree. Le Gros was a Royalist supporter during the civil wars and fought side by side with Thomas Knyvett's son. See B. Schofield, *The Knyvett Letters, 1620-1644* (Norwich: Norfolk Record Office Publications, 1949), 160. The gauge of literacy is normally taken to be the ability to sign a name on the deposition.
[39] NRO, DN/DEP/46/50, fol. 277r, 7 April 1663. Thomas Le Gros v. Thomas Ramsey.
[40] NRO, DN/DEP/46/50, fol. 339r, 7 April 1663. Thomas Le Gros v. Thomas Ramsey.
[41] NRO, BL/Y 1/2, 1 November 1661. Declaration by Thomas Ramsey of Crostwick, clerk, that he has defamed and slandered Sir William Paston of Oxnead by his letters, all copies of which have now been burnt; witnessed by Thomas le Gros, Thomas Falke, Henry Lucie, Thomas Bradford, Edward Barber and Ben Cooper.
[42] Ibid.
[43] Rumours that royalist Mayor Utting was to be removed from his post and sent to appear before parliament in London sparked an angry mob to gather arms in his defence. The near revolt ended in premature disaster when Norwich's gunpowder storehouse was accidently set alight, destroying a large part of the city centre.
[44] NRO, MC 98/1/16, Letter from Thomas Ramsey, Parson of Crostwick, to John Utting, Mayor of Norwich.
[45] NRO, DN/DEP/46/50, fol. 277r, 7 April 1663.

[46] NRO, DN/DEP/42/47A, fol. 59r, June 1636. Sherwood v. Bery. Blomefield records that Nicholas Sherwood was the Rector of All Saints in Earsham from 1618. He was ejected in 1643 by the Earl of Manchester, but subsequently restored, remaining there until his death in 1671, three days before his wife. Blomefield also mentions Thomas Berry whose memorial stone is laid at the door of the north porch, dated 17 April 1653. Both the stone and its position suggest Berry was an affluent man. See, F. Blomefield, *An Essay Towards a Topographical History of the County of Norfolk: Humble-yard. Depewade, Earsham, Henstede* (1806), 316-17.

[47] NRO, DEP/45/48b, fol. 116v, 23 March 1640. Locke v. Kinge. King is mentioned in J. Wilson, *The Wymondham Town Book, 1585-1620* (Norwich: Norfolk Record Office, 2006), 14-15.

[48] "Knave" was a serious insult and a common reason to instigate defamation proceedings. It was a broad term, covering dishonesty, criminality and even sexual immorality, see Williamson, *Aspects of Social Relations,* 146-53.

[49] NRO, DN/DEP/46/50, fol. 361r, July 1663. John Parker v. Alexander Kirby.

[50] Ibid.

[51] NRO, DN/DEP/42/47A, fol. 630r. William Jobb v. John Utting.

[52] Steve Hindle and Laura Gowing both discuss the mixed response to women appearing in court to pursue allegations of sexual crimes against them. There was always a risk that taking a man to court with an allegation of sexual misconduct would backfire and destroy the woman's reputation in the process. See S. Hindle, "The Shaming of Margaret Knowsley: Gossip, Gender and the Experience of Authority in Early Modern England", *Continuity and Change* 9:3 (1994): 391-419 or Gowing, *Domestic Dangers.*

[53] NRO, DN/DEP/42/47A, fol. 630r. William Jobb v. John Utting.

[54] Church of England Clergy Database: http://eagle.cch.kcl.ac.uk:8080/cce/persons

[55] The witnesses against Utting were on the whole at a higher or at least comparable status, including one gentleman, a blacksmith, a miller, several yeomen, husbandmen, alehouse keepers and a parson.

[56] Naunton was also the author of "Fragmenta Regalia" published posthumously in 1641, six years after his death.

[57] NRO, DN/DEP/44/48A, fol. 163r, 2 October 1639. Mr Naunton v. Robert Longe.

[58] William Lodge was rated at six hearths and Henry Tubby at seven, indicating they were both very wealthy. P. J. Seaman, *Norfolk and Norwich Hearth Tax Assessment: Lady Day, 1666* (Norwich: Norfolk and Norwich Genealogical Society, 1988), 8-9.

[59] NRO, DN/DEP/47/51, fol.177r, April 1665. Robert Gilbert v. William Lodge.

[60] NRO, DN/DEP/47/51, fol.177r, April 1665. Robert Gilbert v. William Lodge and John Soanes v. Henry Tubby.

[61] "Belonging" was a key feature of early-modern parishes. This was partly because of suspicion of strangers, but, also because poor relief was based on parish residency. Brodie Waddell discusses the importance of belonging in his essay in

this collection: "Neighbours and Strangers: The Locality in Later Stuart Economic Culture".

[62] NRO, DN/DEP/36/39, fol. 241v, 1614. Samuel Hooke v. Thomas Chapman.

[63] NRO, DN/DEP/41/46, fol. 518r, 22 November 1635. Isack Welham v. Mary wife of Thomas Love.

[64] NRO, DN/DEP/37/40, fol. 191v, 15 December 1617. Wilson v. Leste. The connection between a refusal to perform infant baptism and Puritanism can be looked at in detail in Maltby, *Prayer Book and People*, 52-6.

[65] NRO, DN/DEP/38/43, fol.389r, 15 October 1629.

[66] H. Le Strange, ed., *Norfolk Official Lists*, (Norwich, 1890), 203.

[67] NRO, DN/DEP/38/43, fols 389r-90r, 15 October 1629.

[68] K. Wrightson and D. Levine, eds, *Poverty and Piety in an English Village: Terling, 1525-1700* (Oxford: Oxford University Press, 1979), 160-72. This section of Wrightson and Levine's micro-history discusses Stalham's later life and the religious situation in Terling in more detail. Stalham continued to face persecution for his views, but predominantly from the Church authorities rather than his new congregation. In 1636, 1638 and 1639 in particular, he was called before the archdeacon to answer for acts of non-conformity, such as not wearing the surplice, not reading royal proclamations, or railing in the communion table. Stalham later recorded that he had lived "in weaknesse and in fear and in much trembling" during this time.

[69] The symbolism of sacred space is considered in C. P. Graves, "Social Space in the English Medieval Parish Church", *Economy and Society* 18:3 (1989): 297-322; C. Marsh, "Sacred Space in England, 1560-1640: The View from the Pew", *Journal of Ecclesiastical History* 53:2 (2002): 286-311; C. Marsh, "Order and Place in England, 1580-1640: The View from the Pew", *Journal of British Studies* 44:1 (2005): 3-26 and R. Tittler, "Seats of Honour, Seats of Power: The Symbolism of Public Seating in the English Urban Community, c. 1560-1620", *Albion* 24:2 (2002): 205-223.

[70] NRO, DN/DEP/42/47A, fol. 5r, 4 April 1635. Witherell v. Harris.

[71] DN/DEP/43/47B, fol. 78v, 30 May 1638. Theoderick v. Bude.

[72] NRO, DN/DEP/43/47B, fol. 99v, 12 July 1638. Theoderick v. Bude.

[73] NRO, DN/DEP/51/55, fol. 1r, 13 October 1680. Shuckford v. Gilbert.

[74] H. Lefebvre, *The Production of Space,* trans. D. Nicholson-Smith (Oxford: Blackwell, 1991), 239. Ceremonies such as Rogation extended this concept into the wider community, symbolizing the social order in the allocation of processional places. For more on ceremonies and their importance see V. Turner, *Image and Pilgrimage in Christian Cultures: Anthropological Perspectives* (Columbia: Columbia University Press, 1995). Also refer to Brodie Waddell's essay and the introduction in this collection for a brief explanation of *habitus*.

[75] As Spaeth suggests, in the Norwich Diocese suits were often brought by richer parishioners, but then supported by people of the same or lesser status. See Spaeth, *The church in an Age of Danger,* 91.

[76] Margaret Spufford challenged the idea that it was only the "godly elite" who had a stake in parish moral reform. See M. Spufford, ed., *The World of Rural Dissenters, 1520-1725* (Cambridge: Cambridge University Press, 1995).

NEIGHBOURS AND STRANGERS: THE LOCALITY IN LATER STUART ECONOMIC CULTURE

BRODIE WADDELL

Belonging to a local community was a vital part of "making-shift" in later Stuart England. To be a "neighbour" or "inhabitant", rather than a "stranger" or "foreigner", had a profound effect on one's economic situation. For instance, gaining "settlement" in a parish or becoming a "freeman" in a town brought with it a range of important rights and privileges, whereas being branded as a "vagrant" or "intruder" could have dire consequences. The culture, institutions and practices of localism shaped the English economy in ways that are often impossible to measure but equally impossible to ignore.

Of course, local communities took many forms during this period. They varied considerably in size and strength, including boroughs, parishes, manors, townships, districts, and neighbourhoods. But whatever their extent or complexity, they shared several key features. First, they were all based on particular territorial spaces, with borders that might be tangibly etched onto the landscape with walls, fences or boundary markers. Second, they normally had some degree of self-government and an ability to police their own borders, leading contemporaries to refer to them as "little commonwealths".[1] Third, and most importantly, they always depended on a basic division between insiders and outsiders, between "us" and "them". As will be seen, these attributes made the locality a central site in the endless battles over economic resources, especially in moments of crisis. As semi-autonomous spaces, limited more by geography than by wealth or status, local communities offered independence and power to people who lacked the political influence of the landed and mercantile elite.[2]

Previous scholarship on these issues is hardly difficult to find. The historiography has, however, developed several tendencies to which this chapter is a response. Specifically, for many decades this scholarship built on a simplistic model of decline – crudely summarized as a shift from "community" to "society", from *Gemeinschaft* to *Gesellschaft* – inherited from nineteenth-century social theory.[3] Although more recent research has effectively demolished the most blatantly wrong-headed assumptions associated with this theory, very few scholars have focused on the continuing economic relevance of the local community in the half-century or so after 1660.[4] This chapter is thus an attempt to examine the strength of "localist" mentalities during this period through an investigation of later Stuart popular culture, whilst also synthesising the scattered existing research on this topic. Rather than expounding on a particular type of locality (e.g. the parish or the borough) or on a particular type of economic relationship (e.g. poor relief or land use), this essay is intended to provide a more holistic analysis of the logic that underlay these various sources of identity, solidarity and conflict.

The chapter begins with an exploration of the many ways in which loyalty to the locality – as well as the vilification of outsiders – was disseminated through popular media, especially the sermons, ballads, oaths, festivals and rituals that communicated these messages to people in every corner of England. The second part of this chapter focuses on more concrete manifestations of local community, including formal institutions and habitual practices. While showing the extensive variety of material support available to insiders, it also shows how outsiders were systematically disadvantaged and sometimes excluded entirely from local economic life. The third part is an analysis of the violent collective responses that sometimes erupted when external agents threatened the economic welfare of a community. This shows how bloody riots could be sparked by the very same set of assumptions that inspired informal charity and parochial processions. Finally, the chapter concludes with a brief review of the effects of locality on popular agency and a survey of the basic contours of change over the period. It emphasizes the diversity of stories that can be told about the influence of local community in later Stuart England, noting that while the effects of localism on economic relations cannot be ignored, neither can they be reduced to a straightforward narrative of rise, decline or continuity. This chapter thus reveals the profound impact of this type of community but also its undeniable variability and complexity.

I. Culture and Identity

Thou shalt love thy neighbour as thy self.[5]

If thou sell ought unto thy neighbour, or buyest ought of thy neighbour's hand, ye shall not oppress one another.[6]

Thou shalt not remove thy neighbour's landmark.[7]

Woe unto him ... that useth his neighbour's service without wages, and giveth him not for his work.[8]

The King James Bible of 1611 enjoined its readers again and again on the subject of economic relations. It instructed them on the necessity of charity, on commercial dealings, on land disputes, and on employment practices. And, as the passages above indicate, it did this using the idiom of "neighbours" and "neighbourliness", ensuring that these concepts became an intrinsic part of contemporary thinking about economic affairs. Naomi Tadmor, after examining this issue in detail, has concluded that the reworking of ancient scriptural injunctions to fit the "social world" of early modern England "helped to underpin contemporary norms of Christian neighbourliness and endow them with fresh significances".[9] Moreover, the "language of neighbourly love" was constantly re-interpreted and continually communicated through media like catechisms, sermons, cheap print and proverbial wisdom – as a result, it infused everyday interaction in both towns and villages.[10]

Of course, one should not assume that the connection between this abstract concept and the neighbourhood economy was unambiguous. In fact, contemporary moralists usually tried to dissuade their audiences from reading the idiom too literally. For example, Isaac Barrow, like most preachers, reflexively used the phrase "poor neighbour" to refer to *any* suitable objects of charity, irrespective of locality.[11] In his sermon on the subject, published in 1680, he argued that neighbourly love and charity were "duties of common humanity", because Christ's blood had "demolished" the "wall of partition" which had separated the "holy neighbourhood" of Jews from the gentile "strangers and foreigners", thus ensuring that "neighbourhood is universal and unlimited".[12] Other clergymen – from Thomas Manton, an influential nonconformist, to Anthony Harneck, a preacher at the Savoy Chapel – argued for a similarly expansive definition of "neighbour".[13] According to them, a poor family on the other side of the country had no less claim to neighbourly benevolence than one living next door.

This was the interpretation offered by most later Stuart preachers, but not all were quite so unequivocally anti-literal. White Kennett's sermon at the London mayoral election of 1711, for instance, must have left a slightly different impression. Although he denounced those who used the notion of "neighbour" to act uncharitably towards outsiders, he also acknowledged that some people were "our more especial Neighbours, [which] do entitle them to our more peculiar Care and Love". More specifically, he singled out fellow Protestants, fellow British subjects, and fellow Londoners.[14] So, despite his protestations, Kennett ultimately condoned a more exclusive conception of "neighbourhood", one that would have been much more comprehensible to those already inclined to favour the local poor over distant "strangers".

Loyalty to the local community often cut through the ties which supposedly bound together all of humanity. Laypeople almost invariably prioritized the place they regarded as "home"–whether a neighbourhood or village, or a more institutionalized entity such as a parish or urban corporation. In part, this resulted from the many practical concerns and interests that neighbours tended to share, but these identities also drew much of their strength from the fecund soil of a popular culture which promoted localized mutuality and solidarity against economic "interlopers".[15]

In the case of London, the grandest of all these "little commonwealths", this mentality found expression in popular broadsheets. The city's printers produced several later Stuart ballads extolling its wealth and prosperity, including one entitled *Londons Praise* which stands out thanks to its especially communal tone.[16] Like others of the genre, *Londons Praise* emphasised the strength of the urban economy and the virtues of its "good substantial" citizens; yet it also repeatedly lauded civic unity and equality. For example, the balladeer specifically acknowledged the horizontal ties which bound together all the city's freemen by claiming that the magistrates defended "their Neighbours" from malefactors and

> every year they change Lord Mayor,
> to shew their mutual Love,
> And that in power they equal are,
> and none the other above.

So, while not neglecting to extol the stately grandeur of the mayor and aldermen, this panegyric simultaneously called attention to the presumed solidarity, perhaps even egalitarianism, inherent in urban citizenship. Moreover, in order to enjoy the economic rights that came with this civic "freedom", one had to swear the freeman's oath. For Londoners, this meant vowing to uphold "the Franchises and Customs" of the city and "bearing your part as a Free man ought to doe".[17] New freemen also swore to use civic institutions, rather than the royal courts, to solve commercial disputes whenever possible. In other words, attaining the "freedom" required defending, supporting and utilising the institutions of the local community. The oath served as a ritualized recitation of the importance of civic strength and local autonomy, schooling freemen in the values essential to life as an upstanding Londoner.

This communal mentality similarly imbued the economic culture of England's other cities and towns. Jonathan Barry has provocatively described it as "bourgeois collectivism", arguing that townspeople tirelessly promoted "all those qualities, such as thrift, respectability, and industry, often labelled the Protestant work-ethic and seen as the foundation of individualism", but "their success was assumed to depend on *collective* rather than individual action" and "they were matched by a set of overtly collective virtues, of sociability and good fellowship".[18] The instruments used to propagate these ideals were manifold. Not only did freemen directly instruct their children and apprentices in the virtues of civic mutuality, they also attempted to give their imagined community physical form though elaborate pomp and ceremony on special occasions. Ritualized urban festivities – such as the Lord Mayor's Show in London and "guild day" in Norwich – revived markedly after 1660, and their undeniable elements of hierarchy should not blind us the fact that, at the same time, they clearly celebrated urban unity and local identity.[19] In many cases, the participants in these civic events reiterated their loyalty to such ideals by twinning their symbolic displays with practical expressions of mutuality. Corporate feasts, for example, often ended with a distribution to the town's poor, and Lammas Day celebrations in late seventeenth-century Coventry coincided with the regulation of common lands.[20] Moreover, these practical adjuncts to urban festivity were only small parts of the extensive systems of material support and relief established by townsfolk to protect the welfare of fellow inhabitants. Access to these communal resources could itself become a cultural signal, what Phil Withington has called "a badge of communal belonging".[21]

The same mix of revelry, ritual and commensality helped to define local communities in rural areas as well. Villagers developed much of their sense of locality from the many seasonal celebrations which filled rural calendars, and this had tangible effects on the nature and dynamics of everyday social relations. According to Robert Malcolmson, "popular recreations" of this sort "celebrated those ideals which transcended self" and "served to foster social cohesiveness and group unity" – they could even temporarily create "a rough and ready social equality" which cut across differences in wealth and status.[22] The particular form taken by such festivities varied considerably, though most seem to have included some type of feasting, gift-giving or charitable collection. Ronald Hutton, the pre-eminent historian of seasonal customs, has found evidence of these features in numerous cases from the late seventeenth and early eighteenth centuries, especially in the customs associated with Christmas, New Year, Plough Monday, May Day, sheep-shearing and harvesting.[23] Even newly invented holidays sometimes included elements of mutuality. At Ashby Folville in Leicestershire, for example, the churchwardens feasted "the neighbours" on Restoration Day.[24]

The parochial perambulations during Rogation week offer perhaps the quintessential example of this process of defining and promoting community through ritualized festivity.[25] Historians have long emphasized the social, economic and cultural importance of this yearly event, and recent research indicates that "beating the bounds" became more elaborate and more widespread after the Restoration.[26] For instance, some perambulating parishioners carried banners, others wore coloured silk ribbons, and at least one group sang a brief rhyme describing their route.[27] Such visual and aural expressions of locality encouraged participants to focus on collective, rather than individual, concerns – a perspective suggested more explicitly in the "Exhortation" appointed by the church for this exact purpose. As preparation for the Rogation march, the clergyman would tell his flock that "it is the part of every good Townsman, to preserve as much as lieth in him, the Liberties, Franchises, Bounds, and Limits of his Town and Country", though without causing a breach in "Love and Charity" through thoughtless strife. The perambulation was, according to the "Exhortation", an opportunity to discover and condemn those "greedy men" who "plough and grate upon their Neighbours Land" or who encroach on "the common balkes and walkes"; they ought to be "admonished, and charitably reformed, who be the doers of such private gaining, to the slander of the township, and the hindrance of the Poor". In addition, the minister would remind parishioners of their collective duties, including mundane responsibilities such as maintaining the local highways and, of course, relieving the local poor.[28] Indeed, the events themselves often became occasions for communal feasting and hospitality, while younger participants sometimes received treats.[29] The economic welfare of the community and its members was thus central to the ritual, rhetoric and reality of perambulation.

Yet, these sorts of festivities expressed exclusion as well as inclusion. The "beating of the bounds", for example, explicitly marked out the spatial limits of parochial community, thus deepening the division between insiders and outsiders. Moreover, the stream of favours shared among locals had a sinister undercurrent, for it emerged not only from mutuality between neighbours but also from hostility to strangers. After all, it would have seemed obvious to most people that members of one's own community should be privileged – both formally and informally – in day-to-day economic dealings. For example, returning for a moment to the ballad discussed in the preceding section, London was depicted as praiseworthy in part because of its unapologetically exclusionary economic policies:

> No forraigner can set up there,
> the orders are so strong,
> In Shop they must not sell no ware,
> least they the Free-men wrong.[30]

This division had even more force at the parochial level where legal distinctions between "settled" inhabitants and "foreigners" were compounded by long-standing cultural traditions. The "impermeability" of village dialect and proverbs, the ubiquity of colourful localist insults, the violence of inter-parish football matches – all of these contributed to the strength of "local xenophobia" in the seventeenth and eighteenth centuries.[31]

A stranger from another village could face considerable economic disadvantages when competing with locals, but the situation was worse still for someone who appeared to lack a "home" entirely. A dark cloud of suspicion had hung over poor itinerants since at least the Reformation and, despite lightening somewhat over the course of the seventeenth century, it continued to follow this sort of traveller in the later Stuart period.[32] For example, some clergymen preaching on charity showed a decidedly uncharitable attitude toward such people, calling them "constant Wanderers from Place to Place, [who] can never settle themselves to any Trade or Labour, but love to live idly, and to do nothing".[33] They saw this seemingly nomadic existence as a threat to good order and government, a danger that could only be countered with the whip and the stocks. They were not alone. Other educated commentators did their best to convince their audiences that there were "some thousands of wandring persons that go from door to door, to the great dishonour & disadvantage of the Nation"; thus necessitating "publick Work-houses ... for Vagrants, and sturdy Beggars, who have no habitation, and must be held to their Labour, as Gally-slaves are tied to their Oars".[34] The image that emerges is one of ceaseless transience, of shadowy figures moving at the edge of the community "from Place to Place" and "from door to door".

A slightly less threatening portrayal can be found in contemporary ballads, perhaps because those who bought them had more in common with vagrants than did most ministers and pamphleteers. Yet, despite their comedic style and upbeat mood, these songs show a similar antipathy to wandering mendicants. Taking on the voice of "a jovial Beggar bold", the balladeer invariably described a life which mixed rambling around the country with innumerable petty crimes and deceits.[35] His constant mobility meant spending nights in barns, under hedges or even inside "a Hollow Tree"; and, in turn, this lack of a fixed locale ensured that he would "pay no rent", guaranteed a fresh supply of gullible benefactors, offered new targets for theft, and helped him avoid hostile officials. For instance, one band of "Merry" beggars reported that

> we do pass from Town to Town;
> but for a time we stay,
> Least the Magistrates hear of us,
> and Whip us thence away.[36]

According to the popular stereotype presented in these ballads, the vagrant's irregular movement "from Place to Place" indicated that he actually belonged to *no place* at all, not merely excluded from a particular local community, but lacking both locality and community entirely. Although in practice this strict dichotomy between the "placed" and the "displaced" rarely withstood close examination, its presence in sermons, pamphlets and ballads framed many people's perceptions of poor travellers.

This imagined rift – with settled householders on one side and incorrigible vagabonds on the other – was part of a much longer and deeper fissure which split the economic landscape of early modern England into two supposedly distinct territories. Ultimately, in the minds of many, one either belonged to a particular locality or one did not. The shared sense of place which bound together fellow "citizens", "inhabitants", "parishioners" or "neighbours" necessarily involved excluding those regarded as outsiders, and this process of unifying the community while defining its limits was clearly visible in the many popular expressions of solidarity discussed above.

But this localist culture was not a timeless set of customs and beliefs, continuing unchanged throughout the seventeenth and eighteenth centuries. Instead, several aspects of it seem to have experienced both a revival and a decline during the period considered here. For instance, under the later Stuarts, the number of localities celebrating annual festivals reached proportions not seen since the sixteenth century, including a temporary revival of parish wakes.[37] After suffering considerable cultural attrition at the hands of would-be reformers under earlier regimes, the Restoration enabled towns and villages once again to reinforce communal ties with revelry and generosity. This festive culture, which was so crucial to reinforcing local identity, had been largely suppressed in the 1640s and 1650s, but re-emerged as a powerful social force under Charles II. Likewise, contemporary religious idioms continued to promote an "ethos of communalism" among neighbours, leading Keith Wrightson to note that "reports of the death of neighbourliness in early modern England would appear to have been greatly exaggerated".[38]

That said, the revival was sometimes temporary. In urban settings, it could not avoid being gradually undermined by social and political divisions which emerged in many towns, sometimes appearing as early as the 1670s. At Oxford, for example, the custom of ritually riding the bounds of the city led to openly partisan disputes that peaked during the reign of William III, and at Norwich "guild day" celebrations became an occasion for party politics when the mayor decided to decorate his door with pictures linking the Whigs with Oliver Cromwell in 1715.[39] In rural England, villagers of all ranks appear to have embraced communal festivities in the late seventeenth century, but here too the re-emergence of this localist culture was eventually followed by its diminution. From the early eighteenth century, the wealthy and the educated again began to oppose such revelry. The magistrates in Gloucestershire, for example, banned "unlawfull Wakes and Revells" in 1710, because these "Disorderly meetings" were said to promote immorality and "the General Impoverishment of many good Subjects".[40] Moreover, although parish perambulations became more common after 1660 and continued to be popular until disrupted by parliamentary enclosure in the late eighteenth century, both participation and the accompanying charity may have became more restricted by the end of the later Stuart period.[41]

Nonetheless, it would be misleading to dismiss this whole era as one in which partisanship and polarisation simply fractured local communities. In fact, the culture of festive mutuality seems to have been stronger under Charles II than it had been in at least a generation and perhaps even a century or more. Even when some of these customs began to weaken in the decades that followed, others remained fairly widespread. Moreover, as will be shown in next section, the reinvigoration of many localist celebrations coincided with several changes in the way towns and villages enforced the boundaries of this geographically circumscribed conception of community. Cultural manifestations of economic localism overlapped with more practical aspects of inclusion and exclusion.

II. Structures and Institutions

The bonds of local community – forged through shared identities and cultures – provided an invaluable defence against economic threats for many people in later Stuart England. Those who "belonged" benefited from informal support and communal resources, whilst those who did not suffered restriction and exclusion. The structures erected to maintain and defend the collective economic welfare of the locality both expanded the range of options open to insiders and narrowed those available to outsiders. This meant that an individual's ability to act as an independent economic agent often hinged on belonging to a particular community.

For those who suffered immiseration, membership in a community made it possible to request – perhaps even expect – support from their fellows. Casual assistance, for example, circulated most readily within the confines of the street, the parish, the village, or similarly limited spaces. Even in London, the loose bonds that formed between neighbours could provide an efficient support system. Historians have uncovered innumerable examples of poor men and women relying on these localized networks of charity for both minor favours and major help in times of hardship, but of course access to help depended on maintaining a reputation as a "good neighbour".[42] For example, while many paupers could report having long survived "on the charity of good neighbours", Janet Nicholson of Greystoke, Cumberland, found that neighbourly support dried up after parish officers declared her undeserving of relief in 1700.[43] A ballad published around 1685 told a less disheartening tale. In it, a poor man from Somerset became unable to pay his rent after the death of his wife and a sudden rise in the price of corn. His merciless landlord imprisoned him, but his neighbours – including "a poor Widow" – heard of his suffering and took pity. They raised money amongst themselves and "quickly releas'd their poor Neighbour from thrall". Unsurprisingly, the ballad reported that God rewarded the virtuous husbandman and his supporters while punishing the "cruel Oppressor" with madness.[44] So, although Keith Wrightson has recently argued that "obligations of neighbourliness perhaps became more narrowly defined and ... more restricted in their accessibility" over the early modern period, both the culture and the customs of the time indicate that this avenue for redress remained open for many poor people in later Stuart England.[45]

The lack of direct evidence makes drawing firm conclusions about trends in "neighbourliness" impossible, but historians have much more systematic records about institutionalized forms of community-based support and these sources reveal a clear upward trajectory. The most striking development was an expansion in the reach and depth of parochial relief. Almost every parish in the country collected funds for this purpose by the end of the seventeenth century, and the sums involved grew increasingly large.[46] Of course, under this system, only those regarded as full members of the community had access to communal resources. The first criterion was legal residence: one needed to have earned "settlement" in the parish, usually through paternity, marriage, year-long employment or apprenticeship. This understanding of "settlement" – codified in 1662 and reinforced thereafter – arose mostly from practical concerns, but it also helped to ensure that no one who claimed relief would be a stranger to other parishioners.[47] The second criterion was moral rather than legal: one had to display the requisite virtues of godliness, industry, thrift, sobriety, respectfulness, honesty, and so forth. Only by living within the bounds of the "moral community" could the poor hope to receive relief from their fellow parishioners.[48] These two preconditions imposed obvious limits on the provision of communal aid, blocking access for those regarded as outsiders or deviants.

The poor themselves were well-aware of these limits. When seeking help from magistrates, they emphasized the length of their residency and their good standing among their neighbours, sometimes including testimonials to their honest reputations.[49] But if they met these criteria – if, in other words, they could prove that they "belonged" – many of the poorer sort appear to have expected relief forthwith. Of course very few claimants actually used the language of "rights" – after all, membership in the "moral community" of the parish was predicated on a humble, respectful attitude.[50] Still, as the system of local welfare expanded, the poor may have increasingly felt a sense of "entitlement" and begun to see parochial relief less as a gift from "superiors" and more as a resource shared among notional equals.[51] Perhaps this is why, from the 1670s onward, villagers could be heard singing about time spent "on the parish" as a normal part of growing old and dying:

> A Fig for care, why should we spare
>   The Parish is bound to find us,
> For thou and I and all must dye,
>   And leave the world behind us.
> The Clark shall Sing, the Bells shall Ring
>   And the Old Wives wind us;
> Sir John shall lay our Bones in Clay,
>   Where no body means to find us.[52]

No ratepayer or overseer would have smiled on such a presumptuous (if fatalistic) attitude towards institutionalized relief, but it may have been a commonplace among many potential paupers.

For residents of towns and cities, the economic support attached to membership in the local community was broader still. In addition to the well-established structures of parochial support, townspeople might have access to free schools, sponsored apprenticeships, charitable loans, short-term aid, and long-term pensions.[53] Here, "belonging" was usually contingent on holding "the freedom of the city", a privilege often assumed to be rather restricted. However, the proportion of freemen in the urban population actually expanded in the later Stuart period, and even in the notoriously oligarchic City of London about three-quarters of male householders were freemen in 1675.[54] Moreover, while access to subsidized education and pensions was usually limited to the families of freemen, other forms of civic relief were offered to the town-dwellers more generally. So, poor relief and charitable loans certainly "reified civil and communal boundaries", but the span of the urban community could often be very wide indeed.[55]

Common rights offered another form of support that did not reach beyond the boundaries of the locality.[56] Restrictions on these rights varied considerably from place to place: often they included only manorial tenants or urban freemen, but sometimes they encompassed all settled "inhabitants" of a particular village or town.[57] Moreover, the strength of custom ensured that many of the landless poor came to believe that the access to commons "was a right equal in rank and value to the property rights so assiduously defended by the gentry", even when they had no legal claim.[58] The resources available to "commoners" gave many a chance to make ends meet when they might otherwise fall into inescapable penury. So, although commentary on commons and enclosure was comparatively rare in the late seventeenth and early eighteenth centuries, these "rights" remained a vital part of the economy of makeshifts in many areas. Even in 1720, for example, around ninety per cent of the population of Northamptonshire lived in unenclosed parishes, and at least 180 English towns had commons or common rights at that time.[59] This meant that vast numbers of poor families had access to local communal resources, including pasture, firewood, timber, turf, bracken, reeds, sedge, wild fruit and nuts, fish, wildfowl, and gleaned corn. But the limits of this "communal economy" must be reiterated: it was "parochial and exclusive" rather than "generous and universalistic".[60]

These various sources of support – neighbourly charity, parish relief, common rights – formed only one part of the complex framework that structured local economic relations. The main pillars in this edifice were the range of legal institutions that provided a degree of self-government to the people of each particular territorial unit: the borough, the manor, the parish, the port, the forest, the mine, and so forth.[61] The power invested in these bodies varied greatly, but they often ensured that the community could shape the economic landscape by influencing land allocation, regulating highways and waterways, enforcing by-laws regarding crops and livestock, or simply systematically privileging their constituents over outsiders.[62] An obvious example of the effect of localized jurisdiction can be seen in the rules and by-laws issued by most boroughs, whereby the freemen enjoyed considerable practical advantages over the non-freemen who lived among them. Those who had not acquired the "freedom of the city" were officially excluded from guild-controlled trades, limited to buying and selling only at certain times, and liable to various special tolls or duties.[63] Moreover, urban citizens devoted much energy to protecting their economic privileges. John Miller has noted that towns both large and small – including Cambridge, York, Norwich, Oxford, Leicester, Penrith, Wootton Bassett, Tiverton, Wilton, and Maidstone – sought to prevent "foreigners" from encroaching on the crafts and trades of freemen.[64] In some cases, the efforts of urban corporations often coincided with craft fraternities. Hence, in July 1712, the London Corporation issued a new Act of Common Council for the prosecution of "foreigners" who "use any manual occupation or handicraft or to sell or put to sale any Wares or Merchandizes by Retail in any Shop inward or outward" which led many companies to enforce their regulations concerning foreigners "with renewed vigour", though some faced resistance from their targets.[65] Here, as elsewhere, the defensive mentality fostered by urban citizenship strengthened the ability of workers to police the boundaries of their trade.

In some respects, this routine process of exclusion mirrored the action taken against the "stranger" or "vagrant" poor. Steve Hindle and Keith Snell have shown how parishes systematically "removed" relief claimants who lacked "settlement", a process which became increasingly pervasive in the late seventeenth century.[66] Indeed, at the beginning of the eighteenth century, when the yeoman Richard Gough wrote his history of the parish of Myddle, Shropshire, he devoted an lengthy appendix to documenting the many attempts by local communities to exclude paupers who they regarded as "foreign".[67] For those classified as "vagrants", the experience was even worse. When caught, they were often whipped, sometimes imprisoned "at hard labour" for several days, and then sent back to their last place of "settlement".[68] Proclamations issued from this period confirm the prevalence of this attitude. "Rogues, Vagabonds, Beggars, and other idle Persons" were plaguing London, claimed a royal proclamation in 1661; they should not be relieved "to the wrong of the native poor" but rather "openly whipped, and sent away".[69] Likewise, in 1676, the Lord Mayor of London demanded that civic officers immediately take severe action against the "inordinate liberty now used by vagrants and common beggars to wander about and pester the streets and common passage of this city".[70] These sorts of extraordinary measures, alongside the ceaseless grind of the machinery of the poor law, ensured that the indignant suffered a constant risk of expulsion if they dared to cross into the civic or parochial space reserved for local paupers.

However, to focus exclusively on evidence confirming the exclusionary power of these localities would leave an overly uniform impression of their fortunes over the course of the later Stuart era. In the case of towns, a more realistic portrait would instead include both their surge of strength under Charles II and the multiplying signs of weakness that they began to show in the latter part of this period. Their regulatory regimes seem to have been least effective during turmoil and disarray of the 1640s and 1650s.[71] In the 1660s, however, they vigorously re-established their economic authority and, as indicated in the examples outlined above, they generally maintained it for decades thereafter. Yet, in the years that followed, these bold efforts to shut out outsiders sometimes began to falter. Because their prohibitions on unfree workers and traders were only rarely buttressed by Acts of Parliament, towns could face an increasing number of challenges to their authority. Norwich, Oxford and other towns discovered that legal ambiguity made fining and suing interlopers ever more difficult. Although they responded by passing by-laws to strengthen their position, lawyers continued to undermine the effectiveness of civic attempts to prevent unfree trading by emphasising the uncertain legal status of such prohibitions.[72] Elsewhere, enforcing exclusionary policies proved less problematic. At York, for instance, the community's relentless defence of its economic monopoly lasted long after the later Stuart period and, in 1736, an observer complained that freemen "have for many years last past, by virtue of their charters, as it were locked themselves up from the world, and wholly prevented any foreigner from settling any manufacture amongst them".[73] In most towns, however, concerted action against unfreemen became more infrequent and ineffective after the burst of energetic enforcement which followed the Restoration.

In contrast to this pattern of revival and decline, a few local institutions simply experienced a continual and unmitigated loss of economic influence over the course of this period. Manorial courts, for example, retained a degree of relevance well into the eighteenth century in some areas, but their overall impact was undoubtedly declining over the long term.[74] This may, in part, have been a consequence of the increasing integration of the national economy, whereby towns and manors become submerged in larger networks circulating goods, labour and capital.[75] However, other local institutions followed an opposite trajectory. The most important of these was the parish. As an economic institution, it went from strength to strength under the later Stuarts. Parochial poor relief became essentially universal throughout England during the seventeenth century and it accounted for a constantly increasing proportion of the local economy. As a result, parishioners policed the territorial boundaries of their community ever more closely and "settlement" became a crucial factor in the economic lives of the labouring poor. When one sets these three types of local communities – the town, the manor, the parish – alongside each other, the problems inherent in any unilinear history of economic localism became obvious.

III. Collective Violence

State officials generally regarded these expressions of collective agency – charity, prosecution, expulsion – as harmless at worst and useful at best. In some cases, the authorities clearly welcomed these associational activities because they seemed to contribute to the maintenance of social stability and order. Yet, many other communal efforts at economic redress received a much less favourable reception. Some were simply legally dubious, but others directly targeted representatives of the state or involved riotous campaigns of violence. Over the course of the later Stuart period, some groups resorted to methods that put them in direct opposition to legal authority, even when they continued to deploy the idiom of "law" to justify their actions. The issues involved varied widely, but this section will address four particularly revealing examples: taxes, debt, land, and food. In each of these cases, the spatial boundaries of the locality became flashpoints for violent resistance to outsiders.

Despite both the ever-increasing levels of revenue collected by the national government and endemic rates of individual tax evasion, organized resistance to state impositions was decidedly rare. When it did occur, local solidarity appears to have been perhaps the most important factor. It seems likely, for example, that popular resistance to the hearth tax resulted as much from animosity towards the intrusions of non-local collectors as from opposition to Charles II's government. If so, these crowds – sometimes supported by magistrates – believed that they were defending their whole community when they drove off and stoned "Chimney-men" in St Neot's, Newcastle, the North Riding, Hexham, Hereford, Banbury, Pewsey, Winchcombe, Weymouth, Bridport, Marlborough and Tauton in the late 1660s.[76] Likewise, opposition to the excise – which "threw into stark relief the potential conflict between centre and locality" – and to the destruction of illegal tobacco crops spurred violent rioting in the mid-seventeenth century, and resentment continued to simmer in the decades after the Restoration.[77] This hostility to state intrusion also partly explains the "communal solidarity" found in some coastal villages confronted by officials seeking to suppress smuggling.[78] Although violent reactions to centralized taxation undoubtedly stemmed from a variety of different causes, the bonds of locality may well have been the determining factor in many of these incidents.

The attacks on outsiders caused by conflict over debt are much less widely known. Insolvent debtors normally relied on support from their friends and neighbours to make ends meet, but sometimes they actually banded together with other debtors to form permanent territorial communities in the "liberties" of London.[79] One such organisation emerged in the district of Southwark known as "The Mint", which seems to have become formalized in the late seventeenth century. According to a series of complaints to Parliament in 1706, "the said Minters have several Clubs, and a Chairman presiding amongst them, being attended by Beadles and Constables of their own making, by whom they send for the Offenders of their Laws", for which they even established their own "Gaol".[80] They tenaciously defended each other from outsiders by regularly fighting off groups of invading constables, rescuing captured Minters, and subjecting many hostile intruders to extremely unpleasant punishments. Specifically, they ritually "pumped" outsiders by ducking them in water ("the Law of the Mint") or threw them into sewage ditches ("the Law of the black Ditch"). For example, they seized a borough officer who had helped convict a Minter of murder, "and pumped him at ten Pumps, and at six of them twice, and then threw him five Time into the black Ditch". The officer was then forced to vow never to return:

> they made him lay his Hand upon a Brick, covered with Sir Reverence, and upon his Knees made him swear in these Words: "I Francis Smith am a Rogue in grain: And God damn my Body and Soul, if ever I come into the Mint again:" and made him kiss the Brick, and drove him out of the Mint in a miserable Condition, with Scorn and Derision.

The mock solemnity of the occasion – exemplified by their use of a filth-covered brick as a bible – could not disguise the ferocity of the assault. In addition to violently excluding outsiders, they also targeted any member of their self-declared "honourable Society" who dared to collaborate with external authorities. When a local brewer and tavern-keeper aided some constables, they "voted him out of their pretended Society; and such of them as were his Debtors ... bound themselves under an Oath, that they would never pay him one Farthing of their Debts; which will prove his Ruin". It was only in 1722 that an Act of Parliament effectively disbanded this unlawful community.[81] A combination of desperate economic situations and legal ambiguity made the creation of these "Clubs" possible, but they were maintained by much more than mere practicality. Here, solidarity required both a shared commitment to violent mutual defence and an alternative understanding of "law" and "honour".

The defence of "The Mint" as a particular territorial unit mirrored, in some ways, the collective actions undertaken to defend various other types of land. Intruders were expelled, and local people protected from outside prosecution. However, the central object in these conflicts was the preservation of a common resource, so the participants could often appropriate existing organisational structures rather than building entirely new ones. Urban common lands, for example, were often managed co-operatively using civic ordinances and customs. Hence, when Charles II tried to give a loyalist named Robert Townsend control over Cheylesmore Park in 1661, the citizens of Coventry – who had long managed the land themselves – responded with a series of acts of collective resistance.[82] They destroyed "new inclosures" several times in the 1660s and then, in January 1689, they marched in "a great rabble" led by burgesses to drive the encloser from his house, and destroy his fences and ditches. More "Ryots & Tumults" followed in the 1690s and by 1705 the Coventry citizens regained legal control over the park. Perhaps unsurprisingly, these protests not only sometimes involved burgesses – a group of men who supposedly represented the community as a whole – but they also seem to have occasionally coincided with the Lammas Day ceremonies that customarily signalled the opening of the commons for grazing. Both the patterns of participation and the timing of these actions thus implied a conflict between a defensive local citizenry and an encroaching outsider.

In contrast to these "civic" protests, the defence of commons in fens and forests was often more violent. Riots at the Hatfield Level, which lay at the borders of Yorkshire, Lincolnshire and Nottinghamshire, typify the sort of direct action that some fen-dwellers employed to defend their territory from intruders. Although the first protests had began in the 1620s, unrest continued on a regular basis into the eighteenth century. On several occasions after the Restoration, groups of commoners – sometimes led by local gentlemen and supported by a "common purse" – showed their collective strength and determination through a variety of tough tactics: they assaulted the drainer and his agents; seized livestock and crops; burnt building supplies; levelled fences and ditches; destroyed a windmill and houses. Indeed, they conveyed their message especially clearly in the summer of 1660 when they targeted the church used by recent settlers by smashing the windows, destroying the furnishings, and driving a flock of maggoty sheep into the nave. It was not until the 1710s that the commoners were finally quieted by a combination of concessions, judicial settlement and military force.[83] Likewise, in the Forest of Dean, long-running disputes over land-use resulted in several violent protests in the decades that followed the Reforestation Act of 1668. Here too the commoners repeatedly destroyed enclosures, felled trees and broke into the pound. In 1688, they chose more prominent targets when they attacked the site of the Verderer's Court and pulled down two forest keepers' lodges – thus directing their collective ire at the bridgeheads of distant authority.[84] The objects targeted by these various groups of commoners – the encloser's fence, the settlers' church, the keeper's lodge – clearly embodied the very essence of "alterity", a symbol of foreign encroachment erected within the bounds of the local community. By levelling or desecrating these physical emblems of intrusion, those who "belonged" collectively reasserted their claims over the land.

Like the battles over land use, communal responses to dearth often hinged on the division between insiders and outsiders. Indeed, widespread assumptions about local entitlement ensured that, in times of sudden distress, the needs of each "little commonwealth" could take precedence over the supposedly universal reach of the law of property. When examining grain riots, it is usually impossible to disentangle the influence of this logic from that of simple necessity; however, many incidents in the later Stuart period demonstrate the strength of these assumptions. Just before Christmas in 1662, for example, five hundred women raised "a tumult at Weymouth, because a quantity of corn was bought for transportation; the people seized it, and kept guard that it should not be shipped in the night".[85] Their willingness to set guards rather than merely pillaging the captured grain indicates that the primary objective of "the people" was to keep the grain within the locality, not to satisfy the immediate hunger of the rioters themselves. Several similar events occurred in early 1674 when "the poorer sort of people" in Stratford-upon-Avon prevented the departure of corn barges and crowds in Colchester seized grain being shipped from the port.[86] In some cases, protests began in response to the arrival of corn dealers from outside the locality during dearths. Hence, Dutch factors caused a "mutiny" when they tried to buy up foodstuffs in Colchester in 1692, and Bristolian merchants faced a similar reaction in Worcester the following year.[87] Throughout this period, the "exportation" of corn – whether shipping it overseas or simply carrying it to different town – could provoke riots by hungry locals. Put simply, this was regarded as a betrayal of one's "home". The anger created by such behaviour was exemplified in the two-hundred armed women of Kelvedon and Coggeshall who, in 1709, threatened to shoot several men and burn down their houses "by reason they have been dealers in corn to London".[88] The regularity with which such attitudes appeared during the grain riots of these years indicate that, in times of severe economic distress, the needs of the locality could easily trump the law of property.

Indeed, this tendency can be seen in practically every attempt at redress which built on the logic of communal solidarity. Each of these cases – from tax resistance and debtors' groups, to riots about commons and corn – emerged from a division between insiders and outsiders. Hence, resolving the grievance apparently necessitated supporting or defending "neighbours", while excluding or expelling "strangers". More importantly, participants imagined that the "agent" in these actions was the community itself. This was obviously a fiction – after all it was usually a tiny minority of the whole that actually made key decisions or engaged in agitation – but it was a vitally important one, as it vested these attempts at redress with the legitimacy they needed if they were to have any hope of succeeding. The fiction of unanimity also empowered ordinary people to take the law into their own hands or even create their own pseudo-laws. Following the model of self-government set out in the charters of incorporated towns and craft guilds, these men and women collectively asserted their right manage the local economy. This meant protecting common resources while punishing trespassers and traitors according to standards set by the community. In short, ordinary people showed a remarkable measure of confidence and autonomy by collectively asserting their control over a particular territorial space that they regarded as their own.

IV. Conclusions

Both the history and historiography of local communities are complex, but it may nonetheless be useful to reflect here on the broader implications of the specific examples discussed in this essay. Put simply, the evidence examined in this chapter points to two conclusions. The first relates to the link between space and agency. The second relates to the inadequacy of previous narratives of the history of "community".

As the Southwark Minters knew well, social strength sometimes depended less on *who* than on *where*. The obvious inequality of power between a constable and an insolvent debtor could be reversed within the confines of a territorial "liberty" or "sanctuary" like the Mint. The economic communities that arose within particular localized spaces – whether conventional types such as towns or parishes, or unconventional types such as free-mining districts or debtors' sanctuaries – could multiply exponentially an individual's ability to redress grievances. Explicit spatial boundaries made the division between insiders and outsiders seem much more visible and, in turn, this apparently unambiguous dichotomy rendered collective action all the more effective. Using locality as a foundation, local people could attempt to defend their welfare and advance their livelihoods, while isolating or excluding opponents and competitors.

One of the wellsprings for this form of agency was communal culture. It sustained the local identities and emotional solidarities that proved essential to more practical manifestations of community, and it had a mutually reinforcing relationship with the institutions reviewed in section two. Indeed, these local institutions were the other vital impetus for collective action. They gave these communities a structural strength and durability that they would otherwise sorely lack. This combination of culture (festivals, ceremonies and beliefs) and institutions (corporate bodies, laws and courts) created a framework within which ordinary people could gain a degree of control over their economic lives. Yet, although the locality might provide substantial resources to poor members and also pull individuals together in order to pursue common aims and protect themselves from outsiders, it should not be romanticized. The crowd actions inspired by such territorial solidarities were often violent and xenophobic. After all, sometimes the defence of "community" was simply a matter of an angry group of poor people beating up a "foreign" pauper. In 1664, for example, women at Thorpe Market (Norfolk) assaulted a woman who tried to glean after she had been refused permission.[89] Still, the economic impact of spatial conceptions of locality cannot be ignored. They bound together insiders, dehumanized outsiders, and gave many seemingly powerless people a weapon in the struggle over scarce resources.

The influence of these communities was not, however, an unchanging feature on the social landscape. One must attempt to account for shifts over time. The traditional model used to describe these permutations is "the dissolution of community", a fact long considered to be self-evident. Thus, when Ferdinand Tönnies wrote his powerful elucidation of *Community and Society* in 1887, he assumed that the latter inevitably lost ground to the former. The decaying culture of *Gemeinschaft* – i.e. co-operation, commonwealth, concord, and rural folkways – was gradually subsumed by the developing culture of *Gesellschaft* – i.e. contracts, calculation, competition and urban cosmopolitanism.[90] This simple notion of "development" offered an endlessly flexible explanatory model that has, in turn, influenced the work of practically every historian of early modern society.

The problems with the narrative of *Gemeinschaft* to *Gesellschaft* are obvious. Indeed, this chapter only adds another voice to the ever-growing chorus of revisionists who have critiqued these sorts of teleological assumptions.[91] Specifically, the preceding sections have shown that the later-Stuart period actually witnessed a heightened awareness of locality in some important respects. Communal festivities, including Rogation processions, revived markedly in many villages, and this coincided with the expansion of parochial poor relief and disputes about "settlement". Likewise, the strength of "bourgeois collectivism" seems to have been reinvigorated by the outburst of civic festivity and corporate regulation after 1660. Even "neighbourliness", a phenomenon that is admittedly difficult to measure, did not appear to simply wither away in response to the growth of "modernity". Such localist conceptions of economic community were not a moribund relic of a bygone age. Nor can they be easily reduced to a narrative of continuity. Some features undeniably diminished significantly over this period; some revived under Charles II only to start slowly waning in later decades; some grew continually stronger even in the early-eighteenth century.[92] Hence, as Keith Wrightson has recently argued, our justifiable scepticism has allowed us to knock down previous models, but "we have stumbled over the question of change".[93] The sheer complexity and diversity of the elements involved make any attempt to offer an all-embracing narrative of changes in economic culture look foolhardy.

Perhaps, then, all we can learn from this account is that the impact of locality on later Stuart economic relations was deep but also uneven. Despite this somewhat inconclusive result, one implication is clear: localized communities empowered people who might otherwise have had "neither voice nor authority in the commonwealth".[94] Those who were normally disenfranchised due to their poverty or gender could thrust themselves on to the public stage, whereupon paupers became "parishioners", debtors became "Minters", artisans became "freemen", women became "neighbours". As members of a community, they could no longer be ignored.

Notes

* I am grateful for the invaluable comments from Steve Hindle and Mark Hailwood on earlier versions of this chapter.
[1] For the use of terms like "this little commonwealth" to refer to parishes and cities, see Steve Hindle, *On the Parish?: The Micro-Politics of Poor Relief in Rural England, c.1550-1750* (Oxford: Oxford University Press, 2004), 334; Phil

Withington, *The Politics of Commonwealth: Citizens and Freemen in Early Modern England* (Cambridge: Cambridge University Press, 2005), esp. 10-11.

[2] In the terminology of Michel de Certeau, these communities allowed for "strategies" rather than mere "tactics", as they provided "a *place* that can be delimited as [the subject's] *own* and serve as the base from which relations with an *exteriority* composed of targets or threats ... can be managed": *The Practice of Everyday Life* (Berkeley, etc., 1984), Ch. 3, quotation at 36. The effects of this enhanced autonomy can be seen in Section III, below.

[3] Ferdinand Tönnies, *Community and Society* (Mineola: Dover Publications, 2002).

[4] For a fuller discussion of this historiography, see below: Section IV.

[5] Leviticus 19:18, Mark 12:31, Romans 13:9.

[6] Leviticus 25:14.

[7] Deuteronomy 19:14.

[8] Jeremiah 22:13.

[9] Naomi Tadmor, "Friends and Neighbours in Early Modern England: Biblical Translations and Social Norms" in *Love, friendship and faith in Europe, 1300-1800*, eds, Laura Gowing, Michael Hunter, and Miri Rubin (Houndsmills; New York: Palgrave Macmillan, 2005), 151. The fruitful mistranslation of "friend" as "neighbour" was essentially canonized in the Authorized Version of 1611.

[10] Tadmor, "Friends and Neighbours", 158-62, 164; Ian Green, *The Christian's ABC: Catechisms and Catechizing in England, c.1530-1740* (Oxford: Clarendon Press, 1996), 451, 460-6; Keith Wrightson, "The 'Decline of Neighbourliness' Revisited" in *Local Identities in Late Medieval and Early Modern England*, eds, Norman Jones and Daniel Woolf (Basingstoke: Palgrave Macmillan, 2007), 22, 25, 30; Morris Palmer Tilley, *A Dictionary of Proverbs in England in the Sixteenth and Seventeenth centuries* (Ann Arbor: University of Michigan Press), 494-6.

[11] Isaac Barrow, *The Duty and Reward of Bounty to the Poor* (1671); idem., *Of the Love of God and Our Neighbour* (1680). All primary sources published in London unless otherwise noted.

[12] Barrow, *Of the Love of God and Our Neighbour* (1680), 79-83 (on Matt. 22:39).

[13] Thomas Manton, "Sermon XVII [on 1 John 11]" in *A Fifth Volume of Sermons* (1700), 699-700; Anthony Horneck, "Sermon XXXIV" in *Several Sermons on the Fifth of St. Matthew* (1698), II, 420-1, 426-7, 432.

[14] White Kennett, *A Sermon Preach'd in the Church of St. Lawrence-Jewry* (1711), 17-23. Many catechisms, including the official Church of England catechism, also allowed for a more literal interpretation of "neighbour" as they left the term undefined: "Catechism" in *The Book of Common Prayer* (1662); Thomas Comber, *The Church-Catechism With A Brief and Easie Explanation Thereof* (1681), 20.

[15] In some ways, one might argue that "local culture" was "interchangeable with "popular culture": Andy Wood, *The Politics of Social Conflict: The Peak Country, 1520-1770* (Cambridge: Cambridge University Press, 1999), 27.

[16] *Londons Praise, or, The Glory of the City* (c. 1666-89) in *The Pepys Ballads*, ed. W. G. Day (Cambridge: D. S. Brewer, 1987), IV, 339. For songs lauding the city in more general terms, see ibid., I, 188-9; IV, 274. For a discussion of London as a self-defined "moral community", see Joseph Ward, *Metropolitan Communities:*

Trade Guilds, Identity and Change in Early Modern London (Stanford (CA): Stanford University Press, 1997), esp. 11-26.
[17] Richard Garnet, *The Book of Oaths* (1649), 22-4.
[18] Jonathan Barry, "Bourgeois collectivism? Urban Association and the Middling Sort", in *The Middling Sort of People: Culture, Society and Politics in England, 1550-1800*, eds, Jonathan Barry and Christopher Brooks (Basingstoke and London: Macmillan and St Martin's Press, 1994), 98.
[19] Ronald Hutton, *The Rise and Fall of Merry England : The Ritual Year, 1400-1700* (Oxford: Oxford University Press, 1994), 230; J. Ellis, "A Dynamic Society: Social Relations in Newcastle upon Tyne, 1660-1760", in *The Transformation of English Provincial Towns, 1600-1800*, ed. Peter Clark (London: Hutchison, 1984), 200-1; Peter Burke, "Popular Culture in Seventeenth-Century London", *London Journal* 3:2 (1977): 151-2. Even two historians who have emphasized the social and political divisions found in some later Stuart urban festivity, have also noted ways that it might also promote unity: Peter Borsay, "'All the town's a stage': Urban Ritual and Ceremony", in *Transformation of English Provincial Towns*, ed. Clark, 239-43; John Miller, *Cities divided: Politics and Religion in English Provincial Towns, 1660-1722* (Oxford: Oxford University Press, 2007), Ch. 4.
[20] Ilana Krausman Ben-Amos, *The Culture of Giving: Informal Support and Gift-Exchange in Early Modern England* (Cambridge; New York: Cambridge University Press, 2008), 217-20; *Victoria County History* (hereafter *VCH*): *Warwickshire*, VIII, 204. For examples of "unusually inclusive" corporate feasting, which could include subsidies for freemen and "the commons", see Miller, *Cities Divided*, 95. For Lammas Day more generally, see Ronald Hutton, *The Stations of the Sun: A History of the Ritual Year in Britain* (Oxford; New York: Oxford University Press, 2001), 331.
[21] Withington, *Politics of Commonwealth*, 184-6. For the structures of practical support, see below: Section II.
[22] Robert Malcolmson, *Popular Recreations in English Society, 1700-1850* (Cambridge: Cambridge University Press, 1973), Ch. 5, esp. 81, 84-5. Of course, like Malcolmson, I would note that they could also become focal points of social conflict; they were not inherently forces of cohesiveness.
[23] Hutton, *Rise and Fall of Merry England*, Ch. 7; idem., *Stations of the Sun*, 19-20, 61-5, 127, 229-33, 242, 322, 334.
[24] Quoted in Hutton, *Rise and Fall*, 250. For a more subversive, carnivalesque celebration of locality, see the Hocktide mock-mayoral elections in the weaving village of Randwick (Gloucestershire) discussed in David Rollison, *The Local Origins of Modern Society: Gloucestershire, 1500-1800* (London: Routledge, 1992), 211-18.
[25] Manorial perambulations served a similar function and these continued in some regions into the nineteenth century: Bob Bushway, *By Rite: Custom, Ceremony and Community in England, 1700-1800* (London: Junction, 1982), 88-100.
[26] Much of the inspiration for this work came from Keith Thomas, *Religion and the Decline of Magic: Studies in Popular Beliefs in Sixteenth and Seventeenth Century England* (1971; London: Penguin, 1991), 71-4. For the importance of Rogation in

the later Stuart period, see Steve Hindle, "Beating the Bounds of the Parish: Order, Memory, and Identity in the English Local Community, c. 1500–1700", in *Defining Community in Early Modern Europe*, eds, M. Halvorson and K. Spierling (Aldershot and Burlington: Ashgate, 2008), 205-28; Hutton, *Rise and Fall*, 247-8; Hutton, *Stations of the Sun*, Ch. 26, esp. 285-6; Keith Snell, *Parish and Belonging: Community, Identity, and Welfare in England and Wales, 1700-1950* (Cambridge: Cambridge University Press, 2006), 37-40; David Fletcher, "The Parish Boundary: a Social Phenomenon in Hanoverian England", *Rural History* 14:2 (2003), esp. 183-6; Nicola Whyte, "Landscape, Memory and Custom: Parish Identities, c. 1550-1700", *Social History* 32:2 (2007): 175-80.

[27] Hindle, "Beating the Bounds", 223.

[28] "An Exhortation to Be spoken to such Parishes where they use their Perambulation in Rogation Week" in *Certain Sermons or Homilies Appointed to be Read in Churches* (1673), II, 303-7.

[29] Hindle, "Beating the Bounds", 213-16, 218; Fletcher, "Parish Boundary", 185-6.

[30] *Londons Praise, or, The Glory of the City* (c. 1666-89) in *Pepys Ballads*, IV, 339. Similarly, those taking the London freeman's oath swore to "cullour no Foraigne Goods under or in your name" and "know no Forraigner to buy or sell any Merchandise with any other Forraigner": Garnet, *The Book of Oaths* (1649), 22-4.

[31] Rollison, *Local Origins*, Ch. 3, esp. 68-9; Snell, *Parish and Belonging*, Ch. 2.

[32] For perceptions of vagrancy prior to 1660, see Paul Slack, *Poverty and Policy in Tudor and Stuart England* (Harrow: Longman, 1988), 22-7, 98-9; A. L. Beier, *Masterless Men: The Vagrancy Problem in England, 1560-1640* (London: Methuen, 1985), Ch. 1; Patricia Fumerton, *Unsettled: The Culture of Mobility and the Working Poor in Early Modern England* (Chicago: Chicago University Press, 2006), Ch. 3; Hindle, *On the Parish?*, 73-5, 104, 107.

[33] Thomas Lynford, *Charity-Schools Recommended: A Sermon* (1712), 8. For other instances of preachers demanding punishment rather than relief for "Vagrants and common Beggars" who "pass from Town to Town", see Peter Nourse, *Practical Discourses* (1708), I, 121; William Stainforth, *The Duty of Doing Good Recommended and Press'd In a Sermon* (York, 1711), 9.

[34] Richard Haines, *The Prevention of Poverty* (1674), 5-6; Thomas Furmin, *Some Proposals For the Imployment of the Poor* (1681), 5.

[35] This paragraph is based on a group of ballads which shared similar themes (and sometimes whole verses): *The Beggars Song, Both in City and Country* (1685-88), in *Pepys Ballads*, IV, 250; *The Beggers Chorus, In the Jovial Crew* (c. 1684-96), in *Pepys Ballads*, IV, 251; *The Merry Beggars of Lincolns-Inn-Fields* (1685-8), in *Pepys Ballads*, IV, 252; *The Beggars Delight* (n.d.), in *Pepys Ballads*, IV, 253; Anon., *The Jovial Beggars Crew* (1684); "A Beggar I'll Be" (c. 1660-3) in *Musa Pedestris: Three Centuries of Caning Songs and Slang Rhymes (1536-1896)*, ed. John Farmer (London, 1896), 26-9.

[36] *The Beggars Song, Both in City and Country* (1685-88), in *Pepys Ballads*, IV, 250. Interestingly, in one verse of this particular ballad, the beggars admit that they

"come home at night" to see their families, yet the rest of the song focuses on their mobility.
[37] Hutton, *Rise and Fall*, ch. 7, esp. 229-30, 238-9; Felicity Heal, *Hospitality in Early Modern England* (Oxford: Clarendon, 1990), 358-65.
[38] Wrightson, "Decline", 21; Tadmor, "Friends and Neighbours", 152.
[39] Miller, *Cities Divided*, 104. In London, although processions continued long after, the last Lord Mayor's Show was held in 1702. Moreover, Peter Borsay has shown that much of the culture of the post-Restoration "urban Renaissance" was restricted to the elites: Borsay, "All the town's a stage"; idem., *The English Urban Renaissance: Culture and Society in the Provincial Town, 1660-1770* (Oxford: Clarendon, 1989), Ch. 11.
[40] Malcolmson, *Popular Recreations*, 146.
[41] Hindle, "Beating the Bounds", 212, 215-16.
[42] Hindle, *On the Parish?*, 58-81; Ben-Amos, *Culture of Giving*, 64-9; Bernard Capp, *When Gossips Meet: Women, Family and Neighbourhood in Early Modern England* (Oxford: Oxford University Press, 2003), 55-7; Wrightson, "Decline", 24-5. Although focused on the early seventeenth century, an excellent study of "neighbourly" economics in London can be found in Jeremy Boulton, *Neighbourhood and Society: A London Suburb in the Seventeenth Century* (Cambridge and New York: Cambridge University Press, 1987), Ch. 9-10, esp. 236-47. Perhaps the most pervasive form of neighbourly help was the extension of credit within "the moral community" of the locality: Craig Muldrew, *The Economy of Obligation: The Culture of Credit and Social Relations in Early Modern England* (Basingstoke: Macmillan, 1998), 298.
[43] Hindle, *On the Parish*, 61-2.
[44] Anon., *The Cruel Land-Lord: Or, The Fortunate Husband-man* (1685?).
[45] Wrightson, "Decline", 38.
[46] Hindle, *On the Parish?*, 255-6, 262-82; Slack, *Poverty and Policy*, 169-82; Jeremy Boulton, "Going on the Parish: The Parish Pension and its Meaning in the London Suburbs, 1640-1724", in *Chronicling Poverty: The Voices and Strategies of the English Poor, 1640-1840*, eds, Tim Hitchcock, Peter King, and Pamela Sharpe (Basingstoke and London: Macmillan, 1997), 22-5. As Hindle has shown, the range of support funded by parish rates was extensive. It included not only long-term pensions and short-term relief, but could also include housing, stocks of raw materials, medical care, etc.
[47] One could also earn "settlement" by renting at £10 per annum or more, serving in a parish office, paying of local taxes, owning immoveable property, or simply by birth in the case of illegitimacy. For post-1662 "settlement" more generally, see Snell, *Parish and Belonging*, Ch. 3 ("heads" of settlement at 85-6); Keith Snell, *Annals of the Labouring Poor: Social Change and Agrarian England, 1660-1900* (Cambridge: Cambridge University Press, 1985), 71-3, 99-100; Hindle, *On the Parish?*, 304-5; Slack, *Poverty and Policy*, 194-5. This issue was complicated by non-resident relief for certificate holders, but this only became common in the later eighteenth century.

[48] For the virtues expected of the poor, see Hindle, *On the Parish?*, 379-98. For the "moral community" of the parish, see Keith Wrightson, *English Society, 1580-1680* (London: Unwin Hyman, 1982), 53-4.

[49] Hindle, *On the Parish?*, 410. For later examples of paupers emphasising their ties to their "home" parish, see Snell, *Parish and Belonging*, 87-9.

[50] For exceptions to this rule, see Hindle, *On the Parish?*, 416-17.

[51] For growing "assumptions about entitlement" and "the right to relief", see Slack, *Poverty and Policy*, 190-2; Snell, *Annals of the Labouring Poor*, 72-3, 112; Tim Hitchcock, Peter King, and Pamela Sharpe, "Introduction", in idem., *Chronicling Poverty*, 10-12. For a critique of this historiographical "consensus", see Hindle, *On the Parish?*, 398-405, 446.

[52] Anon., *Merry Drollery* (1670; reprinted 1691), 217. This song (or at least the opening couplet) was regarded as "famous" by the eighteenth century and was still irritating the elite in the mid-nineteenth century: *The Spectator* (1712-15), III, 358 (no. 232; 26 Nov. 1711); J. S. Mill, *Principles of Political Economy* (1848), I, 331. For a brief discussion of this text, see Hindle, *On the Parish?*, 416.

[53] Barry, "Bourgeois Collectivism?", 95-6, 99; Withington, *Politics of Commonwealth*, 180-6. Also, many new inter-parochial "Corporations for the Poor" were founded in the late seventeenth century, which strengthened city-wide economic ties: Paul Slack, *From Reformation to Improvement: Public Welfare in Early Modern England* (Oxford: Clarendon Press, 1999), Ch. 5; Miller, *Cities Divided*, 71-3.

[54] In other towns, the proportion of male householders who were freemen could also be large: more than two-thirds in York in the 1660s; over half in Newcastle in c. 1660-1740; around 30 percent in Norwich in the 1690s: Jonathan Barry, "Civility and Civic Culture in Early Modern England: the Meanings of Urban Freedom", in *Civil histories: Essays presented to Sir Keith Thomas*, eds, Peter Burke, Brian Harrison, and Paul Slack (Oxford: Oxford University Press, 2000), 184; Phil Withington, "Public Discourse, Corporate Citizenship, and State Formation in Early Modern England", *American Historical Review* 112:4 (2007), 1033; Ellis, "Dynamic society", 201, 223 n. 31. In contrast, over the early modern period as a whole, freemen may have been "commonly between a quarter and a half of male householders in the larger English towns": Paul Slack, "Great and Good Towns, 1540-1700", *The Cambridge Urban History of Britain*, ed. Peter Clark (Cambridge: Cambridge University Press, 2000), II, 363.

[55] Withington, *Politics of Commonwealth*, 184.

[56] Unless otherwise noted, this paragraph is based on E. P. Thompson, *Customs in Common* (New York: The New Press, 1991), Ch. 3; Hindle, *On the Parish?*, 27-48; Sara Birtles, "Common Land, Poor Relief and Enclosure: The Use of Manorial Resources in Fulfilling Parish Obligations, 1601-1834", *Past & Present* 165:1 (1999): 74-106; John Broad, "Parish Economies of Welfare, 1650-1834", *Historical Journal* 42:4 (1999): 998-1001; J. M. Neeson, *Commoners: Common Right, Enclosure and Social Change in England, 1700-1820* (Cambridge: Cambridge University Press, 1993), Ch. 2, 6; Peter King, "Customary Rights and Women's Earnings: The Importance of Gleaning to the Rural Labouring Poor,

1750-1850", *Economic History Review*, 2nd ser., 44:3 (1991): 462-6, 469-70; Henry French, "Urban Agriculture, Commons and Commoners in the Seventeenth and Eighteenth Centuries: The Case of Sudbury, Suffolk", *Agricultural History Review* 48:2 (2000): 171-99; Withington, *Politics of Commonwealth*, 180-1; Barry, "Bourgeois Collectivism?", 95-6, 99.

[57] In the south-east, for example, it appears that most agricultural labourers lacked common rights even before the mid-eighteenth century: Leigh Shaw-Taylor, "Labourers, Cows, Common Rights and Parliamentary Enclosure: The Evidence of Contemporary Comment, c.1760-1810", *Past & Present* 171 (2001): 95-126.

[58] Birtles, "Common Land", 96.

[59] Neeson, *Commoners*, 58-9; French, "Urban Agriculture", 172.

[60] Thompson, *Customs in Common*, 179.

[61] These included borough sessions, court leet (manor), court baron (manor), parish vestry, market court, portmote (port or borough), swainmote (forests), woodmote (woods), barmote (mines), etc.

[62] For jurisdictions, see Angus Winchester, *The Harvest of the Hills: Rural Life in Northern England and the Scottish Borders, 1400-1700* (Edinburgh: Edinburgh University Press, 2000), Ch. 2, 7; J. A. Sharpe, *Crime in Early Modern England* (London: Longman, 1984), 25-6; Andy Wood, "Custom, Identity and Resistance: English Free Miners and their Law, c.1550-1800" in *The Experience of Authority in Early Modern England*, eds. Paul Griffiths, Adam Fox, and Steve Hindle (Basingstoke: Macmillan, 1996), 256-73. Wood notes that the free-miners courts "granted a peculiar autonomy and sense of collectivity to free miners which made them unusually assertive of their rights": ibid., 153. See also his study of the influence of local jurisdictional changes on social relations in the Peak district: Wood, *Politics of Social Conflict*, esp. 28-36.

[63] Withington, *Politics of Commonwealth*, ch. 6; Barry, "Civility and Civic Culture", 186, 190.

[64] Miller, *Cities Divided*, 82-6.

[65] John Kellet, "The Breakdown of Gild and Corporation Control over the Handicraft and Retail Trade in London", *Economic History Review*, 2nd ser., 10 (1958): 386-8. For other examples of urban corporations such as Bristol, Coventry, Oxford and Newcastle reinforcing regulations against "strangers" in the eighteenth century, see M. J. Walker, "The Extent of Guild Control of Trades in England, c.1660-1820: A Study Based on a Sample of Provincial Towns and London Companies" (PhD diss., Cambridge University, 1985), 124.

[66] For the exclusion of non-parochial poor, see Hindle, *On the Parish?*, Ch. 5; Snell, *Parish and Belonging*, Ch. 3, esp. 139-43.

[67] Richard Gough, *The History of Myddle*, ed. David Hey (Harmondsworth: Penguin, 1981), 251-64.

[68] Nicholas Rogers, "Policing the Poor in Eighteenth-Century London: The Vagrancy Laws and their Administration", *Histoire Sociale / Social History* 24 (1991), esp. 131-2, 139-41

[69] *A Proclamation For the Due Observation of Certain Statutes made for the Suppressing of Rogues, [etc.]* (1661).

[70] *By the Mayor: The Right Honourable the Lord Mayor of the City of London, Taking Especial Notice of Inordinate Liberty* (1676).
[71] Margaret James, *Social Problems and Policy during the Puritan Revolution, 1640-1660* (1930; London: Routledge & Kegan Paul, 1966), Ch. 5; John Shedd, "The State Versus the Trades Guilds: Parliament's Soldier-Apprentices in the English Civil War Period, 1642-1655", *International Labor and Working-Class History* 65 (2004): 105-16.
[72] Miller, *Cities Divided*, 82-5; Joanna Innes and Nicholas Rogers, "Politics and Government, 1700-1840", in *Cambridge Urban History*, ed. Clark, II, 543-8.
[73] Francis Drake, *Eboracum* (1736), 239-49, quoted in *VCH: Yorkshire – The City of York*, 215. Moreover, this level of enforcement continued throughout the century: ibid., 215-18.
[74] Sharp, *Crime*, 83.
[75] For a summary of this process of economic integration, see Keith Wrightson, *Earthly Necessities: Economic Lives in Early Modern Britain, 1470-1750* (London: Penguin, 2002), Ch. 10.
[76] L. M. Marshall, "The Levying of the Heath Tax, 1662-1688", *English Historical Review* 51 (1936): 632, 635-6; *Calendar of State Papers: Domestic* (hereafter *CSPD*), *1666-7*, 327, 330-1, 336; *CSPD, 1667-8*, 222, 224; *Calendar of Treasury Books* (hereafter *CTB*), II, 69, 79, 81; III, 71, 406; V, 318-19; Historical Manuscripts Commission (hereafter HMC), *Twelfth Report: Appendix VII (Le Fleming)*, 47; Michael Braddick, *Parliamentary Taxation in Seventeenth-Century England: Local Administration and Response* (London: Royal Historical Society, 1994), 252-66; Tim Harris, *London Crowds in the Reign of Charles II: Propaganda and Politics from the Restoration until the Exclusion Crisis* (Cambridge: Cambridge University Press, 1987), 205-6. For negative representations of hearth tax collectors in ballads, see *Pepys Ballads*, IV, 308-9.
[77] Braddick, *Parliamentary Taxation*, 285-6; Joan Thirsk, "New Crops and their Diffusion: Tobacco-Growing in Seventeenth-Century England", in *Rural Change and Urban Growth, 1500-1800: Essays in English Regional History in Honour of W.G. Hoskins*, eds, Christopher Chalklin and Michael Havinden (London: Longman, 1974), 95-7. For excise riots in Somerset (1675), Shropshire (1699), and various places in Wales (1699, 1704, 1712), see P. J. Norrey, "The Restoration Regime in Action: the Relationship between Central and Local Government in Dorset, Somerset & Wiltshire, 1660-1678", *Historical Journal* 31:4 (1988): 801; Max Beloff, *Public Order and Popular Disturbances, 1660-1714* (1938; London: Frank Cass & Co., 1963), 94-5.
[78] Paul Monod, "Dangerous Merchandise: Smuggling, Jacobitism, and Commercial Culture in Southeast England, 1690-1760", *Journal of British Studies* 30 (1991): 181. For violent clashes between smugglers and government officers, see Beloff, *Public Order*, 95-8.
[79] These "places of pretended privilege" included "that in the Minories; those in and near Fleet-street, as Salisbury-court, White-friars, Ram-alley, and Mitre-court; in Holborn, Fulwood's Rents, and Baldwin's-gardens in Gray's inn-lane; in the Strand, the Savoy; in Southwark, Mountague-close, Deadman's-place, the Clink,

and the Mint". Parliament attempted to suppress them in The Escape of Debtors Act of 1696, 8 & 9 Will. III, c. 27 (*Statutes of the Realm*, VII, 271-5). For the context of this Act and its successor in 1722, see John Noorthouck, *A New History of London* (1773), 284, 322.

[80] Unless otherwise noted, all information and quotations in these two paragraphs are from the committee report in *Journal of the House of Commons*, XV, 169-70 (23 Feb. 1706). See also *CSPD: Anne*, IV, 85, 92, 103.

[81] "The Mint in Southwark Act", 9 Geo. I, c. 28 (*Statutes at Large*, V, 470-2). However, even then resistance continued in some liberties. In 1724, for example, the inhabitants of the Wapping Mint sanctuary organized resistance to intrusion with such violence that it resulted in an execution: Peter Linebaugh, *The London Hanged: Crime and Civil society in the Eighteenth century* (London: Allen Lane, 1991), 56-8.

[82] For the Cheylesmore enclosure riots, see *CSPD, 1667-8*, 435; *CSPD, 1668-9*, 438; Coventry Council Minutes, Coventry History Centre, BA/H/C/17/3, p. 55 (Sept. 1699); *VCH: Warwickshire*, VIII, 204.

[83] In the later Stuart period, there were incidents in 1660-1, 1664, 1668, 1682, 1684, 1691, 1697 and 1712. All the information on the Hatfield Level has been drawn from Keith Lindley, *Fenland riots and the English revolution* (London: Heinemann, 1982), 233-52. For more examples of later Stuart riots in the fens, see ibid., Ch. 7.

[84] For the various protests in the Forest of Dean during this period, see *CTB*, III, 457; ibid., IX, 586-7, 1495; *CSPD, Anne*, III, 59; Cyril Hart, *The Commoners of Dean Forest* (Gloucester, 1951), 72-7; idem., *The Free Miners of the Royal Forest of Dean and Hundred of St. Briavels* (Gloucester, 1953), 171, 184-6, 189, 192-3. "Tacit support for the rioters came from some local gentry": *VCH: Glocestershire*, V, 368.

[85] *CSPD, 1661-1662*, 602 (25 Dec. 1662). I have only included examples in which the transport or export of corn was clearly central. There were many other later Stuart food riots (whose details are obscure) which may or may not have focused on this issue.

[86] Nicholas Fogg, *Stratford-upon-Avon: Portrait of a Town* (Chichester: Phillimore, 1986), 76; John Walter, "Faces in the Crowd: Gender and Age in the Early Modern English crowd" in *The family in Early Modern England*, eds, Helen Berry and Elizabeth Foyster (Cambridge: Cambridge University Press, 2007), 116.

[87] Narcissus Luttrell, *A Brief Historical Relation of State Affairs from September 1678 to April 1714* (Oxford, 1957), II, 629 (1 Dec. 1692); III, 29 (4 Feb. 1693). For other reports about the arrival of factors (including Dutch, Quakers, and unspecified "foreigners"), see ibid., III, 20, 32; VI, 494.

[88] Nicholas Corsellis to Lord Rivers, 16 May 1709, in HMC, *Eighth Report: Appendix I (Marlborough)*, 46.

[89] Quoted in Hindle, *On the Parish?*, 38. For later cases of often violent "collective sanctions" against gleaning interlopers or those who ignored local customs about timing, see Peter King, "Gleaners, Farmers and the Failure of Legal Sanctions in England, 1750-1850", *Past & Present* 125 (1989): 132-3.

[90] Tönnies, *Community and Society*, esp. 231-5.
[91] Both the previous historiography and its critics are ably surveyed in Wrightson, "Decline"; idem., "Mutualities and Obligations: Changing Social Relationships in Early Modern England", *Proceedings of the British Academy* 139 (2006): 157-94; Alexandra Shepard and Phil Withington, "Introduction", in idem., *Communities in Early Modern England: Networks, Place, Rhetoric* (Manchester and New York: Manchester University Press, 2000), 1-15; Richard Smith, "'Modernization' and the Corporate Village Community in England: Some Sceptical Reflections", in *Explorations in Historical Geography: Interpretative Essays*, eds, Alan Baker and Derek Gregory (Cambridge: Cambridge University Press, 1984), 140-79.
[92] These contrasting histories are discussed more fully above, but the first category would include manorial self-government, the second category would include urban corporatism and certain village festivals, and the third category would include the secular parish.
[93] Wrightson, "Mutualities and Obligations", 161.
[94] William Harrison, *The Description of England* (1577), ed. George Edelen (Washington and New York: Folger and Dover, 1994), 118.

CUSTOM, MEMORY AND THE OPERATIONS OF POWER IN SEVENTEENTH-CENTURY FOREST OF DEAN

SIMON SANDALL

This paper explores the relation between popular agency, local community and customary senses of the past during the late sixteenth- and seventeenth-centuries. In considering the practical and multi-faceted meanings of power, my analysis is informed by Antonio Gramsci's assertion that hegemony does not simply involve the threat of coercive force, but also the cultural negotiation of consent. The analysis that follows argues that this "organisation" of consent appears to consist, in large part, of competition over the perceived legitimacy of collective ways of remembering and the world views supported by such. Pursuing this integral link between conflicting legal understandings and hegemonic competition over collective memory strategies, my primary focus is the free mining community of the Forest of Dean in Gloucestershire. I pay particular attention to the Mine Law Court through which a jury of twelve, twenty-four or forty-eight miners exercised a strict monopoly of jurisdiction over regulation of the body of customary law which governed their industry and attempted to resolve conflicts between fellow miners or between such miners and other parties. It is important to remember, however, that those engaged in this mining industry were part of an extremely litigious forest community on a wider scale and, in this regard, I consider the relation of customary mining practice to more general rights to common within the forest. A cultural perception of legality was reflected in the criteria for entry into this community as it was necessary for a free miner to be able to demonstrate that he had been born within the hundred of St Briavels, that he was the son of a free miner and that he had worked in a mine for a year and a day.[1] Through this local study and a brief consideration of the wider context of early seventeenth-century England, I explore how the study of custom can highlight the extent to which law was a local and culturally mediated experience during this period. It was an experience which appears to have been more socially inclusive than the formal written codes and practices of central equity litigation which were gaining prominence during this period.

Writing in 1696, William Carter explained that "A Custom .... being only matter of Fact, and consisting in Use and Practice, it can be recorded and registred no where but in the Memory of the People. For a Custom taketh beginning and groweth to perfection in this manner". His description, whilst highly idealised as will be discussed, does point to a perception of custom as *lex loci*; a body of local legal practices whose dependence upon an "unwritten" collective memory and the social relationships within which it developed and operated facilitated a broad participation in local popular political culture. In outlining the understandings of legality which seem to have underwritten the popular political culture of Dean, my paper ultimately seeks to examine the difficulties inherent in attempts to formalise such collective ways of remembering during the seventeenth-century. The most prominent difficulty in this respect, it would seem, was that these customary senses of the region and its past were very much embodied in the everyday practices of those that constituted this forest community; practices that were, to a large extent, invoked and perpetuated by the kind of bodily mnemonic traces that Paul Connerton has termed "habit memory".[2]

Seventeenth-century Dean saw much conflict in reaction to what was popularly perceived as a large scale assault on local custom. As part of an early Jacobean drive to rationalise and maximise income from royal demesne lands, many forest inhabitants were made to feel increasingly insecure over their rights of access to land, the tenure of which had previously been regarded as secure through continued and ancient use. It is a historical commonplace that upon accession to the throne of England in 1603, James I inherited severe fiscal difficulties from the regime of his predecessor. In May 1602, Lord Treasurer Buckhurst had implored that "it was fittest to have peace with Spain before we be too far spent, for he [Spain] hath a spring that yieldeth continual supply, his Indies, & we are like a standing water, which war will exhaust & make dry & barren".[3]

Predominant in attempts to address such concerns was an awareness that many areas of the Crown's estates had been allowed to develop into relatively autonomous systems of local governance within which rents had been allowed to remain at lower and outdated levels. The profits from these estates had thus been relatively unaffected by the vast upheavals in land ownership and inflationary growth of the sixteenth-century, lending credence to Buckhurst's description of England's "standing water". Richard Hoyle warns against simplistic readings of the efficacy of

Elizabethan land sales, noting that these make "no allowance for inflation; in real terms the value of the estates was progressively reduced".[4] By the time James came to the throne, his regime was struggling against both the effects of inflation and the consequences of Elizabethan policy regarding the management of royal estates. Perhaps because many of the key innovations in estate management (including the 1554 integration of the Court of Augmentations within the Exchequer) had taken place before Elizabeth acceded to the throne, her policy seems to have been aimed largely at maintaining such income at a stable level whilst transferring as many costs as possible to the tenants of her land. As such, the Jacobean administration was left with the task of attempting to squeeze more income from lands whose terms of tenure had effectively been frozen by the policies of the Elizabethan government. Hoyle notes that under Elizabeth, "customary tenants were offered confirmations of their customs or preferential leasehold arrangements for taking upon themselves the expense of repairing river banks and coastal defences..... without wages" so it was, under James, "no longer possible (if it ever had been) to alter significantly the terms and conditions by which customary tenants held their lands".[5]

Whatever the complex and often contradictory reasons, after approximately two centuries of relative autonomy, these areas were becoming increasingly subject to the scrutiny of the Crown or agents thereof. In view of the difficult situation regarding the perceived legitimacy of customary rights in these areas after such a sustained period of largely uninterrupted practice and the consolidation of many such usages under Elizabethan governance, the attentions of the Crown turned increasingly towards undermining such security of tenure through the concerted scrutiny of title. For this purpose, many "private men" of no particular qualification were recruited to carry out searches of "concealments" which, generally speaking, consisted of land which had been assarted from royal forest without being disclosed. Philip Petitt confirms that "Otto Nicholson was formally engaged in this service in July 1605, when he was appointed receiver of all money accruing from the improvements of assarts – other than their annual rent". In November 1606, he was offered a more lucrative arrangement whereby he was to receive "one-fifth of all fines and profits arising after his appointments", a deal which apparently did little to dampen his zeal.[6] His name is, unsurprisingly, prominent in many Exchequer records relating to Dean during the first three decades of the seventeenth-century.

In 1613, for example, John Sallens confirmed that for the "space of manie years last past [he] was lawfullie seised in his demeasne ... time out of mind", and that he "had and used to have within the said fforrest aswell com[m]on of pasture".[7] John Sallens and his co-plaintiffs had taken this case to equity as the lands and rights for which they had apparently compounded with Nicholson were being contested by reason of a grant of forest resources made to William Herbert, the third Earl of Pembroke. Sallens et al were complaining that this disputed land was "p[re]tended by the said Otho Nicholson to bee assarted (which in truth were not)". These plaintiffs did, however, submit "themselves & theire estate to his mercy and the said Otho Nicholson did p[ro]mise and contract with the said Inhabit[an]ts that compounded" that they would not lose:

> theire Com[m]ons, estovers, botes p[ro]fits or com[m]oddities w[i]thin the said fforrest but that they might enjoy the same in such mann[er] and forme as they within Fortie years before the said Composic[i]on did and might have enjoyed the same as if noe such Composic[i]on had bene made the benefit of which promise and contract the said plts humblie pray maie bee allowed unto them.[8]

This testimony clearly illustrates the uncertainty and insecurity engendered by such quests to uncover "defective" title, particularly when, as appears from this case, the authority of those who were responsible for such searches was questionable at best and often in conflict with the interests of other "private men". Joan Thirsk summarises the issue thus:

> No matter how cautiously matters were planned in the Exchequer, no matter how much diligent scheming went into ensuring that tenants were gently cajoled into paying composition to their gracious King, the whole edifice of reform rested on individual projectors, who, when once they were let loose in the counties, were incapable of being restrained except by adverse reports from local dignitaries. Their livelihood depended on wringing as much cash as possible out of the King's tenants, and their earnings were inextricably tied with those of the Crown.[9]

During the early seventeenth-century in the Forest of Dean we can see the increasing involvement of "projectors" and other agents of the Crown, acting to blur the division between the public interest of the Crown and "common weal" and that of "private men".

It was in such a context in 1611, that James I bestowed control of a large part of the Forest resources upon William Herbert, Earl of Pembroke. Under the terms of this grant, Pembroke was to receive 12,000 cords of wood per year and £33.6s.8d per year towards enclosing the areas which had been cut. These areas were to be enclosed for twenty-two years and, during this period, no other persons were to be permitted ironworks in the forest or to take wood, ore, timber or cinders without the Earl's permission. This grant together with the more general drive towards "improvement" of the Forest during the first half of the seventeenth-century obviously encroached upon local customary use rights at all levels of the social scale and, quite predictably, exacerbated tensions within the forest.

In 1607, local landowner and ironmaster Sir Edward Winter had complained to Star Chamber regarding the riotous behaviour of those that he understood to be free miners. Suggesting that the men had played upon fears that he was gaining an unauthorised foothold in the local mining industry, Winter claimed that they had pursued such a course:

> well knoweinge that in the myndes of the vulgar sort (of that country especiallye) there is not anything that leaves a deeper impression of hatred and malice then a conceipt once strongly apprehended by them of beinge abridged by any man of such freedoms and liberties as they challenge and doe pretend to have.

Winter's evidence thus worked to construct an opposition between the legitimacy of his rights which attached to the office of Constable of St. Briavels, and the "pretended custome" which existed only "in the myndes of the vulgar sort". Such stereotyping persisted in his description of the alleged "Ryotors", "most of them beinge men of verie lewde conversation and the aptest p[er]sons in that countrey to attempt or Commyt any outrage or misdemeanour". Winter protested that these offences were not to be suffered in a "well governed Commonweale" adding, in a fashion which echoed a common elite anxiety, that they were "the more heynouse and intolerable in that they were committed and executed in your Ma[ies]ties Forrest and that in the night time".[10] Not only had these defendants been unnaturally committing their crimes on a "Saturdaye betweene eleven and Twelve of the Clocke in the night (when good subiects should be in bedd)", but they were heavily armed and disguised with "vizards and scarfes"; this final point being very strenuously denied by all of the defendants. Winter's bill to Star Chamber, then, apparently sought to contrast his quiet legal possession of rights with the armed and aggressive attempts of the defendants to claim their "pretended" custom. He also contrasted the legitimate, open and daylight proceedings of his employees with the "unnatural" nocturnal activity of this group which contained, contrary to his language of social description, five yeomen of Newland and two gentlemen including Richard Katchmaye "of late advanced to the Capteynshippe of one of the trayned bandes in that division of the forest". According to Winter this group were "all or the most of them for many years together being knowen to be the most sedytiouse, turbulent and dangerouse spirits of that Countrye".[11]

Through such polarised thinking, then, Winter's apparently strategic testimony worked to construct a series of oppositional relations which ultimately combined to represent him as the conduit of orderly governance whilst his opponents were, thus, cast as a disorderly and furtive threat to such. His apparent interpretation of the situation is interesting in its implication that custom was very much about cognition. The evidence of these proceedings suggests that custom was related to a traditional "way of seeing" or "being" in the forest; as such, it would seem that particular worldviews supported particular understandings of legality.

Winter's language of social description set up an opposition between his own social group, the "greater gentry" of the region who exercised more "formal" use rights and the "vulgar sorte" who clung desperately to their "pretended customs". This language appears to have been used in papering over certain cracks and simplifying a very complex set of relations; there is much evidence to suggest that the local industrial gentry were far from unified in purpose. Winter's language nevertheless points to a burgeoning process of social polarisation whereby less formal claims to customary rights were being ascribed to those increasingly identified as the "vulgar sorte" of the Forest.

Competing definitions of customary use rights within the forest were central to many disputes during the first forty years of the seventeenth-century. In August 1612, the Earl of Northampton complained about the detrimental effects of such sustained and exclusive wood-cutting. In doing so, he made some interesting observations regarding the disturbances; in particular, how they were perceived by the rest of the forest community. Such cutting, he said, had caused "some fifteen desperate knaves" to set fire to piles of cordwood and then:

> dancing about the fire cried God save the King; they still walk the wood with weapons and oft I hear weak shot; they call their neighbours cowards for not assisting them; they give out that they look for more help; the Justice has given order for their apprehension but the country [i.e. the local plebeian population] favour them

These "desperate knaves" seem to have been very active in their attempts to recruit foresters in resisting "improvement" of the region. Northampton stressed the need for the local gentry to take control from the "odious" Pembroke as they would be far better situated to temper the "wild humours of those Robin Hoodes".[12]

The leaders of these "riots" were not, of course, facilitating the authorities' attempts at identification so it is difficult to point to the mining community with any certainty. There is reasonably convincing evidence, however, to suggest the integral nature of their involvement in the organisation and leadership of collective resistance into the late 1620s. In violation of an Exchequer decree of 1628 which granted quiet possession of Mailescott Woods to Lady Barbara Villiers, for example, a number of inhabitants of the forest continued to mine and to pasture cattle on this land. All of the defendants, as inhabitants of the hundred of St Briavels, asserted that they had the right to common of pasture and the right to mine in the wastes of the forest. They stated flatly - in their answer to the Attorney General - that they would not be bound by an Exchequer decree that recognised the right of the King and his grantees to enclose Mailescott and other lands in Dean. Mailescott, and all of these other lands had their enclosures and fellets destroyed in the riots that ensued. The connection between loss of mining rights and the outbreak of riots is clearly demonstrable, as before the enclosures were able to proceed, Lady Villiers had to make one concession – to permit the mining of iron ore in Mailescott Woods as freely as before the decree of 1628. Buchanan Sharp observes that this concession did not completely pacify the forest but it seems that, once the miners' demands had been satisfied, only minor riots occurred.[13]

During these disturbances in protest against the encroachment of Villiers and her agent Sir Giles Mompesson in Dean, the "rioters" acted:

> By sound of drum and ensigns in most rebellious manner, carrying a picture or statue apparelled like Mompesson and with great noise and clamour threw it into the coalpits that the said Sir Giles had digged.

This highlights, once again, the centrality of the mining community to this resistance, but also gives cause to consider the symbolism of these actions. Given the apparent nature of some of these disturbances, perhaps we should not be surprised to learn that the leaders were commonly referred to as "John" or "Lady Skimmington", suggesting that this action was often framed in the idiom of local and popular shaming rituals. Variously known as skimmingtons, charivari or rough music, such rites constituted an important element of the symbolic resources available to the early modern community in highlighting transgressions of local customary norms. In this guise, it seems, "rioters" were looking to legitimise their actions within the context of traditional forms of protest or public mockery. These forms of public theatre had their parallels in, and intertwined with, "official" philosophy in the form of the "world turned upside down" motif of traditional church rituals and agricultural festivals. In this vein, Martin Ingram tells us that "these customs; actually bear witness less to cultural conflict than to areas of shared culture".[14] The symbolism invoked by the "Skymington rioters" suggests that this was not action directed against local gentry but, rather, a call for this group to perform the duty demanded by their position in protecting the resources of the Forest from the encroachments of outsiders.

Through evoking such customary modes of social regulation, the riots highlighted the wedge which was being driven through the community of the forest by such enclosure; a division between those who had tenure of property and those that depended upon less formal access to the forest wastes. Edward Winter's testimony to Star Chamber would suggest that such a division was as much cultural as economic in that his interpretation of legality was defined almost in opposition to that propounded by the "vulgar sort". In alluding to customary social roles in this particular fashion, the "Skymington rioters" were apparently able to foreground the hierarchy of use rights which they evidently felt was being lost through the "improvement" of the forest. In this hierarchy, different social groups certainly operated upon different rungs but they were, at least, on the same ladder. As Sharp suggests, then, the need for customary access to an "open and com[m]onable" forest implied a strong and assertive collective interest of the mining community and the wider group of propertyless forest inhabitants. The following sections of this paper therefore examine the ways in which this local custom was evidenced, aiming to shed some light on the nature of local collective memory practices and their centrality to the negotiation of hegemony in this region during the late sixteenth- and seventeenth-centuries.

I. Mnemonic landscapes: evidence of the material environment

David Rollison identifies a technique of memory which is useful in approaching non-abstract, embodied forms of historical or legal record, recalling the tangible relationship between memory and material environment. Suggesting that the landscape was literally used to store information, he contends that "the land was a memory palace, so that irrevocably to alter or destroy a land form (as in a mining operation, or in enclosure) was to erase a part of the collective memory".[15] The case of Thomas Hall, gentleman of "Heighmeadows", versus Harry Dowle and others "dwellers & inhabitants w[i]thin the said manner of Staunton" effectively demonstrates this relation between the material environment and collective customary legal memory. In 1632, Hall entered a bill complaining that the defendants had broken on to land known as "Stanton's Myne" and had:

> broke down the mounds and hedges of the same (it being well & sufficiently fenced) and have cutt downe and carried away five hundred trees there lately growing and have putt into the said woodground and soyle great store of cattle which have eaten spoyled and consumed the Springes and young wood there and have made the same lye *open* w(i)thout any fence to the said forrest of dean.

According to Hall, Dowle and the others had managed to gain possession of all written documentation relating to the ownership of this land and "pretend that they have some lawfull estate therein, butt refuse to shewe or discover the same". As such, he claimed, these defendants had left him "Remidiles herein by the strict course of the com[m]on law to recover the said writings, deedes, leases and evidences, not knowing the certain dates, or contents of the same nor whether they are contained in bagge box troncke or chest sealed and locked".[16] Hall's dispute with the commoners of Staunton foregrounds the complex interaction of written and oral methods of recall in the legitimation of use rights and, irrespective of the truth of these claims, provides evidence of anxiety regarding such. His reliance on the written evidence of exclusive property ownership seems to have been vulnerable in its abstract nature, whilst Dowle and others claiming common access to this "open" part of the forest were able to call upon the more material and collective resources of the local "memory palace". They argued that this land could not have been "laied open" as alleged in the bill because it had "layen open during all the time wherof the memory of man runneth not to the contrary". More than this, they were able to collectively testify that they could not have removed five hundred trees because:

> There are few or noe trees thereupon growing but only Shrubbes and bushes and underwoddes and that as they verily believe There hath not byn ffyve hundred Trees thereupon groweing w[i]thin the memory of man.[17]

The potential difficulties faced by those attempting to assert exclusive property rights were evidently considerable, particularly when faced with such embodied legal record in its robust expression of local collective memory.

II. The "ancient men" of the forest: custom and women's agency

Alongside the evidence of the material environment, customary usage of this space was defined by continuance of practice and evidenced, at least in theory, by the spoken word of local, predominantly male, inhabitants. In a 1593 deposition to the Court of the Exchequer, Thomas Baker had "heard crediblie from his ancestors" of their rights to common within the forest and stated that they had "lopped treyes" "for all the tyme of his memorie".[18] In 1618, an interrogatory directed from the same court asked each deponent for details of past estovers taken in the region and also asked them to state how they knew such information. John Hannys, a 53 year old labourer deposed that "by the gen[er]all reporte and relac[i]on of ancient men inhabiting within the said Forrest he hath credibly heard" of such.[19] In a boundary dispute between the "surveyor gen[er]all of his ma[ies]ties woodes" and Sir Edward Winter, Treswell indicated the Crown's dependence on local and orally transmitted knowledge in establishing its rights within the forest demesne lands. He suggested that:

> also there be yet lyvinge divers aged and auncyent men whose testimonie is requisite for the Manifesting of the same Land(es) where they bee and of his ma[ies]ties title to the premmises, who yf they should be decease before they be examined might eterne to his ma[ies]ties greate prejudice and hurte.[20]

This oral recall of precedent was evidently problematic for those that found themselves matched against a larger group within the community. Hopewell Fox, the "viccar of Lidney" was evidently experiencing difficulty in his collection of tithes and other customary dues. Entering an Exchequer bill in 1662, he complained of a conspiracy to obscure "the exact certainty or exact particulars of the Tythes and other duties which are severally and respectively due", claiming that he was approaching this court for an "equitable" hearing because "his witnesses to prove the saide are gone unto remote partes unknown to your orator".[21] In the absence of such witnesses to support his claims, Fox evidently felt that he was being left to fend for himself against the confederation of many amongst the community of Lydney as evidenced by his many complaints to the court during this period.

Embodied methods of identifying customary precedent were, therefore, demonstrably integral to the claims of those from all sections of this community, be they representatives of the Crown, clergymen, gentlemen, miners, yeomen or labourers. In terms of such evidence, it is essential to consider custom in its social aspect. Whilst a central body of customary practices directly determined use rights to the material resources of the forest, the density of such core usages trailed outwards into an elaborate web of traditions, norms and perceptions which influenced, structured and were, in turn, structured by patterns of sociality and community relations. At the nodal points between the operations of central courts, local court systems and local custom, perceptions of legitimacy in the maintenance of proper order were profoundly malleable and ambivalent as was evident in Dean's "Skymington riots" of 1628-30. Keith Wrightson speaks of the "wretched village officers" who were "ensnared at the point where national legislative prescription and local customary norms met". Beyond the officially mediated activity of the manor or central court, therefore, was a space where local litigious senses appear to have been embroiled in the patterns and relationships of everyday life. The self-defining "Skymington" disturbances evidently drew on inclusive popular and customary shaming rituals in legitimating their defence of common rights to an "open" forest. These public performances often incorporated pots, pans and other utensils of domestic everyday life in generating the din that was so provocative in the face of ruling class sensibilities regarding the quiet governance of a well-ordered society. [22]

Considered in its social aspect, then, custom broadens the range of everyday activity which can be understood as political in intent and consequence. Wrightson assures us that the defence of custom was "quintessentially local politics", explaining that "localised customary consciousness was just as much a form of political consciousness as the knowledge of national affairs fostered by a developing print culture".[23] This conceptualisation of political activity, therefore, allows a wider and more nuanced interpretation of popular agency. Laura Gowing has underscored the social and economic pressures that shaped lived bodily experience in seventeenth century England but similarly suggested exclusively feminine domains of power that sustained the governance of the female body.[24] These mechanisms of control were perpetuated by the physical and emotional necessities of female touch, intimacy and community, certainly, but also by custom, tradition and inherited cultural understandings of the gendered body and its prescribed social role. Bernard Capp points to contemporary stereotyping of female sociality as "gossip networks" but also provides much evidence that the spread of rumour and consequent public humiliation could be a powerful weapon in the context of an early modern concern for reputation and good credit, particularly in respect of those with trade and business interests in the local community.

Discussing the purely ideological status of claims to uncontested patriarchal domination, Wrightson suggests that a more probable condition was one:

> of dynamic equilibrium between the powerful influence of gender roles as conventionally defined – the only definition available – and the day to day efforts of women to cope, to adapt, to resist, to defend their own space, get their due, and cultivate their own sense of self esteem within the matrix of the existing system of constraints.[25]

Extant documentation from this period suggests that traditionally gendered expectations could often leave wives, mothers and daughters well situated in respect of the organisation and leadership of some grain riots. Aside from the appropriation of patriarchal ideas regarding their role in providing family sustenance and maintaining the interdependence of neighbourly communities, women were those closest to fluctuations in the grain markets during the course of their everyday lives.

At the same time as the miners and commoners of the Forest of Dean were engaged in the "Skymington riots", John Walter notes that the women and children of Maldon in Essex were acting to physically prevent grain being sold for export at a time when the poor of the region were experiencing difficulty in trying to feed their families. In March 1629, he explains, "a crowd of over 100 women with their children boarded a Flemish ship and forced its crew to fill their caps and aprons with grain from the ship's hold". Whilst those involved in this action escaped without punishment a very similar "riot" two months later, this time involving "200 to 300 unemployed clothworkers" including men, ended with the execution of several rioters.[26] There were many factors – amongst which were a potentially aggravated situation and, perhaps, a more ominous defiance of authorities - which contributed to the harsher punishments meted out for the second riot. It seems difficult not to conclude, however, that, in addition to the perhaps less threatening nature of women and children, traditional ideologies and customary expectations which linked the roles of wife and mother to preservation of the domestic economy and provisioning might have lent a greater sense of legitimacy to the earlier action of Maldon's women and children. Capp also notes grain "riots" led by women in Southampton and Dorchester in 1608 and 1630 respectively. Whilst he accepts that such gender ascribed roles would probably have played a part in the female organisation and leadership of some such disputes, he suggests that "it was natural for them to play a prominent role in riots over grain supplies, for they were the main buyers in the local markets, and the first to notice when stocks were diverted to London or overseas".[27] The significant point is that less formal or distinct customary senses of legitimation, whilst often derived from harsh patriarchal tenets, could offer space for the exercise of women's agency in the economic sphere of public life.

In the Forest of Dean, however, the situation was markedly different. The "Skymington riots" in defence of industrial rights and the maintenance of open forest had apparently been organised by the mining community; an occupational group which, as discussed, was exclusively male in composition. Popular senses of the past as they were articulated in the context of disputes in Dean demonstrate that the local collective memory which constituted customary perceptions of a region could very often be the expression of the settled, male adults of that area. The grain riots in Southampton, Dorchester and Maldon, however, suggest that women often had access to such local and customary cultural resources in legitimating their engagement with market forces during the early seventeenth-century.

III. "Jury called the contrey": the social mediation of local justice

I have explained that customary law had always been dependent to some degree on the interplay between oral evidence and the written record of custumals, charters and deeds whilst suggesting the constitutive role of local reputation and the importance of social relationships in the operation of the forest legal system. In resisting John Gyes' attempts, in 1582, to bring legal proceedings through the Court of the Exchequer, "George Cachemayd gent Edmund Cachemayd gent Crystofer Bond John Bond William Heynes & William Kedgewyn" maintained that:

> the custome of the said mannor of St Brevell[es] ys that amercyament[es] and paynes set & taxed by a Jury sworne at the lawe dayes holden in the said mannor may by the custome of the said mannor be affyred myttygated & dymynished by a Jury called the Contrey[28]

These substantial men of the forest, then, emphasised the influence of social relationships and local cultural influence which might inform members of such a jury. In their dispute with Gyes regarding appropriate methods of litigation, the men pointed to a fundamental difference between central and local courts. In the processes of "equity", members of a community were recorded individually by deposition whereas, in a more local court system, the experience of a jury member or that of an "ancient" witness to customary practice could not be isolated from the experience of living within the area thus served.

Transcending the judgement of the "Jury called the Contrey" was perhaps a motive of John Gyes in appealing to this central court. His family was certainly no stranger to the often controversial interplay of oral and written legal culture. In 1574 his brother, Robert Gyes, was the subject of a bill of complaint concerning their deceased father William who had been presented before the same court by Roger Taverner "farmo[u]r to o[u]r sayd soveryn". Apparently, William Gyes "during his lifetime [had] already been called before this court for waistes and spoyles by hym committed within the Forrest and was fyned in the said courte" which fines, Taverner complained, had still not been paid. To make matters worse, he had also "contrary to the usage and aunciect custom of makinge of leases of such her Ma[ies]ties inheritaunces hath proved and gotten wordes putten into the said supposed graunt".[29] This case demonstrates, simultaneously, both the dependence of custom on the written record and scepticism towards the veracity of the documentation involved. John Gyes was, therefore, using the same legal resource through which his father had been prosecuted for the manipulation of written legal evidence. Further, he also seems to have been signalling the intent to escape community censure, the disparity in social standing between him and the defendants and the reputation of his family in the hope of an "equitable" hearing.

Custom's pretence to timelessness and orality apparently aided accommodation of the messy complexities of coincident use rights. As we have seen, the transmission of customary use rights within the forest was dependent upon the social interaction of a defiantly vernacular culture which appears to have stood in stark contrast to the secretive and oligarchic operation of some of those select vestries described in the work of Steve Hindle and Paul Griffiths.[30] Griffiths describes a culture of secrecy in the administration of some London guilds during the seventeenth-century. In its less metropolitan focus, Hindle's study of the state and social change during this period points to the rise of the civil parish and the conjunction of church and state authority in an emergent political culture of the middling sort in some areas of England. Whilst often associated with reformed religious ideals, this culture of the select vestry member was grounded – in many respects – in an acquisition of power through management and distribution of poor relief within the parish. In many areas this appears to have been a prominent influence in an increasing cultural division of the kind implied by Edward Winter's dismissal of the "pretended custom" of the "vulgar sorte".

The most well known record of such burgeoning cultural divisions is, perhaps, the 1596 "articles" of the "chieffe inhabitants" of the parish of Swallowfield in Wiltshire. Noting that the "Josteces are farr of[f]", the document suggests that these inhabitants were announcing themselves as the custodians of local order, agreeing to "keepe all & synguler the artycles her[e] sett dowen", such action being "for the better servynge of her Ma[jes]tie". Amongst various articles apparently aimed at the coherence of this group and the control of settlement within the parish, the twelfth states the necessity for:

> a paper Booke to Regester all o[u]r doynges & by or w[i]th [what] autorety or warrant wee do it consernynge her Ma[jes]ties service & one other Booke for the Churche & the poor.

When it came to their duty of care for the poor, the "chieffe inhabitants" of Swallowfield were, it seems, beginning to make moral distinctions between various categories of those under their supervision. Whilst it was agreed that "all shall do their best to helpe the honest poore, the blynd, the syck, the lame and diseased persons", article [18] decreed that "all shall do their best to suppress pilferers Backbyters hedge breakers, & myscheveous persons, & all such as be prowde, dissentious and arrogant persons".[31] Hindle suggests that:

> The significance of the late sixteenth and early seventeenth centuries for the development of the English state cannot therefore be exaggerated. Enhanced social stratification, and the cultural differentiation which it implied, were the consequences of the pursuit of stability in late Tudor and early Stuart England. In turn, these proved to be powerful influences on the long term incorporation of English political society. By the late seventeenth century, they had found institutional expression in the civil parishes of rural England.[32]

We can see then that such innovation at the conjunction of national and local systems of governance - particularly within parishes which witnessed a shift towards the rule of the select or closed vestry - would often tend towards a significant narrowing of participation in the political life of the community.

The situation within Dean was very different to such areas as Swallowfield and those described by Hindle. The most striking contrast is, perhaps, that a large part of the Forest was extra-parochial. Aside from this, the nature of the conflict over Dean's resources during the first years of the seventeenth-century suggests that "ancient" and customary senses of the region were still very keenly felt amongst the commonalty of the region. In contrast to the forms of record keeping which appear to have prevailed in the civil parish, customary legal memory implied an extremely broad participation in its perpetuation and appropriation, an aspect of forest life which seems to have been central to local popular political culture.

IV. Custom and the written record

In their dependence on local opinion then, popular perceptions of legality were not as useful to those attempting to establish exclusive property rights within the Forest. Processes of state enlargement during this period were not confined to the rise of the civil parish but found expression, also, in the growth of centralised legal hegemony, particularly in respect of equity courts. The bulk of source material examined for this paper was drawn from the records of the Court of the Exchequer. These records, in themselves, speak of the increasing involvement of central courts in forest affairs. As with the rise of the civil parish, however, the increase in equity litigation was a process which seems to have found its main agents in particular inhabitants of these local communities. Many plaintiffs bringing cases from within the Forest were extremely reflexive regarding the process of seeking such legal recourse. Amongst the reasons given for seeking judgement in these courts was the prevalent hope that their dispute would be mediated through "equity and good conscience" outside the influence of local censure, protectionism or partisanship. Many cases were brought in the attempt to resolve conflicting local interests; some related to missing or manipulated legal documentation or, quite simply, a failure to resolve conflicting claims to customary use rights. The plaintiff in one case represented the "common voice" of the "contrey" as an unjust "confederacy" and others aired their suspicions regarding the raising of a "common purse". On many occasions it seems possible that such litigation was being used simply for obstructive purposes.[33]

Adam Fox suggests that "the records of decisions and agreements made locally could be superseded by the decrees of the central common law and equity courts to which increasing resort was being made in the sixteenth and seventeenth centuries", noting that "this development was to have significant effects upon both popular legal consciousness and general perceptions of the written word".[34] Between 1580 and 1680, 34 sets of depositions were given to the court of the Exchequer which related to the forest of Dean. From these, I have retrieved details of 408 deponents, of whom 244 were recorded as being gentlemen, yeomen or husbandmen. Less than five per cent of these deponents were women. Whilst approximately fifteen per cent were engaged in what might be considered artisanal occupations (including 22 miners), those deponents whose voice was heard through such a system constituted a relatively exclusive group, certainly in comparison with the social range of those traditionally called upon to evidence customary usages of the forest. Whilst representing a significant proportion of those seeking equity, the mining community also began adopting more documentary methods of record keeping in the apparent attempt to protect their small scale customary industry. 1610 saw the codification of their Laws and Privileges - probably as the consequence of anxieties regarding Pembroke's imminent grant. These were printed in 1673 and, from 1680 onwards, the proceedings and orders of the Mine Law Court were recorded complete with a chronological schedule. These apparent attempts to resist the encroachment of outside interest, however, actually appear to have rendered the operation, regulation and practices of this industry more rational and legible to outside interests. Through the increasing codification of its practices, the mining industry, like many other aspects of the forest legal culture, was becoming subject to diachronically ordering influences from without.

By the end of the seventeenth-century the Forest was certainly far more penetrable and legible to non-residents. James C. Scott's observation that the state "creates such a system through its ability to give its categories the force of law"[35], however, seems to refer to a far more monologic and deterministic model of state enlargement than appears to have been the experience of changing understandings of custom and legality in this region during the late sixteenth- and early seventeenth-centuries. Even if this local community did not intentionally work to inscribe themselves within the legal hegemony of the burgeoning early-modern English state, this does not necessarily preclude any notion of agency on their part. Whilst Scott is happy to attribute the capacity for agency to the centralising state at least partly through the unintentional consequences of its actions, the process by which the free mining community of Dean became increasingly legible to outside parties during the course of the seventeenth-century demonstrates that this conceptualisation was equally applicable to their actions. Philip Cassell quotes Anthony Giddens' suggestion regarding the "significance of connecting unintended consequences of action with institutionalized practices, those deeply embedded in time"[36] to understanding the processes of "social reproduction" which seem to be at the heart of changing understandings of community and legality. In short, it seems that the free miners of Dean, in attempting to protect the integrity of their customary rights through increasing documentation and recourse to equity courts, unintentionally rendered their industry more legible to those that otherwise lacked the local understanding or recall required to take control of such embodied usages.

In his 1931 work, *Ancient Law*, Henry Maine makes the useful observation that "When primitive law has once been embodied in a Code, there is an end to what may be called its spontaneous development. Henceforward the changes effected in it, if effected at all, are effected deliberately and from without". From Maine's comments, Jack Goody concludes that after the code comes into existence, "legal modification" can be attributed to the "conscious desire for improvement". Such a conscious desire for improvement – in very broad and simplistic terms – implies an analogy between the rationalisation and diachronic ordering of land usages, and the codification of legal practices through which such enclosure and disafforestation was regulated. Both processes imply a shift from legitimation grounded firmly in the material past to a more abstracted world view that looked forward to the "march of progress". These processes of legal and physical enclosure, both related to the fixity of the written word, the statistical chart and the map, appear to have combined in attempts to formalise local collective memory structures and to narrow the base for participation in their construction, perpetuation and operation.

There is no doubt that several projects, both governmental and industrial, were underway during this period which seem to have been directed towards the incorporation of the Forest's population and resources within the bourgeois hegemony that was apparently consolidated in the 1832 Reform Act. In this regard, I have examined the increasing recourse to central equity courts, and its long term effects in rendering the forest and its industries more legible to external interest; a process which appears to have been, at least in part, an unintended consequence of the miners' attempts to preserve their occupational rights from just such "foreign" interests. In 1785, a committee under the direction of Sir George Onesiphorus Paul "secured an act of parliament for building a new gaol at Gloucester and four houses of correction in other parts of the county", one of which being at Littledean.[37] The opening decades of the nineteenth century also witnessed heavy investment in the establishment of a profitable and efficient rail network to service the Forest's increasingly large-scale coal mining operations whilst lengthy discussion ensued regarding the potential local application of the "new poor law".[38] In addition to such debate, the records of the Quarter Sessions for this period contain entries relating to several Acts of Parliament that had been passed to bring the extra-parochial Forest of Dean under "normal jurisdiction".[39]

V. The end of the Mine Law Court

The reasons behind the discontinuance of the Mine Law Court in 1775 remain obscure to this day. Hart quotes several conflicting recollections cited in the records of a commission conducted in 1832 following the "Warren James riots". Amongst these was the statement of James Machen, aged ninety, who believed:

> that the Mine Law Courts dropped because the miners behaved badly, and there was always so much confusion that the gentlemen would not attend; the miners quarrelled amongst themselves and created disturbances.

Thomas Davis, an eighty year-old free miner of Five Acres, on the other hand stated that he had:

> been at Mine Law Courts; while they lasted no foreigner ever thought of having refuge in the Forest. The court was given up because of a dispute between free miners and foreigners whom we did not consider fit to carry on the works.[40]

In 1775, free miners of the Forest of Dean were prosecuted in the Quarter Sessions for cutting timber.[41] That the mining court was discontinued in the same year that its business first started to be prosecuted through the Quarter Sessions of the Assizes suggests the strong possibility that due to the growth of this industry, the changing nature of its regulation and the increasing legibility of such regulatory mechanisms, some of the more powerful interests operating within the Forest felt that they could simply dispense with this vestige of an "irrational" and "protectionist" past. In 1780, Richard Glassonberg of Littledean "Labourer" and James Trigg "the younger of the same place Coalminer" were prosecuted:

> in Pursuance of an Act of Parliament passed in the Ninth Year of his present Majesty King George the third, for cutting downe an Oake Timber tree in the said Forest Contrary to the statute in that case made and provided.[42]

It seems that the miners' customary right to timber from within the wastes and demesne lands of Dean which had long been derived from local precedent was being prosecuted according to the national statute law of central government.

Bob Bushaway quotes the report of a doling custom of St Briavels that was still in practice during the second half of the eighteenth-century. The author noted that:

One of the most strange customs that time has handed down to us prevails at St. Briavels, Gloucestershire. On Whit-sunday, several baskets full of bread and cheese, cut into small squares of about an inch each, are brought into the Church; and immediately after divine service is ended, the churchwardens, or some other persons, take them into the galleries, from whence their contents are thrown among the congregation, who have a grand scramble for it in the body of the church, which occasions as great a tumult and uproar as the amusement of a village wake; the inhabitants being always extremely anxious in their attendance at worship on this day. The custom is held for the purpose of preserving to the poor of St. Briavels at Hewelsfield the right of cutting and carrying away wood from 3,000 acres of coppice land in Hudknolls and the Meend; and for which every householder is assessed 2d, to buy the bread and cheese given away.[43]

Judging by this account, customary practices were still essential to many aspects of forest life. This particular custom, in its provision for the poor, would presumably have been increasingly essential in the face of the loss of common rights through the "improvement" and enclosure of Dean. Through the apparent formalisation of these practices, then, it seems that those customs relating to industrial usages had been emptied of their social content and those which related to the mediation of community interaction, whilst being effectively divorced from their previous litigious efficacy, might have worked to reinforce a division of cultures within this community. Bushaway's example suggests a distinction between those who sought practical relief in such customs and those that regarded them as a seasonal amusement. In this regard, it would seem that the discontinuance of the Mine Law Court was of profound significance to the process whereby this region became inscribed within the centralised hegemony consolidated in the 1832 reforms and defined in terms that made its resources more accessible to the encroachments of "outsiders". The 1834 "Memorial by the Free Miners and their Case against the Foreigners" is extremely illuminating in this respect and demands extensive citation. The miners explained that, in defence against the claims of "foreigners" to "have found a proof of their usage in working the mines as well as free miners", they had "now traced the history of the Mine Law Courts, and of the practice of the free miners, from the reign of King Edward 3, through the reigns of James 1, and Charles 1, to the reign of Charles 2". Regarding the discontinuance of the court, the miners related:

That the foreigners finding the Mine Law Courts an insuperable obstacle to their success, and more particularly that by the orders last quoted of 1775, there was no chance for their being permitted to work in the mines, found that the only means by which they could hope for success was to destroy the Mine Law Courts.

That the documents of this court were always kept in the Speech House in the Forest of Dean, but that after the conclusion of the last court in 1775 some person or persons broke open the chest in which they were contained and removed them.

That the free miners from that period to the present have made repeated applications to the wardens and the gavellers respecting these orders and documents, but that the wardens and gavellers, while they declared that they could not hold the Mine Law Courts as usual without these documents, at the same time denied all knowledge of their existence.[44]

I have demonstrated the emblematic nature of the Mine Law Court and its intimate embroilment within, and articulation of, a fierce popular communalism that was grounded in the pugnacious defence of ancient customary use rights and memories of conflict over such. It seems sensible to concur with many of those questioned in the 1832 commission who suggested that the loss of the Mine Law Court, forty-seven years previously, had rendered forest resources increasingly vulnerable to the encroachments of "foreigners" and the "private man".

VI. Popular resistance in early nineteenth-century Dean

At a discursive level, then, much extant documentation together with the discontinuance of the Mine Law Court in 1775 might imply an increasing formalisation of legal and governmental structures and the historical records which supported them. Because of their integral role in organising resistance to encroachment upon the customary use rights of the Forest, the controversial discontinuance of the miners' court might imply a tendency towards the atomisation of popular collective memory practices which had informed and sustained this local commonalty. Such evidence could suggest the growth of increasingly exclusive legal and governmental mechanisms that were to prove conducive to private capital investment and the processes of state enlargement during this period.

My conclusion, therefore, turns to the "Warren James riots" of 1831 in demonstrating how partial, ineffective or ambivalent such historical processes could be. James' call for resistance in terms which would surely have been recognisable to those that had participated in such action during the seventeenth-century achieved a huge level of support. These riots (a somewhat misleading description) clearly point to the survival of such customary senses of community and legitimacy until well into the nineteenth-century.

On 12 August 1831, James appeared before the assize court at the Shire Hall in Gloucester. The first of the two indictments, relating to a charge of felony grounded in the Riot Act of 1714, declared that "Warren James, together with divers other unknown evil disposed persons to the number of 100 or more, with force of arms did unlawfully, riotously, routously and tumultuously assemble together to the disturbance of the public peace".[45] The dispute related to a perceived breach of the terms under which the forest had been "settled" in 1668. The act passed in that year had stated that half of the 22,000 acres of Dean's central demesne lands could be enclosed to allow for the re-growth of trees planted thus replenishing stocks that were being depleted by industrial and other practices. In 1831, the area that had been enclosed for the previous twenty years was due to be laid open in accordance with the seventeenth-century act and Warren James, it seems, was confident that it would be. He explained:

> that the enclosures had been set up for 20 years, that the period would expire on 8 June and that the enclosures would then be thrown open. He added that if the authorities did not open them up, the foresters would.[46]

When it became apparent that this was not going to happen he wrote to Edward Machen – Deputy Surveyor of the Forest - informing him that the controversial hedges, banks and fences (which were very well established by this point) were to be removed.

When no further action was forthcoming on this matter, it appears that James took the decision to publicise his plans for the commonalty of Dean to "open the Forest" of their own accord. Of this action itself, some surviving contemporary reports suggest a more disciplined and workmanlike operation than that implied by the charge of riotous and tumultuous assembly. During a four day period, and apparently at the instigation of James, up to three thousand inhabitants of the forest had mustered at various locations to begin the arduous task of breaking up enclosures which had become the focus of local antagonism.[47] The *Monmouthshire Merlin* reported that these crowds set about the fences "in the same way as they would have worked on anything else".[48] Even the deposition of John Langham, Machen's assistant, described the disciplined manner in which, as soon as James had "struck the first blow with a

Mattock or hoe and some of the earth fell, the rest of the party immediately commenced working and pulling down the bank".[49]

The apparently disciplined nature of James' involvement and organization belies the conviction of the court that the assembly of forest residents on the morning of 8 June was riotous, tumultuous or a "disturbance of the public peace".[50] In the days before the gathering, Warren James and Edward Machen, Deputy Surveyor of the forest, had each arranged for notices to be pinned to trees throughout the area. James's posters announced the intended meeting, whilst Machen's reply attempted to outline the legal reasons for the legitimacy of recent enclosures making clear, to residents of the forest, his interpretation of such intended activity. His notice explained that "if three or more persons shall assemble for such purpose, all that are present will be guilty of a riot".[51]

These posters rather strikingly illustrate the ideologies which underpinned, on one hand, the "old" customary traditions of local order and methods of protest in support of such and, on the other, the more "progressive" senses of the British polity that worked to represent the claims of the property owning middle classes. Whilst Machen attempted to assure the "inhabitants of Dean forest ... that the Enclosures [were] made under an Act of 48th Geo III. cap. 72, the provisions of which are the same as 20th Charles II. cap. 3", James simply had to announce a meeting of the Free Miners of the locality "for the purpose of opening the forest, and their right of common to the same".[52] Despite the rudimentary nature of his call to action, James received massive support for removing enclosures, the erection of which, had been integral to the recent transformation of the local landscape. If the fears expressed in a letter from concerned magistrates to the Home Office are to be taken at face value, up to three thousand people were eventually recruited to his project.[53] Shortly after the disturbances, in 1838, Dean's free miners were required to register their occupational status in the written records of the Deputy Gavellor. By the end of November 1839, 827 miners had been recorded suggesting that James' call to action had exercised influence beyond those directly employed in the industry.[54] Chris Fisher, quoting the *Gloucester Journal* and the *Monmouthshire Merlin*, notes that, in addition to "Warren James and one or two others who may be identified as the working proprietors of small mines, there were workmen from the larger mines, women and children and men who had land and cottages in the Forest but who did not work as miners".[55] Contemporary estimates of the figures, then, suggest that support was drawn from a wider section of the forest community than the immediate fraternity of free miners on whose behalf James was claiming to speak and act.

Such reports make clear the inefficacy of Machen's call in comparison to James' activity. His mode of articulation would have been very familiar to those that had been involved in similar action during the seventeenth-century. Whilst Machen referenced a list of abstracted parliamentary statutes, James was able to draw his authority from the articulation of deep seated cultural feelings and perceptions simply by utilizing the locally metonymic phrase "open the Forest". This type of unwritten customary "shorthand" contrasted starkly with the verbose and bureaucratically technical list of statutes through which Machen referenced his legal authority. Whilst these regulations were being codified, thereby contributing to the diachronic ordering which would help to consolidate a national hegemony, it seems those legal codes thus referenced were being stripped of the social and material components which aided such a local customary consciousness in its interpellation of the Forest commonalty.

Memories of the loss of the Mine Law Court evidently evoked feelings of vulnerability to outside interests and the forces of a market economy. The cultural and occupational orientation of James and the community of free miners made them particularly suitable agents for the intellectual organization and articulation of collective grievances held by propertyless inhabitants who had anciently been dependent on rights to common within the forest. In a letter dated 1 June 1831, local magistrates (including Machen) wrote to the Home Office explaining that upon being informed that the ground might always be enclosed, James had gained credit amongst the people, entering "thus at length into the history of the Enclosures".[56] The letter also records that:

> Warren James a miner who had taken great trouble about their rights and has obtained considerable influence amongst them by representations such as these and also by stating that he was countenanced by persons high in authority and by the Severn trust itself at length induced them to join in this desperate undertaking and we fully believe that a great majority have joined under an idea that they were asserting a just right.[57]

In the view of events related to the Home Office, certainly, James was both aware of the history of the locality and, whether invented or otherwise, was conscious of the need to demonstrate connections with authority beyond the local magistracy.

James, then, was not simply emulating older traditions of local popular protest. His campaign of publicity and legitimation suggests that his strategy was also informed by an awareness of wider national movements in defence of the rights of England's labouring population. It is entirely feasible, as such, that his proximity to various visiting speakers in Bream might have influenced his understanding of the more radical implications of resisting those agents represented by Machen's attempts to impose the hegemony of statute law upon rights of access to the resources of the Forest. This influence seems evident in the methods by which he organized and articulated such resistance. As the son of a free miner his actions, in themselves, might have constituted a powerful symbolism in articulating collective memories of this community's longstanding centrality to the defence of "open" forest. As a member of the hereditary mining community of Dean, he would also have been culturally situated to understand the local histories of protest together with national perceptions of this region and its relation to wider networks of trade and influence.

It seems likely that the memory of conflict in defence of these rights engendered a collective interest through which James was able to build a broad popular alliance in support of his call to restore the customary landscape which was both symbolically and physically central to the locally shared habitus. Edward Machen, in countering, called upon rational parliamentary statute, the hegemonic apparatus of the burgeoning class of property owner. Whilst James and the free miners received the support of between 2,000 and 3,000 people, Machen's organization of consent became subordinate to the use of coercive force. A further letter from Machen, P.J. Ducarel and George Crawley to the Home Office dated 23 June 1831 read:

> We beg that you will inform Lord Melbourne that since our last communication with his Majesty's Government circumstances have induced us to change our opinion with regard to the removal of the military altogether. The party of the 11th Foot have already left the neighbourhood; and we would suggest that the Dragoons now with us should remain for some time as many prisoners are daily brought before us, and there still appears to be such excitement in the Forest.[58]

This letter makes clear the extent to which Machen and his fellow magistrates felt that the consensual basis of their authority had been undermined following the challenge of James and the free miners.

Fernand Braudel's distinction between differing timeframes and depths of historical consciousness has proved extremely productive in my assessment of the long and short term experience of historical change in Dean.[59] If we look at the short term "accidents and vicissitudes" which constituted the surface level of historical change, it is clear that custom within the Forest was pared down through a series of conflicts and related ideological negotiations during the seventeenth- and eighteenth-centuries. In this respect many social customs were trivialized and relegated to the status of antiquarian curiosity; remnants of a culture to be recorded as it passed into obscurity. Those bodies of customary law which regulated the region's industry, meanwhile, were increasingly reified and emptied of their social content, a process which appears to have reached its culmination in the discontinuance of the Mine Law Court in 1775 and the apparent atomization of this region's popular communalism. The "James" disturbances of 1831 and their aftermath, however, demonstrate that the deeper structures of collective memory, local communalism and the desire to maintain continuity in the traditional patterns and rhythms of Forest life were far more difficult to eradicate.

Notes

[1] The boundaries of St Briavels hundred were almost coterminous with those of Dean's mineral field.
[2] Paul Connerton, *How Societies Remember* (Cambridge: Cambridge University Press, 1989).
[3] Roger Wilbraham, *The Journal of Sir Roger Wilbraham, Solicitor-General in Ireland and Lord of Requests, for the years 1593-1616*, http://www.archive.org/stream/journalofsirroge00wilbrich, 49-50.
[4] Richard Hoyle ed., *The Estates of the English Crown, 1558-1640* (Cambridge: Cambridge University Press, 1992), 12.
[5] Ibid, 31-32.
[6] Philip Pettit, *The Royal Forests of Northamptonshire: A Study in their Economy, 1558-1714* (Gateshead: Northumberland Press for the Northamptonshire Record Society, 1968), 73.
[7] TNA, E112/82/300.
[8] Ibid.
[9] Joan Thirsk, "The Crown as Projector on its own Estates, from Elizabeth I to Charles I," in *Estates of the English Crown*, ed. Hoyle, 346.
[10] Paul Griffiths, "Meanings of nightwalking in early modern England," *Seventeenth Century* 13:2 (1998): 223.
[11] TNA, STAC8/303/7.
[12] TNA, SP14/70/49.
[13] Buchanan Sharp, *In Contempt of All Authority: Rural Artisans and Riot in the West of England, 1586-1660* (Berkeley: University of California Press, 1980), 206.
[14] Martin Ingram, "Ridings, Rough Music and the 'Reform of Popular Culture' in Early Modern England," *Past & Present* 105 (Nov., 1984): 112-13.
[15] David Rollison, *The Local Origins of Modern Society; Gloucestershire 1500 - 1800* (London and New York: Routledge, 1992), 70.
[16] TNA, E112/180/57.

[17] Ibid.
[18] TNA, E134/36Eliz/Hil21.
[19] TNA, E134/14JasI/Hil8.
[20] TNA, E112/82/310.
[21] TNA, E112/403/12.
[22] Ingram, "Ridings, Rough Music"; Chris Humphrey, *The Politics of Carnival: Festive Misrule in Medieval England* (Manchester: Manchester University Press, 2001).
[23] Keith Wrightson, "The Politics of the Parish in Early Modern England," in *The Experience of Authority in Early Modern England,* ed. Paul Griffiths, Adam Fox and Steve Hindle (Basingstoke and London: Macmillan, 1996), 24.
[24] Laura Gowing, *Domestic Dangers: Women, Words, and Sex in Early Modern London* (Oxford and New York: Oxford University Press, 1996).
[25] Wrightson, 'Politics of the Parish'
[26] John Walter, "Grain Riots and Popular Attitudes to the Law: Maldon and the Crisis of 1629" in *An Ungovernable People: The English and their Law in the Seventeenth and Eighteenth Centuries,* ed. John Brewer and John Styles, (London: Hutchinson, 1980), 48-49.
[27] Bernard Capp, *When Gossips Meet: Women, Family, and Neighbourhood in Early Modern England* (Oxford: Oxford University Press, 2003), 312.
[28] TNA, E112/15/9.
[29] TNA, E112/15/5.
[30] Steve Hindle, *The State and Social Change in Early Modern England, 1550-1640* (Basingstoke: Macmillan, 2002); Steve Hindle, *On the parish?: The Micropolitics of Poor Relief in Rural England, c. 1550-1750* (Oxford: Clarendon Press, 2004); Steve Hindle, "Power, Poor Relief, and Social Relations in Holland Fen, c. 1600-1800," *The Historical Journal* 41:1 (Mar., 1998): 67-96; Paul Griffiths, "Secrecy and Authority in Late Sixteenth- and Early Seventeenth- Century London," *The Historical Journal* 40:4 (Dec., 1997): 925-951.
[31] Steve Hindle, "Hierarchy and Community in the Elizabethan Parish: the Swallowfield Articles of 1596," *The Historical Journal* 42:3 (Sep., 1999): 835-851.
[32] Hindle, *State and Social Change,* 237.
[33] TNA, E112 - Bills and Answers to the Court of Exchequer
[34] Adam Fox, "Custom, Memory and the Authority of Writing," in *The Experience of Authority,* ed. Griffiths et al, 89-177.
[35] James Scott, *Seeing Like a State: How Certain Schemes to Improve the Human Condition Have Failed* (New Haven and London: Yale University Press, 1998), 3.
[36] Philip Cassell ed., *The Giddens Reader* (Basingstoke: Macmillan, 1993), 92-101.
[37] ONDB: http://www.oxforddnb.com/view/articleHL/21597?anchor=match (Dec., 2008).
[38] GRO, Q/FAC 1; GRO, D2091/X6 containing 'Legal opinion on application of the New Poor Law to extra-parochial areas of the Forest of Dean, 1834; letter about poor and church rates, 1837; 6 printed orders of Poor Law Commissioners'; GRO, D421/X5.

[39] GRO, Q/RI
[40] Hart, *Free Miners*, 145-6.
[41] GRO, Q/SIa/1775/Epiphany.
[42] GRO, Q/SR/1780/A.
[43] B. Bushaway, *By Rite: Custom, Ceremony and Community in England, 1700-1800* (London: Junction, 1982), 16-17.
[44] Hart, *Free Miners*, 299-303.
[45] TNA, (CL) Assizes 5/151 pt. 1.
[46] Ralph Anstis, *Warren James and the Dean Forest Riots: The disturbances of 1831* (Coalway, 1986), 104.
[47] Estimated numbers are taken from a letter from *Magistrates to Home Office*, 11 June 1831, TNA, HO 52/12.
[48] *Monmouthshire Merlin*, 9 July 1831. Quoted in Chris Fisher, *Custom, Work and Market Capitalism: The Forest of Dean Colliers, 1788-1888* (London: Croom Helm, 1981), 43.
[49] TNA, (CL) Assizes 6/2 pt. 29.
[50] Ibid.
[51] Ibid.
[52] TNA, (CL) Assizes 6/2 pt. 29.
[53] *Magistrates to Home Office*, 11 June 1831, TNA, HO 52/12.
[54] *Roll of Honour: Mining & Quarrie Fatalities in The Forest of Dean With Index of Freeminers*, www.forestofdeanhistory.org.uk
[55] Fisher, *Custom, Work and Market Capitalism*, 38. Fisher notes that 'no more precise account than this may be offered of the composition of the crowd. The reports of the riot which appeared in newspapers used only such general terms as 'workmen' or 'cottagers''.
[56] TNA, HO/52/12. f. 193.
[57] Ibid.
[58] TNA, HO/52/12. f. 195.
[59] Fernand Braudel, *A History of Civilisation* (New York and London: Penguin, 1993).

THE PEDLAR OF SWAFFHAM, THE FENLAND GIANT AND THE SARDINIAN COMMUNIST: USABLE PASTS AND THE POLITICS OF FOLKLORE IN ENGLAND, C.1600-1830

ANDY WOOD

I am grateful to Fiona Williamson for encouraging me to write this chapter; to Dave Rollison and Claire Langhamer for reading earlier drafts; and to Andy Pearmain for making me think again about Antonio Gramsci. The research for this chapter was supported by grants from the Arts and Humanities Research Council and the Leverhulme Trust.

***

On 29 January 1652, Sir William Dugdale wrote to his friend Sir Roger Twysden concerning one of the local traditions that so fascinated seventeenth-century antiquarians.[1] In the first written account of the tale, Dugdale conveyed to Twysden a piece of Norfolk folklore: the story of the pedlar of Swaffham. As Dugdale told the legend, a pedlar called John Chapman from the market town of Swaffham had dreamt that if he went to London, "he should certainly meet with a man upon London Bridge, which would tell him good news". Chapman therefore set off for London "and walk'd upon the Bridge for some hours" until a shopkeeper asked him what he was waiting for. When Chapman explained his dream, the shopkeeper replied

> alas good friend! Should I have heeded dreams, I might have proved myself as very a fool as thou hast; for "tis not long since that I dreamt, that at a place called Swaffham-Market in Norfolk, dwells one John Chapman a Pedlar, who hath a tree in his backside [i.e., in the rear of his house] under which is hidden a Pot of Money. Now therefore, if I should have made a journey to dig for such hidden treasure, judge you whether I shuld not have been counted a fool".

Keeping to himself the significance of the shopkeeper's words, the pedlar replied that he would no longer be so foolish as to heed such dreams. On his return to Swaffham, Chapman dug under the tree and found a brass pot bearing a Latin inscription which contained a large quantity of money. Some time later, a visitor translated the inscription as reading "under that there was another twice as good". Once again, the pedlar was careful with his words, saying "tis very true, in the shop where I bought this pot, stood another under it, which was twice as big". Sure enough, when Chapman dug under the tree for a second time, he uncovered another pot of gold, twice as big as the last. Initially, he concealed his new-found wealth. But then, the people of Swaffham decided to rebuild their parish church, levying a rate on householders according to their individual wealth. Since his good fortune remained unknown, the pedlar was assessed at a low rate. "But he knowing his own ability" paid for the reconstruction of the whole north aisle of the church, and made a substantial contribution to the erection of "a very tall and beautiful tower steeple".[2]

What are we to make of this story? Nothing at all, one historian has answered. For Margaret Spufford, "The whole point of [folkloric tales] is that [they are] useless". Save for religious texts, Spufford saw no sense in the chapbook literature, adding that "It is perhaps helpful to us to realize the fantasy world, and indeed the mental jumble in which most people must have lived, to which the chapbooks are the key."[3] I would like to suggest otherwise. This chapter proceeds from the assumption that "folktales are historical documents"; and that, like all documents, they might yield something about the culture that produced them. As Robert Darnton puts it,

> The peasants of the Old Regime did not think monographically. They tried to make sense of the world, in all its booming, buzzing confusion, with the materials they had at hand. Those materials included a vast repertory of stories derived from Indo-European lore. The peasant tellers of tales did not merely find the stories amusing or frightening or functional. They found them "good to think with".[4]

First of all, I would like tentatively to suggest a historical context in which the story of the pedlar of Swaffham might have emerged; and secondly, to propose some ways in which later generations might have found the story good to think with. Dugdale's named source for the story was that of "the tradition of the inhabitants, it being told to me there". He added that the inhabitants had also pointed to inscriptions in the windows of the north aisle which thanked John Chapman for funding the construction of that part of the church. According to Dugdale's informants, these events had unfolded some time in the reign of Henry VII. In the 1720s, the Swaffham inhabitants showed the antiquary Francis Blomefield the physical evidence which supported the story: not only the windows in the north aisle, but also a medieval bench end which bore a depiction of a man at work in his shop, below which were the letters I.C. (he presumed for John Chapman). On top of the bench end was the figure of a pedlar "with a pack on his shoulders".[5] Documentary evidence confirms that there was indeed a John Chapman, and that he and his wife Catherine had played an important role in the rebuilding of Swaffham church. Undated parochial accounts from the late medieval period record expenses incurred in the reconstruction of the church, which commenced in the mid-fifteenth century. They note that one John Chapman and his wife Catherine paid for "the north yle, with glasyng, stolyng (seating) and pathyng (paving) of the same with Marbyll, and gave £120 in money to the making of the New Stepyll".[6] Coupled with the material evidence which Blomefield observed in the 1720s, we can safely conclude that there was a historical John Chapman who was sufficiently wealthy to contribute substantially to the reconstruction of the church. The carving of the pedlar was either a play upon the man's surname, or a direct reflection of the source of his wealth. Architectural evidence suggests that the north aisle and additions to the steeple were completed in the first years of the sixteenth century.[7]

At the time at which the people of Swaffham started to rebuild their church, they were suffering from the depradations of two of the notoriously violent gentry of mid fifteenth-century Norfolk; Sir Thomas Tuddenham and John Heydon.[8] But the local people did not suffer silently. In 1451, less than a year after the rebellion of the Kentish and Sussex commons led by Jack Cade, they ensured that their complaints reached the ears of the King. Alluding to Cade's rebellion, the Swaffham folk warned that "ther was up in Norffolk redy to rise" unless royal justice was brought to bear against their "ryche extorrssioners and oppressours". They followed this up with a petition to Parliament later that year.[9] Such assertiveness was not the only sign of the Swaffham parishioners' sense of agency. The rebuilding of the parish church was part of a wider phenomenon which historians have linked to a rise in plebeian piety. The financial and moral investment made by such people – especially those enriched by the woollen industry – is seen as a statement not only of religious belief, but also of the rising prosperity and self-confidence of yeomen farmers and tradespeople.[10] Tuddenham and Heydon's aggressive actions expressed the resentment of the traditional ruling class towards this newly assertive group. In this context, the story of the pedlar of Swaffham provided a focus for local plebeian identity: as the historical John

Chapman faded from living memory, later generations recalled his mythical shadow. The story told them that, for all the contempt directed by the shopkeeper towards the pedlar by the shopkeeper on London Bridge, people from rural Norfolk were smart enough to know when to keep their mouths shut. The story told the people of Swaffham that they were lucky; and it showed that it was appropriate to be grateful for such luck: thus, John Chapman's honesty in investing his cash in the new church, from which the whole community benefited. The story was encoded in local place: entering the church, the parishioners saw a sanctified space, an imposing and impressive structure which had been built by local people like them, not powerful gentry like the Tuddenhams and Heydons. The tale of the Pedlar of Swaffham was partly, then, a story about luck; but it was also a story about the wiliness of the rural plebeian, about his generosity to the wider whole, and it told them that wealth was best shared. In all these respects, the story constructed a community.

There was, then, a utility to the tale of the pedlar of Swaffham: local people found it good to think with. Moreover, it was a tale that was not only located within a specific site; it was also embedded within a collective sense of the local past. The story formed, in Commager's phrase, a "usable past".[11] The notion that the past has a social function originated with the French sociologist Maurice Halbwachs.[12] He made three propositions that have been important to the later development of memory studies: firstly, that all memories are, in some form, influenced by the social formations within which they are constructed and invoked; secondly, that memories are often at their most powerful when embedded within distinct physical settings; lastly, that collective memory is central to social identity. Halbwachs' formulation betrays a clear debt to his mentor, Emile Durkheim and has been criticized for its attention to the subtleties of the relationship between subjectivity, memory and the self.[13] Nonetheless, his work remains a powerful touchstone for those interested in social memory.

This interest in memory and the construction of the past has been, for some historians, somewhat frustrating. Are not memories subject to distortion, or even to deliberate invention? What is the point of studying folklore or collective memories when they are factually unreliable, even flagrantly inaccurate? Such questions are generated deep within the collective psyche of the historical profession. In their early training, historians are often taught to test the "validity" or "accuracy" of a document, to search it for bias or distortion.[14] Judged by such standards, folklore and collective memory will always be found lacking. But my interest here is not in the possibility that folklore and memory might form neutral carriers of an undiluted and untainted historical "truth". Rather, I am interested in what the stories ordinary people told one another might reveal about their mental worlds. In particular, this essay is concerned with what we might call "oppositional" constructions of the past – that is, shared memories (however, from an empiricist point of view, "invented" or "distorted") that can be deployed to criticize the social order and (perhaps) to provide a basis for popular solidarity and action. In this respect, then, I am interested in collective memory as a source of agency.

One of the terms that will recur throughout this piece is "tradition". Raymond Williams has argued that tradition is an "actively shaping force ... [a] deliberately selective and connecting process which offers an historical and cultural ratification of a contemporary order".[15] An influential collection of essays edited by Eric Hobsbawm and Terence Ranger has adopted a similar approach to what they called the "invention of tradition".[16] I want to suggest here that tradition could be mobilized to other purposes. Whether consciously and deliberately "invented" or not, in the sprawling historical period I focus on here (what we might impudently call the "very long early modern period"), tradition helped to define collective identities amongst subordinated groups and to provide legal sanction to their claims to rights, resources and space. One very obvious way in which tradition did so was in the form of customary law.[17] For all that law courts were turning against it, oral tradition could still be invoked in the eighteenth and nineteenth centuries as the legal basis for use-rights or communal boundaries. These things mattered to common people. Thus, for instance, in 1739 the 80 year-old husbandman Thomas Smith provided an account of the customary regulations and boundaries of a set of villages on the hilly border between Derbyshire and Cheshire. Smith explained that "in his youthfull days" he had shepherded on the wide moorland that separated the settlements, confirming that the townships had at that time intercommoned. Over fifty years before, he had been told by John Hill "who was then One hundred years of age" and by his neighbour Ralph Bowden who was then aged 80 "and have been dead many years" that "the water that falls two ways from the Top of the Mountain near to the ... [hamlet of] Roughlow" formed the boundary between the commons of the villages of Fernilee and Shalcross. This testimony – which rested on a claim to reach back by 150 years – formed the bedrock of Smith's local knowledge.[18] In this respect, Thomas Smith's account formed a part of the usable past of his village, articulating and sanctioning entitlements upon the land within a distinct sense of place.[19]

I am interested here in the meaning of tradition and folklore at the moments at which they were invoked and in their basis within collective memory. Researchers have noted that collective memories often take messy historical episodes and simplify them, attributing an eternal essence to history.[20] Following Clifford Geertz, we ought to see memory as a powerful force in the constitution of culture; for Geertz, culture comprises "webs of significance" which trap the very human beings who have spun them.[21] Social memory, though, is more than this; it has a political, as well as a semiotic, force. Geertz takes us only so far in our investigation of folklore; like other cultural anthropologists – and the cultural history they have has inspired – Geertz's interpretive framework fails to deal with disparities of power. For as the Popular Memory Group put it in 1982,

> all political activity is intrinsically a process of historical argument and definition ... all political programmes involve some construction of the past as well as the future ... these processes go on every day ... [hence] political domination involves historical definition. History – in particular popular memory – is a stake in the constant struggle for hegemony.[22]

Arguably, the same is true of folklore. For all its significance, Maurice Halbwachs' conceptualization of memory remains static and implicitly functionalist. Like Durkheim before him, Halbwachs focused on group consciousness: in this case, the normative and integrative function of collective memory. In Halbwachs' account, collective memory therefore appears as homogeneous and as lacking a history. How, then, do ideas about the past change? How do these relate to wider political and social frictions? What is the place of collective memory in the contestation or defence of authority? Halbwachs does not provide us with answers to these questions. But if we combine Halbwachs' sense of memory as a unifying, collective force and as something embedded in discrete material environments with Antonio Gramsci's recognition that culture comprises a field of contestation we are provided with a more dynamic and historical model of social memory.

Dialectical materialism has been out of academic fashion for about a generation. But Antonio Gramsci still has a lot to teach social historians. His notion of "integral history" anticipated the development of the "new" social history by half a century. As Marcus Green puts it, for Gramsci "the "integral historian" is not just a historian who documents historical developments in some sort of positivistic manner, but is one who understands the socio-economic, political and cultural implications of such developments - how particular historical events relate to broad socio-political contexts".[23] Within this conception, the figure of the subaltern – that is, those in a subordinated position within a given social order – occupied a central place. Like later practitioners of "history from below",

Gramsci recognized that historical sources concerning subalterns would be hard to find and even harder to interpret. This was the case, he suggested, because such sources would be likely to have been produced by elites, or at least would be inflected with their ideas.[24] Given that much of Gramsci's writings are concerned with historical periods in which only a small minority of the population were literate, he recognised that for the "integral historian" to gather information on subalterns, she or he had to be wide-ranging in their selection of documents and broad-minded and imaginative in their interpretation: as Gramsci put it, "this kind of history can only be dealt with monographically, and each monograph requires an immense quantity of material which is often hard to collect".[25] Thus, for instance, although Gramsci perceived of Shakespeare as hostile to common people, he also saw in Shakespearean drama an "indirect document" on the early modern labouring classes.[26] Like later historians of crowd politics, Gramsci saw in subaltern political action a text for the analysis of their culture, suggesting that "every trace of independent initiative on the part of subaltern groups should ... be of incalculable value for the integral historian".[27]

The approach taken in this chapter is driven by some of the questions that preoccupied Antonio Gramsci. In particular, I am interested in one of his central propositions: that culture represents a field of contest between opposed groups. Gramsci's best-known concept, cultural hegemony, is predicated upon a particular set of assumptions about the nature of power. As a Marxist, Gramsci saw power as based upon economic relations and social structure. But whereas many of his contemporaries (Lenin; Trotsky; Luxembourg) saw power as centred upon the state, Gramsci sensed that (while he knew that the state mattered a great deal), power was too protean and diffuse to be contained within state structures alone.[28] For Gramsci, if there was a key locus within which cultural hegemony operated, it was within the sphere of everyday life. In a successfully integrated hegemony, the coercive role of the state played only a secondary role. It was within civil society that political power, organized through the "educative and formative" functions of the state, operated to greatest effect. Thus, hegemony was at its most effective when it won the "active consent" of the governed.[29] Less all-embracing (but perhaps more typical) hegemonies worked by limiting the possible, imposing boundaries as to what could be said and done. This secured the negative, or passive, affiliation of subalterns to the dominant order. As Edward Thompson puts it with reference to the eighteenth-century English plebeian:

> he wishes to struggle free from the immediate, daily, humiliations of dependency. But the larger outlines of power, station in life, political

authority, appear to be as inevitable and irreversible as the earth and the sky. Cultural hegemony of this kind induces exactly such a state of mind in which the established structures of authority and modes of exploitation appear to be in the very course of nature. This does not preclude resentment or even surreptitious acts of protest or revenge; it does preclude affirmative action.[30]

Effective elite hegemony therefore prescribes the limits of the possible: it is "a lived system of meanings and values ... beyond which it is very difficult for most members of society to move".[31] This is achieved through two processes: firstly, the creation of broad, cross-class alliances that link a ruling class with other social fractions, such that their narrow, corporate interests are transcended; and secondly, through ceding certain rights and spaces to the dominated in order to win their passive consent to the hegemonic order.

This latter process is central to understanding forms of resistance on the part of subordinated groups. Hegemony connects two fields of power relations: relations of production and domination.[32] It is from the crucible of these forces that the subaltern emerges. For Gramsci, the subaltern was a hazier category than, as in classical Marxist thought, that of the "exploited". Rather than being produced from the mode of production, the condition of subalternity emerges from the dull compulsion of economic force acting in concert with hegemony: these combine to limit the autonomy and agency of the subaltern. Gramsci's interest in popular culture lay not only in its relationship to power, but also in its content.[33] His achievement was to recognize that everyday life and systems of belief constitute fields of struggle, within which work the contending forces of subordination, persuasion, consent and resistance. Subaltern politics is, in consequence, defined by the daily intermingling of resistance and acquiescence: as Gramsci puts it: "subaltern groups are always subject to the activity of ruling groups, even when they rebel and rise up".[34] Yet the extent of this subordination is historically specific.[35] Critically, Gramsci saw ideas as the grounds over which opposing groups struggle: that is, "ideologies *create the terrain* on which men move, acquire consciousness of their position, struggle, etc".[36]

Hegemony, then, is never complete. Within everyday life, as Raymond Williams suggests, lie "alternative meanings and values, alternative opinions and attitudes, even some alternative senses of the world which can be accommodated and tolerated within a particular effective and dominant culture".[37] In societies governed by a successfully dominant class, then, cultural hegemony consists of a "play of subordinations and resistance", rather than a static structure in which oppressor struggles with oppressed in a kind of static trench warfare.[38] Thus, since "hegemony and counterhegemony are always interlaced, each hegemonic impulse involves a counterhegemonic impulse. Hegemony cannot exist or be reproduced without the constant, though partial, incorporation of counterhegemony".[39] One way in which the fundamental instability of hegemony is maintained is through limiting those "alternative senses of the world" that Williams mentions.

In early modern England, one of the fundamental limiting forces within popular politics was that of localism. Early nineteenth century working-class radicalism might be seen as an attempt to take key features of that mosaic of local cultures and rework them into a coherent, national political project.[40] But whereas committed radicals of that period sometimes denigrated working-class localism, historians need not do so. In the nineteenth century, as in earlier centuries, local sentiments endured within working-class culture at least in part because it was within the local that they found networks of solidarity and support, and within which they constructed opposition to their rulers. The local had, therefore, the potential to become both a site of struggle and a meaningful unit of political identification.[41] In the early modern period, class identities were sustained within many villages, neighbourhoods and small towns, and endured in the nineteenth century alongside national and international frames of reference.[42] These were the sites within which, in Gramsci's terms, "subaltern groups had a life of their own, institutions of their own".[43] The maintenance of those units of local identification, however defensive it may at times have been, represented an achievement on the part of working people. In focussing upon the embeddedness of folklore and tradition within memory and place, I am seeking to read popular localism within a hegemonic context. I want to suggest that certain tales, such as that of the Pedlar of Swaffham, aided working people in the sustenance of the local identities which so often gave their lives meaning, dignity and order. All of this represented a cultural achievement in a society in which working people were regarded by their rulers as intellectually and culturally inferior: as the "mean" or "vulgar" people. The story of the Pedlar of Swaffham contested such characterizations, suggesting instead that ordinary people could be canny, creative, generous and community-minded. In a society in which the gentry revelled in their sense (however inaccurate) of overwhelming superiority, all of this was important.

In the next tradition on which I focus, I want to suggest that folklore could both shape and transmit a sense of agency and entitlement amongst working people and that collective memory was fundamental to that process. Moreover, I here suggest that folklore traditions emerged out of a ferment of ideas that blend collective imagination with lived experience, everyday social practice, customary law and local memory. The tradition concerns a man (in later traditions a giant) known as Hikifricke (later as Tom Hickathrift). The earliest recorded versions of the tale originate from the Marshland area in the Norfolk fens. When the antiquarian John Weever visited the region in 1631, he came across a wide common called The Smeeth (or Tilney Smeeth), upon which the villagers of seven parishes (Walpole St Mary, Walsoken, West Walton, Terrington, Clenchwarton, Emneth and Tilney) intercommoned. This was a remarkably rich tract of land, jealously guarded by its commoners: William Camden noted in 1586 that what he called "Tilneysmeeth" provided pasture for 30,000 sheep.[44] The local inhabitants told Weever the story of how their ancestors had acquired this valuable common:

> it hath gone by tradition from Father to the Sonne ... that upon a time (no man knows how long since) there happened a great quarrel betwixt the Lord of this land or ground, and the Inhabitants of the forsaid seven villages about the mere-markes, limits or bondaries of this fruitfull feeding place [that is, The Smeeth]; the matter came to a battell or skirmish, in which the said Inhabitants being not able to resist the Lanlord and his forces, began to give backe; Hikifricke, driving his cart along, and perceiving that his neighbours were faint-hearted, and ready to take flight, he shook the Axell-tree from the cart, which he used in stead of a sword, and took one of the cart-wheeles which he held as a buckler; with these weapons (in a furious rage, you must imagine) he set upon the Common adversaries, or adversaries of the Common, encouraged his neighbours to go forward, and fight valiantly in defence of their liberties; who being animated by his manly prowess, they tooke heart to grasse, as the proverbe is, insomuch that they chased the Landlord and his companie, to the utmost verge of the Common; which from that time they have quietly enjoyed to this very day.

Upon visiting the parish church of Tilney All Saints, Weever was shown "a ridg'd Altar, Tomb or Sepulchre of a wondrous antique fashion" in the churchyard "upon which an Axell-tree and a cart-wheele are insculpted; under this Funerall Monument, the Towne-dwellers say that ... Hikifricke lies interred". Moreover, Weever noted that "The Axell-tree and cart-wheele are cut and figured in divers places of the Church, and Church windows, which makes the story, you must needs say, more probable".[45]

Like all folklore traditions, the story had its instabilities and uncertainties: although all other versions of the story identify Hickifricke as the defender of common rights on The Smeeth, William Dugdale's account of 1662 stated that the "tradition" amongst the "common people" was that Hickifricke had been the owner of the land and that he had fought a battle **against** the locals, in which he had used an axle and a wheel as weapons (although, of course, it may be that Dugdale had not accurately recalled the details of the story).[46] In the later seventeenth century, with the publication of an undated chapbook entitled *The pleasant history of Thomas Hickathrift*, the tradition entered print for the first time. This located the story "in the reign before William the Conqueror". For the first time, it was suggested that Hickathrift was himself of prodigious proportions. The chapbook explained that Tom was born to a poor family in the Isle of Ely. A child of prodigious appetite, he grew to a great height and became known for his huge strength. News of that strength "was spread ... in the Country" securing him employment by a King's Lynn brewer "to carry his Beer in the Marsh and to Wisbich". His master warned him "you are to understand, there was a monstrous Gyant which kept some part of the Marsh, and none durst go that way, for if they did, he would keep them, or kill them, or else he would make them Bond-slaves". Upon defeating the giant in a contest in which (once again) it was noted that he used the wheel of his cart as a shield and the axle-rod as a sword, the news of the giant's death "was spread all up and down in the Country ... for the Gyant was a great enemy to all the Country". "By the consent of the Country", Tom took ownership of the giant's cave, which he converted into a fine residence. As to the giant's land, "some he gave to the Poor for their Common and the rest he made pastures of ... and Toms fame was spread both far and near throughout the Country and then it was no longer Tom but Mr Hic-ka-thrift, so that he was the chiefest Man amongst them, for the People feared Tom's anger as much as they did the Gyants before". He then constructed "a famous Church, and gave it the name of Saint James's Church" (the parish church of Marshland St James, abuts onto The Smeeth about three miles south of Tilney St Lawrence).[47]

By the later eighteenth century, Tom had grown into a giant and was roaming far afield. Chapbooks of 1780, 1790 and 1825 detail his actions: he conquered 10,000 rebels in the Isle of Ely; he beat a giant who was ravaging the county of Kent; he was married and knighted; he joined forces with Tom the Tinker, who was eaten by a lion while he and Hickathrift struggled to save the Isle of Thanet from wild beasts.[48] The most articulate voice of the nineteenth-century rural working class, John Clare, testified to the popularity of the Hickathrift print tradition, which he included within his list of chapbooks from which his own literary skills had grown. Clare listed "Tom Hickathrift" amongst the "6py Pamphlets" he bought, adding that they "are in the possession of every door calling hawker and found on every book stall at fairs and markets". He added that the tales "have memorys as common as Prayer books and Psalters with the pesentry such were the books that delighted me and I savd all the pence I got to buy them for they were the whole world of literature to me and I knew no other".[49] He contrasted the chapbooks with the literature of the elite: "I[f] common fame was the highest order of fame I woud rather chuse to be the Author of cock robin the babes in the wood &c than Paradise lost or the Fairey Queen for you cannot find a village in england that owns an old woman to be a stranger to cock robin or the babes in the wood but you may find a thousand w[h]ere even the highest people in it know nothing of Spencer or Milton further then the name & very often not that".[50] This cultural assertiveness, articulated at a time at which popular culture was under organized attack upon a range of fronts, represented a kind of agency. Raymond Williams puts this well:

> Culture is ordinary: that is the first fact. Every human society has its own shape, its own purposes, its own meanings. Every human society expresses these, in institutions, and in arts and learning. The making of a society is the finding of common meanings and directions, and its growth is an active debate and amendment under the pressures of experience, contact, and discovery, writing themselves into the land.[51]

Like Williams, John Clare saw the ordinariness of popular culture as the source of its enduring strength. Yet despite its entry into print, Hickathrift survived within oral tradition: late nineteenth- and twentieth-century folklorists record a wide variety of Hickathrift stories which were sustained without reference to the printed stories. The Norfolk antiquarian H. J. Hillen was told one such story in 1891 by a fenman whom he met on The Smeeth. With marked condescension, Hillen rendered this "supplementary chapter in the Giant-Killer's career ... in the words of the proud narrator":

> Afore laavin' the carcus o' the graat, big giant, Tom kinder thowt, as how for safety, he'd cut out the giant's slavvery tongue. An' so he did. Bimeby another feller lightin' upon the dade body, whippt out a sword an' slashed orf his hid, which he carried to the King, so as tu git the reward, wot a-bin orfered. Well bor, the King bust out a-larfin' fit he split his sides, a-cause he was that de-lighted; then like a raale gen'lman, he outs with his pus an' wos jest in th'act o'givin' him a mint o'money, when up slips Tom in the nick o'time n' ses he: "Beg pardon, but will yer majesty jest for cu'rosity e'samin' the giant's tater-trap". Then some o' the nobs, wot stood naare, catched howd o' the hid, an' arter a dale o' tuggin' they got them thare jars

open, an' dang me, if thare wornt only the stump left! So Tom stuck his hand into his smock-pocket an' out with the graat, big tongue. Thare was a pretty how-de-you-dew, sure-ly! Tom got the reward, an' the imperdent rarscal, as I a-heeard my pore owd farther say scores an' scores o'times, rushed scraamin' away, gettin' a jolly-sight more kicks than har-pence![52]

In 1970, the story of the giant's tongue was told to the folklorist Enid Porter by a Wisbech villager.[53] Another version of the tale states that Hickathrift was able to slay his rival giant, who was overcome by the mere "small beer" he served up.[54] This was one of a number of Hickathrift stories which Porter uncovered at this time, some of them in rhyme and most without any basis in written tradition.[55] Interestingly, in one of the variations on the story recorded by Porter in 1969, Hickathrift's protagonist in the struggle for The Smeeth was remembered as an ordinary human being: in this version, "a rich and powerful lord once lived in Tilney, who was always at loggerheads with the village people" over The Smeeth. One day, the lord lost his temper and instructed his servants to round up the animals of the tenants and hold them until the tenants promised not to trespass again. So the tenants took their farm implements and marched to the lord's house, where they met him and his servants, all of whom (forewarned by one of his servants) were carrying swords. According to Porter's informant, there was then "a right old skirmish, and the villagers were certainly getting the worst of it when who should come along by Tom Hickathrift the giant, who lived not far away, driving the big wagon which he used as a coach". Tom joined the villagers. He turned over his cart and pulled off the axle to use as a sword and a wheel for a shield, and attacked the lord, shouting

> Come on, now, and fight me, man to man, but the lord begged for mercy. "If I do spare your life", said Tom Hickathrift, "you must swear to let my friends here put out their cattle to graze on the common and swear never to steal from them again" ... "I swear it", said the lord, "if only you will let me go". So Tom promised to do and after that the villagers had no more trouble and were able to let their cattle graze in peace for ever afterwards".[56]

Eighty years earlier, H.J. Hillen had been told a similar story concerning Hickathrift's role in the liberation of The Smeeth, in which

> a dispute arose between the fen-dwellers and the lord of the soil, concerning the proper position of some landmarks. The quarrel developed into a fierce skirmish. Hickathrift, luckily coming that way, immediately espoused the cause of the downtrodden villeins. With the usual improvised

weapons [that is, the axle rod and the wheel], he completely routed the lords numerous hirelings.[57]

Over a long period of time then, aspects of the Hickathrift tradition worked their way loose of print, slipping back into an oral culture that was communicated down the generations to the 1970s.

It is noteworthy, given the emphasis that Halbwachs placed upon the material environment as a mnemonic system, that the Hickathrift tradition was embedded within the land and the structures that stood upon it. We have already seen how, in 1631, Weever was persuaded of the validity of the early version of the story by the sight of the carvings of the "The Axell-tree and cart-wheele" on Hickathrift's tomb and within the church of Tilney All Saints. Local inhabitants showed the same emblems to Francis Blomefield in the early eighteenth century.[58] Over the next two centuries, Norfolk folklorists identified a number of sites, structures and objects which had associations with Hickathrift. In the parish church of Walpole St Peter's there are two holes in the exterior wall of the chancel alongside the stone figure said to represent Hickathrift; the holes were made by the impact of a football which the devil kicked at Hickathrift.[59] Damage to the exterior wall of Tilney All Saints was caused by a hammer thrown from six miles away by Hickathrift in a contest of strength with a blacksmith on The Smeeth.[60] At the village of Emneth, Hickathrift House and Hickathrift Farm stand at Hickathrift's Corner. Hickathrift's Field was said to have been the location of a castle built by Tom; in the field, there was also a hollow known as Hickathrift's Washbasin with a tumuli in the centre. By 1974, these had been built over. H.J. Hillen was told in 1891 that Hickathrift's Washbasin was hollow, and that the giant was buried there. Three of the giant's candlesticks remain, taking the form of "the uprights of old market crosses". One is in the churchyard at Terrington St Johns, the other two in the churchyard of Tilney All Saints. One of these has five imprints on it – said to be the imprint of the giant's fingers and thumb.[61] The history of this cross is interesting. Known in 1891 as Hickathrift's Candlestick, it had originally stood on top of the tumuli in Hickathrift's Washbasin. A map of the Marshland region in 1582 depicts the cross standing in on a mound in the middle of the Smeeth.[62]

Folklorists have supplied us with some revealing glimpses of the context within which this oral tradition was sustained: one Norfolk man recalled how as a child in the 1830s in one of the villages bordering on The Smeeth, "when we were good Gaffer Crane would rehearse Tom's achievements".[63] The fenman Arthur Randall, born in 1901, lived all his life in Wiggenhall St Mary Magdalen in the Marshland. In an interview with Enid Porter in 1966 he recalled how, as a child, he and his siblings sat at their parents' feet of an evening

> as our parents talked of a variety of things but nearly always of events or people they could remember or had heard of long ago. You couldn't say that they were all complete or connected stories that we heard, more often it was a casual reference to an almost-forgotten bit of village history which had been called to mind, perhaps because of some more recent happening … The person we most loved to hear stories about was Hickathrift, the Fenland giant who lived hundreds of years ago in Marshland and was, my father always said, a "civilised" giant and a very good man.[64]

Over a long time, therefore – at any point after 1631 – the Hickathrift tradition shifted in and out of oral and written genres. Like many other folktales before it, the Hickathrift tradition had "originally [been] formulated and transmitted orally, then couched in written form … [then] memorized from this new written version and then altered again in the course of oral performance and in its passage through oral tradition".[65] This suggests that the distinction between speech and writing has been overplayed. The literate practices recalled by John Clare, like Arthur Randall's memories of story-telling in Edwardian Norfolk, may well have more in common with each other than either has with the reading practices of the early twenty-first century. David Hall makes this point well: he suggests that we shouldn't confuse what he calls "traditional literacy" with our own reading practices. For Hall, traditional literacy privileged reading over writing. It had a closer proximity to memory, as children were taught to read "by memorizing certain texts". Traditional literacy formed around a limited number of texts – Hall mentions the Bible, catechisms, psalmbooks, almanacs - we might add the generic tales passed on in chapbooks; and the constant circulation (albeit in varying forms) of certain stories. The Hickathrift tradition operated within this cultural world.[66]

What kind of sense, then, can we make of the Hickathrift tradition? Most obviously, the story is rooted in what early modern people called their "country": the area of about ten or fifteen miles' radius that was defined by credit networks, gossip, marriage horizons, kinship, trading patterns, road systems and customary law. Written into this spatial unit was a distinct sense of place: what David Rollison calls "a particular local-historical habitat". Culture, Rollison suggests, was "an incessant dialogue of language and landscape, mediated by the experiences, memories and legends of generations".[67] Specifically, the Hickathrift story spans the area between one of the main market towns of the fens (Wisbech) and the coastal entrepot of the region (King's Lynn). Its epicentre is The Smeeth, around which cluster the seven villages that intercommoned upon that land. At the time at which the Hickathrift tradition emerged, customary law was an important element in this sense of local belonging.[68] Beyond the seven villages, the story ranges within a broader area, covering the Norfolk Marshland and the Cambridgeshire fens. Once again, villages within this locality were united through intercommoning arrangements and collaborative fen by-laws.[69] The story remains written into the local landscape, organized around churches, gravestones, landscape features and road networks. For those who were in the know, such mnemonic cues called forth the Hickathrift tradition, allowing them to read the land as a repository of local legend and tradition. Local identities remained powerful in East Anglia and the fens for much of the twentieth century, but only now are starting to find their historians. Such identities were sustained by the stock of common stories that define any culture: the Hickathrift tradition represented one such stock, bonding the neighbourhood as a speech community.[70]

The regulations which governed The Smeeth drew the seven villages which intercommoned upon it into daily concourse, defining them as a meaningful entity. Custom, then, was about much more than shared economic interests: it was also about agency, identity, and a distinct sense of the past, in which earlier forms of communal organization and struggle fed into the present. In the seven villages of the Marshland, both customary law and the Hickathrift tradition plotted memories and identities within the same space: The Smeeth. The seven villages possessed a common interest in The Smeeth since at least the thirteenth century. The "strong unity of the Marshland" noted by one medieval historian was founded upon a common administrative system that transcended manorial distinctions.[71] An early seventeenth-century document noted that by 1336, a commission of the Sewers had been formed around the seven villages, in which it was laid down that "the Landholders of ev[er]y towne was authorised to chose dich Reaves for the safetye of the every the said townes and the said dichreaves to have authoryty to compel by distresse & sale ev[er]y pson to paye such Taxes acreshotts & other charges as were for the defence of the sayd Townes". By 1474, a custom had been established whereby "the greatest Landholders" were "somened to meet at Tilney church by the dichreaves ev[ery] mundaye next after Easter there to chose a Jury called headborowes & out of the same to chose iii dichreaves & to have the accompt of the old dichreaves of the yere past".[72] By 1614, when a set of regulations drew together earlier practices, the seven villages had long been united in their common interest in the preservation of The Smeeth.[73] According to the regulations, a jury consisting of "three of the sufficientest Freeholders" of each parish met "at the Smeath Crosse on Tuesday in Easter weeke". This was the cross that was later to become known as Hickathrift's Candlestick, and which was noted as the centre of The Smeeth in the map of 1582. The jurors, together with the fen reeves whom they appointed, maintained a system of by-laws which punished trespasses by "cattle of any other Country", limited hunting and fishing and prevented overstocking and the excessive removal of turf and reeds. The churches which bordered The Smeeth – also to become key locations in the Hickathrift tradition – were important sites in the sustenance of custom: the fen reeves were to bring attention to unmarked stray cattle "in every Churche and Chappel of the Country"; likewise, it was in the parish churches that the reeves announced the days on which turf might legally be cut on The Smeeth.

Underlying the by-laws was a distinct sense of moral economy, in which the smallholder was protected by the limitation of the size of sheep flocks on The Smeeth and preventing larger householders from employing any more than two of their servants in digging turves. The penetration of market values into The Smeeth was hedged about by a by-law which prevented any inhabitant from selling his or her common rights "to any person dwelling out of the Country". The intention was to employ the resources of The Smeeth in the maintenance of a semi-autarchic local economy in which it was still possible for the poor householder to prosper. The enforcement of the by-laws generated a stock of funds that was managed collectively by the seven villages. Fines were to be paid to the "commonage to the Country". Fen reeves were to receive a quarter of the yearly fines for their troubles; the rest was to "be accompted for the Country". This collective fund provided a means of defending the laws and offices of The Smeeth: if a fen reeve was taken to court for enforcing the by-laws of The Smeeth, his defence was to be funded "out of the common purse of the Country for the Fenne and Smeath". All of this was expressed within the legitimating language of custom, calling in the past to ratify the present. The by-laws of 1614 were presented as adding seamlessly to earlier practice: they supplemented rules made "in former times very anciently they have been used". Similarly, the customs operated "for the good of the Country"; they had been drawn up "for the commodity of the Countrey and the commoners thereof".

The seven villages in which the Hickathrift tradition was born, then, were linked through their common interest in The Smeeth, their articulation of common memory, and their common employment of some of the landscape mnemonics of the Hickathrift tradition – Smeeth Cross, the parish churches – in the use of The Smeeth. Significantly, despite manorial boundaries, other aspects of customary law were identical across the seven parishes.[74] The term "Country" recurs throughout the 1614 by-laws, denoting place and communal interest. Importantly, in certain contexts the term was a synonym not only for locality, or neighbourhood; but also for common people.[75] In this way, a specific social group was grafted into a particular landscape. It will be recalled that, at a key point in the text – Hickathrift's defeat of the giant of The Smeeth – the author of *The pleasant history of Thomas Hickathrift* harped on the term: the news of the defeat of the giant "was spread all up and down in the Country … for the Gyant was a great enemy to all the Country". "By the consent of the Country", Tom took over the giant's cave; in the end, "Toms fame was spread both far and near throughout the Country".[76] Tom, then, can be seen as the hero of both the locality and of the common people. As a product of subaltern culture, we can see in the Hickathrift tradition the unity of the local and the popular. In the story, Hickathrift asserts agency – defeating an enemy of the commons (be that a giant who wished to make "bondslaves" of the people, or an oppressive lord) and affirms popular rights – but he only does so *within a limited domain*. In this respect, he represents the personification of the subaltern politics identified by Antonio Gramsci. The Smeeth was more than just a piece of land; it represented a key site within local culture. For The Smeeth was not merely a site of shared interest that linked the seven adjacent villages; it had once been the site of an attempted rebellion.

The attempted rebellion in question lay within the memory of the oldest inhabitants of the locality at the time at which Weever was told about Hickifric. In early August 1553, in the chaos that attended upon the seizure of power by Mary Tudor, the Marshland region had been the location for a large gathering of would-be rebels. As the Queen's Council learnt in a letter of 7 August 1553, there was a popular conspiracy afoot to

> make an insurreccon in Wysbyche in thylde of Elye and that ther was of the same confederacye the nombre of Fyve thousand p[er]son[e]s or mor the whiche intended to assemble that nyght or the next nyght at Wysbyche aforseid and that they wold take all the Jentylmen into ther Rule & Custodye ontyll redress war hadd of ther wrong[e]s done at the Quenes grac[e]s hand and that they wold Campe them selphes in a s[er]teyne place in marchlonde called Tylney Smethe[77]

These events unfolded only four years after the rebellions that had gripped East Anglia and southern England – a sequence of risings known to their participants as the "camping time". The term defined the summer of 1549 as the time at which camps of angry commoners were organized, demanding redress of their grievances against the gentry. It also employed the East Anglian dialect term for football ("camping"), a hurly-burly game played by violent young men in early summer.[78] In naming themselves the "camp men" (for so they were known), the rebels of 1549 identified themselves both as inhabitants of an orderly camp and also as participants in the disorderly action of violent play. The fact that the would-be rebels of August 1553 intended to "Campe them selphes" had a very powerful resonance for a gentry still traumatized by the camping time of 1549.

But why should "a s[er]teyne place in marchlonde called Tylney Smethe" form the locus for the camping time of 1553? Two answers suggest themselves. Firstly, the narrow neck of land around The Smeeth commanded the main route from the North into Norfolk, and as such was a sensitive spot within the political geography of the region.[79] Secondly, The Smeeth had a notable similarity with the best-known of the rebel camps of 1549, that at Mousehold Heath on the eastern edge of Norwich. Both Mousehold and The Smeeth intercommoned by a range of settlements, and so provided an established focus for the "country". Like Mousehold, The Smeeth was therefore the location of the continuous articulation of common interest on the part of a number of neighbouring settlements and the site of the assertion of mid sixteenth-century popular rebellion. Reverberations of those rebellions were still to be felt in the 1614 by-laws that governed The Smeeth. In an echo of the Norfolk rebel articles of 1549, which demanded that priests withdraw from the village economy and look instead to their educational and spiritual duties, the 1614 by-laws laid down that "every Inhabitant dwelling within the townes of Tilney with Islington Terrington Wallpoole Westwalyon Walsoken Emneth and Clenchwarton being married men widowers or widows are lawfull commoners and none others so that they be not spirituall persons or having spirituall promotions or be dwelling in Vicarage or parsonage houses".[80] Perhaps most importantly, The Smeeth was defined by an absence of lordship. That tract of land did not fall into any particular manor, but rather was governed by the seven parishes entirely for their own purposes. In this respect, The Smeeth realized the demand of the 1549 rebels that "no lord of no mannor shall comon upon the Comons".[81]

At the time at which the Hickathrift story entered the written record, then, memories of The Smeeth as the site of rebellion were still alive in the villages around it; moreover, the laws which governed the use of The Smeeth echoes some of the demands of the 1549 rebels.[82] This memory, like the folklore tradition it generated, made sense to the inhabitants of the fenland region in the early seventeenth century. At the time at which Weever was taking evidence concerning the hero Hickifric's struggles with the lord of Tilney, the people of the fens were tenaciously defending their rights against those entrepreneurs and lords who sought to drain and enclose the fens. A story which told of how common land had been gifted to the "Country" at the hands of a valiant man, defeating a lord/giant who wished to make "bondslaves" of them, may well have made sense to the people of the seventeenth-century fenland. Finally, the story embedded a certain truth in the minds of fenland folk: that they were not to be reckoned with. This sense of collective self endured over a very long period of time. In 1966, the 65-year-old Arthur Randall recalled for Enid Porter how

> In the old days the people who lived on the other side of the Ouse river were called High Norfolk folk; those on the other side where my parents were born were called Fen Tigers. The ways and customs and speech of the Fen Tigers, even the work they did on the land, were quite different from those of the High Norfolk people who were always referred to as "Foreigners" by the Tigers.

In her editorial note, Enid Porter explained Arthur Randall's meaning: "Fen Tigers was the name acquired by the Fenmen when they opposed, sometimes with violence, the drainage operations carried out in the seventeenth century".[83] Readings of the land depended upon a distinct sense of the past, one that shaped working people's sense of the land upon which they laboured: in 1925, at a time at which the ditches and banks which protected The Smeeth were threatened with large-scale alteration, a commission was empowered to hear the opinions of inhabitants. Asked by the hearing to comment on the age of the banks, one local replied:

> Oh they are old banks, hundreds of years old. I might add that they were built and put up by our forefathers for the purpose of keeping out the sea waters. The river [Ouse] at this point was formerly a mile wide and the banks were erected and strengthened from time to time to keep out the sea water. That is in the olden time.[84]

Memories lasted for a long time in the fens.

The Hickathrift tradition, then, celebrated the assertion of common rights over tyrannical powers. It was not the only folkloric memorialization of popular struggles. In the Lancashire mill town of Ashton-under-Lyne in the late eighteenth and nineteenth century, dark memories of feudalism were constructed by the radicalized working class. These memories stand at variance to the notion that the ordinary people of this period held a romanticized, nostalgic vision of English society before the Industrial Revolution.[85] Here, the local past was constructed within a ritual known as

"Riding the Black Lad" or (less often) as "Riding the Black Knight". The ritual projected an image of the lord as an enemy of popular liberties and of seigneurialism as an oppressive social system. Moreover, by comparison with the traditions we have so far considered, the Riding of the Black Lad was far more embedded within an overt social conflict and expressive of an assertive, pugnacious working-class culture.[86]

The origins of Riding the Black Lad remain obscure: the earliest mention dates from dates from 1795; in 1898, it was described as an "immemorial custom".[87] By contrast, no nineteenth-century description of Ashton-under-Lyne was complete without its inclusion. Before we consider the ritual and its meaning, it is essential to place the Riding of the Black Lad in its social and political context. Like other mill towns in late eighteenth and early nineteenth-century south-east Lancashire, Ashton-under-Lyne was deeply divided, its small but wealthy middle class of factory owners living well away from the tightly-packed quarters inhabited by the textile workers. The working class of Ashton was increasingly pulled into politics: at first, in the 1790s, in Jacobin agitation, then from the beginning of the next century in trade unionism, which provided the basis for frequent and bitter strike action. In the 1830s and 1840s, Ashton was an important centre of Chartist agitation. The town was, then, the archetype of the radicalized working-class community of the early Industrial Revolution: the union leader John Joseph Betts remarked of his native Ashton that "There seems to my eye's judgement hardly any proportion of the middle class of society in this community. The grinders and the ground make up the bulk of its inhabitants".[88]

The Riding of the Black Lad centred around the symbolic humiliation and destruction of a semi-mythical feudal lord, Sir Ralph de Assheton, who had held the manor of Ashton in the late fifteenth century and was popularly supposed to have been oppressive and violent.[89] According to local tradition, the ritual commemorated Sir Ralph's murderer, who was said to have been "shot as he was riding down the principal street of the town, on one of his Easter-Monday visitations, and the inhabitants to have taken no trouble to discover the assassin".[90] The Riding of the Black Lad took place on the afternoon of Easter Monday. In the ritual, an effigy of Sir Ralph de Assheton – the Black Lad or Black Knight – was paraded about the town. The effigy was made from straw, mixed with gunpowder; the arms were sticks; the head was wooden with a black helmet on top. "On the back were put the initials of the last couple married in the parish church in the Old Year. (As the year drew to a close there was great competition to avoid this distinction.)". Starting at Gallows Field, beside the Old Hall, the figure was carried about the town on horseback; lads rattled moneyboxes as they went, inviting "'passers-by to contribute to the "Blake Lad", i.e., to give them money for drink'".[91] When the Black Lad reached the market cross, "where the Black Knight is said to [have] receive[d] his death wound from a woman's hand", his head was thrown into the crowd; whoever caught it gained a monetary reward. The Black Lad would then be shot at until he burst into flames, following which the sluice of an adjacent marl-pit was opened. As the water gushed down the lane, people would dip cloth into the stream, and throw them about, "bemiring more especially women, but also any strangers or respectable-looking people".[92] Outside observers noted the proletarian nature of the crowd: in 1827, William Hone observed that "The greatest heroes" of the crowd "are of the coarsest nature".[93] In 1842, Edwin Butterworth described the audience to the ceremony as "a coarse vulgar crowd".[94] The older Ashton folk to whom F.H. Griffith spoke in 1895 confirmed this picture: "'each assured me that everybody connected with the rites was "very low", that the whole thing had been "a disgrace to the place" and some added that "the sooner such things were forgotten the better". So my informants, being all "decent folk" had never been allowed by their parents and guardians to take place in the performances'".[95]

The Riding of the Black Lad proceeded on the basis of a distinct reading of the historical and social geography of Ashton-under-Lyne. The location for the commencement of the ritual – "a meadow well known by the name of Gallows-field" – was popularly assumed to be "the place of execution when the lord of Ashton had powers of life and death". Alongside Gallows Field stood Ashton Hall; the seat of Ralph de Assheton. Writing six years after the French Revolution, John Aiken noted that "it was formerly regarded by the inhabitants as a sort of Bastille". A wing of the Hall was "a strong rather small building, with two round towers overgrown with ivy, called the dungeons". In the dungeons were "handcuffs, fastened to the wall".[96] Proceeding from this ominous site, the Black Lad was led "through the old - the roughest - parts of the town", before arriving at the marketplace, where he met his fate.[97] The spatial context of the ritual is worth pausing over. In an important essay, Marc Steinberg has recently suggested that the ritual can be read as a deliberate transgression of spatial order, noting the manner in which the local authorities (dominated by the employing class) were anxious to preserve the orderliness of the streets and marketplace. In Steinberg's account, the conclusion of the ritual represented the deliberate reversal of that normal order, with "respectable-looking people" becoming the targets for the crowd.[98] I would like to add something to Steinberg's perceptive analysis. The ritual involved not only the transgression of the bourgeois space of the marketplace, but also of another overlapping process: the inclusion of the "roughest" parts of the town in the ritual brought the embodiment of former feudal authority from his Bastille, via the Gallows-Field, to face the justice of the working class. In this reworking of the mythic end of Ralph de Assheton, the radicalized proletariat of Ashton-under-Lyne stood in for the oppressed peasantry which they imagined had preceded them, on whose behalf they wreaked a terrible revenge upon the Black Lad.

Nineteenth-century accounts are clear that Sir Ralph de Assheton was remembered as a tyrannical figure, and as such seemed to be the local manifestation of gentry power – a constituent element of the forces of Old Corruption against which working-class radicals felt themselves to be fighting. In 1842 – the year of the Plug Riots - Edwin Butterworth noted that "At the present day the name of the Black Boy excites feelings of horror, and tradition has indeed perpetuated the prayer which was fervently ejaculated for a deliverance from his tyranny: -

> Sweet Jesu, for thy mercy's sake
> And for thy bitter passion
> Save us from the axe of the tower
> And from Sir Ralph of Assheton".[99]

In his account of the Riding of the Black Lad, the prominent Mancunian radical Samuel Bamford suggested that "The ceremony at Ashton would seem to be expressive of hatred and contempt", the cause of which was "severe and arbitrary exaction" on the part of the "Black Knight".[100] Six years earlier Edwin Butterworth addressed the ritual in similar terms: it "is said to have arisen from there having been formerly a Black Knight who resided in these parts, holding the people in vassalage, and using them with great severity".[101] Looking back into the past, the old people whom Griffiths interviewed in 1895 agreed, adding a few details to the picture of Sir Ralph de Assheton:

> The tradition has been that he was a great oppressor of the tenantry – in this all agree. Some give details: he kept his prisoners in dungeons beneath the two old round towers (pulled down only a few years ago), with serpents and toads; he used to put people – sometimes women – in barrels spiked inside, and roll them from the top of the steep hill on which the Hill stood overlooking the river, down the ascent to it known as Ann's Brow.[102]

So, why did the Riding of the Black Lad endure? What, if anything, did it mean? Most obviously, from the point of view of the participants, it was fun: a way of cocking a snook at the authorities and at the mill-owners for a day. In this respect, it represented a very obvious transgression of a public order which was felt to be imposed by an oppressive ruling class. But the ritual was not only about the social conflicts of the early Industrial Revolution; for the figure of the Black Lad raised longer memories: of an even darker period when lords oppressed peasants, threw them into dungeons, rolled them down hills in spiked barrels and hanged them. And if any of this were to be doubted, the evidence was still there to be seen: the Dungeons, the Hall, Ann's Brow, Gallow's Field. The past was a present force in early Victorian Ashton, embedded in place-names, buildings and local memory. In this respect, it represented a finely-tuned local variant upon the radical vision of national history, one populated by oppressive lords and cruel masters, against which working people were pitched constantly in struggle.[103] The past – however simplified or invented – was therefore invoked to ratify present struggles, thickening the context and deepening the meaning of working-class radicalism.

For generations of historians, anthropologists and folklorists, the local seemed always to be in retreat.[104] As John Aubrey remembered things from the distance of the late seventeenth century, "When I was a little boy (before the Civill Warrs)", folklore traditions and customs had been widely practised. But as Aubrey recalled, over the course of his life this had become part of a world he had lost. The main driver of this change, Aubrey thought, had been the printing press:

> Before printing, Old Wives Tales were ingeniose and since Printing came in fashion, till a little before the Civil warres, the ordinary sort of people were not taught to reade and now-a-dayes Books are common and most of the poor people understand letters: and the many good Bookes and the variety of Turnes of Affaires, have putt all the old Fables out of dores: and the divine art of Printing and Gunpowder have frighted away Robin-good-fellowe and the Fayries.[105]

Two centuries later, Francis Grose also felt that he was witnessing the dying days of oral culture. In 1790, he recorded a sequence of local proverbs, noting that

> As the Local Proverbs all allude to the particular history of the places mentioned, or some ancient customs repecting them, they seem worth preserving, particularly as both the customs and many of the places alluded to are sliding silently into oblivion.[106]

This essay has sketched a different picture. It contradicts Aubrey's account on a key point: the assumption that literacy necessarily overwhelms oral culture. It has also suggested that Grose was wrong to predict the imminent death of local culture. It would, after all, be rather difficult to suggest that seismic transformations occurred over the course of the very long period covered by this essay; but for many people localism and oral culture remained powerful forces. Nor were local and oral traditions mere archaic survivals of an earlier mind-set. Rather, they twisted and mutated within an ever-shifting relationship with the apparently modernizing forces of literacy, education and urbanization.[107] Indeed, they continue so to do: at the time of writing, Tom Hickathrift has a presence on the Internet, as does the Pedlar of Swaffham and the recently-revived tradition of the Riding of the Black Lad.

This essay has argued that the local world provided a conceptual milieu within which oppositional ideas might emerge. Of course, this was not the **only** way in which folklore made sense. My aim has not been to impose a single, trans-historical meaning upon the traditions at which we have looked. Rather, what I have tried to show is that social relations and local conflict formed one element of the nexus within which the local world could be comprehended. In this respect, I have here tried to present a corrective to much recent cultural history. But however we understand folklore traditions, what is striking is the sheer **originality** of the collective imagination from which they emerged. Raymond Williams is surely right to suggest that it is in its very ordinariness that popular culture finds its living force. Yet folklore contained the extraordinary within the ordinary: Kate Edwards, a fenwoman born in 1880, put this well when she was interviewed by her daughter in the 1960s:

> Living as we did and how we did, we used to make the most of anything a bit out o' the ordinary, and we looked for'ard to from one special day to the next. Looking back on it now, I'm surprised to see how many high days and holidays there were during the year that we kept, and we certainly made the most of any that children could take part in.[108]

This was as true of storytelling as it was of the ritual year: the local world formed a space within which the popular imagination worked, populating the landscape with lucky pedlars, oppressive lords and brave giants. There was no single author to the tales we have studied; but there were, none the less, generations of individual men and women who told and retold these stories, adding their own twists to the narrative patterns they inherited. Their names have mostly been lost. But their cultural achievement remains lodged in the historical record: they invested their land with meaning; they enriched and added to the cultures they knew, giving life and shape to their world. They took their subalternity and they did something different with it. Can we say as much?

Notes

[1] On antiquarianism and popular tradition, see D. R. Woolf., "'The 'Common Voice': History, Folklore and Oral Tradition in Early Modern England'" *Past and Present* 120 (1988): 26-52.

[2] Francis Blomefield, *An Essay Towards a Topographical History of the County of Norfolk* 11 vols (1739-75; 2nd. ed, London: William Miller & Co., 1807), VI, 212-13. The story, again validated with reference to "constant tradition" is retold with some variations in *The Diary of Abraham de la Pryme, the Yorkshire Antiquary*, Surtees Society 54, ed., Charles Jackson (Durham: Andrews & Co., 1870), 219-20. For the elaboration of the story in the late Victorian period, see J. Glyde, *A Dyshe of Norfolke Dumplings* (London: Jarrold and Sons, 1898), 68-70, where the evidence in the church was said still to be "sufficient to establish the truth of the legend in the minds of the credulous of the district". By the late twentieth century, it was an established nursery tale. See most recently P. Pearce, *The Pedlar of Swaffham* (London: Scholastic, 2001). For similarity to folktales elsewhere, see E. Sidney Harland, "The pedlar of Swaffham" *Folklore* 19: 3 (1908): 333-36. For dreams of mineral wealth in sixteenth century Cornwall, see Richard Carew, *The Survey of Cornwall* (1602; repr., Launceston: Tamar Books, 2004), 21, mentioned in Thomas Fuller, *The Worthies of England* (London: Allen and Unwin, 1952), 86.

[3] Margaret Spufford, *Small Books and Pleasant Histories: Popular Fiction and its Readership in Seventeenth-Century England* (Methuen: London, 1981), 249.

[4] Robert Darnton, *The Great Cat Massacre and other Episodes in French Cultural History* (London: Allen Lane, 1984), 21, 70.

[5] Blomefield, *An essay*, VI, 212-13.

[6] J.F. Williams, "The Black Book of Swaffham" *Norfolk Archaeology* 33 (1962-5): 252.

[7] Nicholas Pevsner, *The Buildings of England: North-West and South Norfolk* (Penguin: Harmondsworth, 1962), 331.

[8] Philippa Maddern, *Violence and Social Order: East Anglia, 1422-1442* (Oxford: Oxford University Press, 1992).

[9] Norman Davis, ed., *Paston Letters and Papers of the Fifteenth Century*, 3 vols. (Oxford: Oxford University Press, 1976), II, 60, 528-30.

[10] For the local context, see T.A. Heslop, "Swaffham Parish Church: Community Building in Fifteenth-Century Norfolk", in *Medieval East Anglia*, ed. Christopher Harper-Bill (Woodbridge: Boydell Press, 2005), 246-71.

[11] Henry Steele Commager, *The Search for a Usable Past and other Essays in Historiography* (New York: Knopf, 1967).

[12] See his two posthumously-published works: Maurice Halbwachs, *On Collective Memory* (Chicago: University of Chicago Press, 1992); Maurice Halbwachs, *The Collective Memory* (New York: Harper & Row, 1980). The term is from Eric J. Hobsbawm "The Social Function of the Past: Some Questions" *Past and Present* 55 (1972): 3-17.

[13] For Halbwachs and Durkheim, see Barbara Misztal, "Durkheim and Memory", *Journal of Classical Sociology* 3: 2 (2003): 123-43. For subjectivity and collective

memory, see Susan A. Crane, "Writing the Individual Back into Collective Memory", *American Historical Review* 102: 5 (1997): 1372-85. For an assessment of the relationship between collective memory and the self which comes closer to Halbwachs' formulation, see Elizabeth Tonkin, *Narrating our Pasts: the Social Construction of Oral History* (Cambridge: Cambridge University Press, 1991), 128-36.

[14] The classic statement of this view remains Geoffrey Elton's *The Practice of History* (London: Methuen, 1967). Many historians would today distance themselves from this book; yet the empiricist principles articulated herein remain embedded in the genetic code of the discipline.

[15] Raymond Williams, *Marxism and Literature* (Oxford: Oxford University Press, 1977), 115-6.

[16] Eric Hobsbawm and Terence Ranger, eds., *The Invention of Tradition* (Cambridge: Cambridge University Press, 1992)

[17] For my earlier (perhaps rather rosy) thoughts on this, see Andy Wood, "The Place of Custom in Plebeian Political Culture: England, 1550-1800" *Social History* 22: 1 (1997): 46-60.

[18] The National Archives, DL4/143/1739/1.

[19] See also Nicola Whyte, *Inhabiting the Landscape: Place, Custom and Memory, 1500-1800* (Oxford: Windgather, 2009); Steve Hindle, "Beating the Bounds of the Parish: Order, Memory and Identity in the English Local Community, c. 1500–1700" in *Defining Community in Early Modern Europe*, eds M. Halvorson and K. Spierling (Aldershot: Ashgate, 2008), 205-27.

[20] James Fentress and Chris Wickham make this point with the greatest force; see their joint work *Social Memory* (Oxford: Blackwell, 1992). See also Roland Barthes, *Mythologies* (1957; Eng. Trans., London: Cape 1972), 142-3. For memory and the constitution of meaning, see Elizabeth Jelin, *State Repression and the Labors of Memory* (Minneapolis: Latin American Bureau, 2003), 18, 21.

[21] C. Geertz, *The Interpretation of Cultures: Selected Essays* (London: Hutchinson, 1975), 5, 89.

[22] Popular Memory Group, "Popular Memory: Theory, Politics, Method", in *Making histories: Studies in History Writing and Politics*, eds R. Johnson, G. McLennan, B. Schwarz and D. Sutton (London: Hutchinson, 1982), 213.

[23] M. Green, "Gramsci cannot speak: Presentations and Interpretations of Gramsci's Concept of the Subaltern", *Rethinking Marxism* 14: 3 (2002): 9. For the resemblance of "integral history" to the new social history that emerged in the West after the 1960s, see ibid., 14-5.

[24] For an important discussion of the problem of locating the subaltern voice in records generated by repressive institutions, see J.H. Arnold, *Inquisition and Power: Catharism and the Confessing Subject in Medieval Languedoc* (Philadelphia: University of Pennsylvania Press, 2001). This can usefully be read alongside F.E. Mallon, "The Promise and Dilemma of Subaltern Studies: Perspectives from Latin American History", *American Historical Review* 99: 5 (1994): 1506-7. Gayatri Chakravorty Spivak has condemned the view that "the oppressed can know and speak for themselves", seeing in this the danger of

reintroducing what she calls "the constitutive subject": G.C. Spivak, "Can the subaltern speak?" in *Marxism and the Interpretation of Culture*, eds C. Nelson and L. Grossberg (Urbana: University of Illinois Press, 1988), 279, 283. I find Spivak's critique unduly negative, tending as it does towards the conclusion that histories of subordinated groups cannot (and/or should not) be written. Any history of subalterns will always be partial and many of the sources upon which such a history might depend will most likely be coloured by the interests of the more powerful; but it does not follow from this that such an enterprise is therefore futile.

[25] Antonio Gramsci, *Selections from the Prison Notebooks* (London: Lawrence & Wishart, 1971), 55, hereafter *SPN*.

[26] Antonio Gramsci, *Selections from Cultural Writings* (London: Lawrence & Wishart, 1985), 241.

[27] *SPN*, 55.

[28] There is a certain parallel here with the writings of Michel Foucault. Although Gramsci differed from Foucault in that he saw power as less than impregnable, both understood power as difficult to pin down, leeching into civil society and everyday life.

[29] The best starting point remains R. Simon, *Gramsci's Political Thought: An Introduction* (London: Lawrence & Wishart, 1982). For Gramsci on hegemony, see especially *SPN*, 12, 181-2. For Gramsci on the state and hegemony, see especially *Cultural Writings*, 191; *SPN*, 242-4. For the origins of hegemony in early twentieth-century linguistics, see Peter Ives, *Language and Hegemony in Gramsci* (London: Pluto, 2004). For misreadings of hegemony, which present the concept as "simply the name Gramsci gave to this process of ideological domination", see James C. Scott, *Weapons of the Weak: Everyday Forms of Peasant Resistance* (New Haven: Yale University Press, 1985), 315; David Arnold, "Gramsci and Peasant Subalternity in India" *Journal of Peasant Studies* 11 (1984): 171, 174; Mark Goldie, "The Unacknowledged Republic: Officeholding in Early Modern England" in *The politics of the excluded, c. 1500-1850*, ed. Tim Harris (Basingstoke: Palgrave, 2001), 155. Contrast these views with that of Jackson Lears: "Whether one imagines hegemony to be relatively open or relatively closed, the essence of the concept is not manipulation but legitimation": T.J. Jackson Lears, "The Concept of Cultural Hegemony: Problems and Possibilities", *American Historical Review* 90: 3 (1985): 330. For an overstatement of the efficacy of hegemony, see Ives, *Language and Hegemony*, 79-80.

[30] Edward P. Thompson, *Customs in Common* (London: Merlin, 1991), 43; see also 86-7.

[31] Raymond Williams, *Keywords: A Vocabulary of Culture and Society* (London: Fontana, 1976), 110.

[32] Simon, *Gramsci's Political Thought*, 21.

[33] The complex nature of folklore led Gramsci to some contradictory formulations: see *Cultural Writings*, 189, 194; *SPN*, 323.

[34] *SPN*, 55. See also Alberto Cirese, "Gramsci's observations on folklore" in *Approaches to Gramsci*, ed. Anne Showstack Sassoon (London: Writers and Readers, 1982), 221.

[35] Thus, the different perspectives of Knight and Arnold are as much empirical as theoretical: Arnold, "Gramsci and Peasant Subalternity in India", 170; A. Knight, "Weapons and Arches in the Mexican Revolutionary Landscape", in *Everyday Forms of State Formation: Revolution and the Negotiation of Rule in Modern Mexico*, eds G.M. Joseph and D. Nugent (Durham, NC: Duke University Press, 1994), 53.

[36] *SPN*, 377, my emphasis. See also Chantal Mouffe, "Hegemony and Ideology in Gramsci", in Martin James, ed., *Antonio Gramsci: Critical Assessments of Leading Political Philosophers. Volume II: Marxism, Philosophy and Politics*, 4 Vols (London: Routledge, 2002), 302.

[37] Raymond Williams, "Base and Superstructure in Marxist Cultural Theory" *New Left Review* 82 (1973): 10.

[38] Richard Maddox, "Bombs, Bikinis and the Popes of Rock n' Roll: Reflections on Resistance, the Play of Subordinations, and Liberalism in Andalusia and Academia, 1983-1995", in *Culture, Power, Place: Explorations in Critical Anthropology*, eds Akhil Gupta and James Ferguson (Durham, NC: Duke University Press, 1997), 286.

[39] F.E. Mallon, "Reflections on the Ruins: Everyday Forms of State Formation in Nineteenth-Century Mexico", in *Everyday Forms of State Formation* eds Joseph and Nugent, 70-1.

[40] See for instance I. Dyck, "Local Attachments, National Identities and World Citizenship in the Work of Thomas Paine", *History Workshop Journal* 35 (1993): 117-35.

[41] On the interlocked strengths and weaknesses of local identification, see Richard Maddox, *El Castillo: the Politics of Tradition in an Andalusian Town* (Urbana: University of Illinois Press, 1993), 9, 11.

[42] This is the central argument of my first book, *The Politics of Social Conflict: the Peak Country, 1520-1770* (Cambridge: Cambridge University Press, 1999).

[43] *SPN*, 54.

[44] W. Camden, *Britannia* (1586; new ed., London: F. Kingston et. al., 1637), 481.

[45] John Weever, *Ancient Funeral Monuments within the United Monarchie of Great Britain, Ireland and the Islands Adjacent* (London: Thomas Harper, 1631), 866. For earlier mention of Weever's tale, see Keith Thomas, *The Perception of the Past in Early Modern England*, Creighton Trust Lecture (London: University of London, 1983), 2-3, 28 and Adam Fox, *Oral and Literate Culture in England, 1500-1700* (Oxford: Oxford University Press, 2000), 223. Thomas suggests that "it is tempting to connect [Hikifricke] with the hero of the popular chapbook, *The History of Thomas Hickathrift*, a giant-killer who gave part of his lands to the poor to be their common", but neither he nor Fox pursue the point. The identification of the Hikifricke of 1631 as the Tom Hickathrift of the later printed tradition is made clear in G.L. Gomme, ed., *The History of Thomas Hickathrift* Chap-Books and Folk-lore tracts, I (London: Villon Society, 1885). For a contemporary map of the area, see William Dugdale, *The History of Imbanking and Draining of Divers Fens and Marshes* (1662; 1777 edition: London: W. Bower & J. Nichols), between pages 244-5.

[46] Dugdale, *Imbanking and Draining*, 24. For a sceptical eighteenth-century account, which none the less identifies Hickifrick as the popular hero, see Blomefield, *An essay*, IX, 79-80.
[47] Anon., *The Pleasant History of Thomas Hickathrift* (London: William Thackeray, no date), 1, 6, 7, 12. Judging from the fashions depicted, the pamphlet was published sometime after 1660. In the parish of Marshland St James, there is still a piece of land called Hickathrift's Field, near the centre of the village, where a boulder landed that had been thrown by Tom in a competition with the giant.
[48] Gomme, ed., *Thomas Hickathrift*, xviii.
[49] E. Robinson and D. Powell, eds, *John Clare by Himself* (Ashington: Carcenet Press, 1996), 68. Elsewhere, he mentioned "rustics" listening to tales of "the Strenth of Hickathrift". G. Deacon, *John Clare and the Folk Tradition* (London: Sinclair Brown, 1983), 42; Hickathrift also features in his poetry: E. Robinson and D. Powell, eds, *The Early Poems of John Clare, 1804-1822*, 2 Vols (Oxford: Clarendon, 1988-9), II, 146.
[50] Deacon, *John Clare*, 44.
[51] Raymond Williams, *Resources of Hope: Culture, Democracy, Socialism* (London: Verso, 1989), 3-14.
[52] Norfolk Record Office, BL/AQ/3/9. [Former reference: NRO, BL XId/18]
[53] Enid Porter, *The Folklore of East Anglia* (London: Batsford, 1974), 180.
[54] East Anglian beer is famously potent. As a personification of masculinity, Hickathrift was expected to hold his drink.
[55] Porter, *Folklore of East Anglia*, 95-102; see also Enid Porter and W.H. Barrett, *Cambridgeshire Customs and Folklore* (Routledge Kegan and Paul: London, 1969), 192-4.
[56] Porter, *Folklore of East Anglia*, 180.
[57] Norfolk Record Office, BL/AQ/3/9.
[58] Blomefield, *An Essay*, IX, 79-80.
[59] Arthur R. Randall, *Sixty Years a Fenman* (Routledge Kegan Paul: London, 1966), 79.
[60] Norfolk Record Office, BL/AQ/3/9.
[61] Elizabeth Wortley, letter, *East Anglian Magazine* 14 (Sept. 1955), 656; Porter, *Folklore of East Anglia*, 95-102; Gomme, ed., *Thomas Hickathrift*, xi-xii.
[62] BL, Add Ms 71126. For copies, see Cambridge University Library, Ms Plans 599; British Library, Cotton MS Augustus I.i., fol. 78. For the context of the production of the map, see P. Eden, "Land surveyors in Norfolk, 1550-1580", *Norfolk Archaeology*, 35 (1973): 474-482. See also R.J. Silvester, "The Fenland Project, No. 3: Marshland and the Nar Valley, Norfolk", *East Anglian Archaeology* 45 (Hunstanton: Witley Press, 1988): 9.
[63] Gomme, ed., *Thomas Hickathrift*, x-xi.
[64] Randall, *Sixty Years*, 72, 79.
[65] F. Canade Sautman, D. Conchada and G.C. DiScipio, "Introduction. Texts and Shadows: Traces, Narratives and Folklore", in *Telling Tales: Medieval Narratives and the Folk Tradition*, eds F. Canade Sautman, D. Conchada and G.C. DiScipio (Basingstoke: Macmillan, 1998), 4.

[66] D. Hall, *Cultures of Print: Essays in the History of the Book* (Amherst, Mass: University of Massachusetts Press: 1996), 57.

[67] D. Rollison, *The Local Origins of Modern Society: Gloucestershire 1500-1800* (London: Routledge, 1992), 67.

[68] S. Hindle, "A Sense of Place? Becoming and Belonging in the Rural Parish, c.1550-1650", in *Communities in Early Modern England,* eds Alexandra Shepard and Phil Withington (Manchester: Manchester University Press, 2000), 96-114.

[69] See, for instance, the customs of 1567: Dugdale, *Imbanking and Draining*, 271. This system originated in the late medieval period and took the regulations of Romney Marsh as its template. See H.C. Darby, *The Medieval Fenland* (Cambridge: Cambridge University Press, 1940), 163-7. Taken together, the area comprises what Charles Phythian-Adams has called a "cultural province": Charles Phythian-Adams, *Re-thinking English Local History* (University of Leicester, Dept. of English Local History, Occasional Papers, 4th ser., No. 1, 1987).

[70] Alun Howkins observes the localism of the rural workers' perspective in the 1920s: *Poor Labouring Men: Rural Radicalism in Norfolk, 1870-1923* (London: Routledge, 1985), xii. See also K.D.M. Snell, "The Culture of Local Xenophobia", *Social History* 28: 1 (2003): 1-30.

[71] David C. Douglas, *The Social Structure of Medieval East Anglia* (Oxford: Oxford University Press, 1927), 195-200.

[72] Norfolk Record Office, BL/DR/10/2.

[73] Norfolk Record Office, BL/DR/8.

[74] Norfolk Record Office, DN/DEP/5/5a, fol. 83v.

[75] For examples, see Keith Lindley, *Fenland Riots and the English Revolution* (London: Heinemann, 1982), 88, 109; *Letters and Papers of Henry VIII*, XII (1), no. 201, iv.

[76] Anon., *Pleasant History*, 6, 7, 12.

[77] Oxburgh Hall, Muniments, Letter: Edward Beawpre to the Council, 7th August 1553.

[78] David Dymond, "A Lost Social Institution: the Camping Close", *Rural History* 1: 2 (1990): 165-92.

[79] See, for instance, the proposal in 1597 that Norfolk rebels should gather at Magdalene Bridge near Tilney Smeeth in 1597: The National Archives, SP12/262/151 (I).

[80] Norfolk Record Office, BL/DR/8.

[81] British Library, Harl Ms 304, fols. 75r-77v.

[82] For popular memories of the 1549 rebellions, see A. Wood, *The 1549 Rebellions and the Making of Early Modern England* (Cambridge: Cambridge University Press, 2007), 241-56.

[83] Randall, *Sixty Years*, 2.

[84] Norfolk Record Office, DB4/41, p.11.

[85] For such a view, see Peter Mandler, "'In the olden time': Romantic History and English National Identity, 1820-50", in *A Union of Multiple Identities: the British Isles, c. 1750-1850,* eds Lawrence Brockliss and David Eastwood (Manchester: Manchester University Press, 1997), 78-91.

[86] For the carnivalesque qualities of the ritual, see M.W. Steinberg, "The Riding of the Black Lad and other Working-Class Ritualistic Actions: Towards a Spatialized and Gendered Analysis of Nineteenth-Century Repertoires", in *Challenging Authority: the Historical Study of Contentious Politics,* eds Michael P. Hanagan, Leslie Page Moch, and Wayne Te Brake (Minneapolis: University of Minnesota Press, 1998), 17-35.

[87] John Aiken, *A Description of the Country from Thirty to Forty Miles Round Manchester* (1795; repr. Newton Abbott: David and Charles, 1968), 226; F.H. Griffith, "The Black Lad of Ashton-under-Lyne" *Folklore* 9: 4 (1898): 379.

[88] Steinberg, "The Riding of the Black Lad": 18-19.

[89] For the medieval context, see J. Harland, ed., *Three Lancashire Documents of the Fourteenth and Fifteenth centuries,* Chetham Society 74 (Manchester, Chetham Soc., 1868), 129.

[90] Edwin Butterworth, *An Historical Account of the Towns of Ashton-under-Lyne, Stalybridge and Dukinfield* (Ashton: T.A. Philips, 1842), 47.

[91] Griffith, "Black Lad": 379-80.

[92] William E.A. Axon, *Lancashire Gleanings* (Manchester: Tubbs, Brook & Chrystal, 1883), 187.

[93] Steinberg, "The Riding of the Black Lad": 26.

[94] Butterworth, *Historical Account,* 49.

[95] Griffith, "Black Lad": 379-82.

[96] Aiken, *Description,* 226; Butterworth, *Historical Account,* 29.

[97] Griffith, "Black Lad": 379.

[98] Steinberg, "The Riding of the Black Lad".

[99] Butterworth, *Historical Account,* 49.

[100] W.H. Chaloner, ed., *The Autobiography of Samuel Bamford,* 2 Vols (1848-9; London: Frank Cass, 1967), I, 141-3.

[101] Butterworth, *Historical Account,* 46.

[102] Griffith, "Black Lad": 379.

[103] R.G. Hall, "Creating a People's History: Political Identity and History in Chartism, 1832-1848", in *The Chartist Legacy,* eds Owen Ashton, Robert Fyson & Stephen Roberts (Rendlesham: Merlin, 1999).

[104] See for instance David Vincent, "The Decline of the Oral Tradition in Popular Culture" in *Popular Culture and Custom in Nineteenth-Century England,* ed. Robert D. Storch (London: Croom Helm, 1982), 20-47.

[105] British Library, Lansdowne Ms 231, fols. 109r, 140r.

[106] Francis Grose, *A Provincial Glossary; with a Collection of Local Proverbs, and Popular Superstitions* (London: Francis Grose, 1790), vi.

[107] For a brilliant discussion of the unpredictable cultural consequences of urbanisation, see Karl Bell, "The Magical Imagination and Modern Urbanisation, c.1780-1850" (PhD diss., University of East Anglia, 2006).

[108] Sybil Marshall, *Fenland Chronicle: Recollections of William Henry and Kate Mary Edwards Collected and Edited by their Daughter* (Cambridge: Cambridge University Press), 199.

DEATH AND THE JARVISES: PUBLIC SPACE, PRIVATE SPACE AND THE POLITICS OF RESISTANCE IN NINETEENTH-CENTURY NORFOLK (AND BEYOND)

ROB LEE

A landowner (let's call him the fourteenth Earl) apprehends a poacher on his land:

"This is my land," says the fourteenth Earl, as if that settles everything.
"So where did you get it?" asks the poacher
"From my father, of course, the thirteenth Earl. I inherited it when he died"
"And where did he get it?"
"From his father, the twelfth Earl"
"I see. And where did *he* get it?"
"Listen, you impertinent man. This land has been in my family for fourteen generations, ever since the first Earl"
"Yes, I see your argument," says the poacher, reasonably, "But where did the first Earl get it?"
"He *fought* for it!" says the fourteenth Earl, flinging out his arms in a gesture of exasperation.
"That sounds fair enough to me," says the poacher, "I'll fight *you* for it".[1]

The encounter between the poacher and the fourteenth Earl is, regrettably, unlikely to be true. It nevertheless neatly captures a mood that was gaining momentum in the latter half of the nineteenth century: one that was beginning to challenge and question some of the old mechanisms of deference, and one that manifested itself in a politically motivated reduction in forelock-tugging. I want to explore something of that mood in this chapter, and explain how it can be traced as an undercurrent to the social relationships of the 1850s and 1860s, which are otherwise thought of as a period of relative political quietude in the countryside.[2] Falling between the activism of the "Swing" Riots and Chartism in the 1830s and 1840s and the resurgence of agricultural trade unionism in the 1870s, these were the decades when engines of social authority like the New Poor Law moved most smoothly through the gears; when the Gothicised "architecture of moral authority" rose most purposefully above customary landscapes; and when the depradations of infant mortality swept through insanitary housing, all too often unremarked and unchallenged. Viewed from this perspective the relative political quiet of the mid-nineteenth century begins to look rather more complex: a period of "paternalistic neglect", perhaps, in which many of the keystones of paternalistic power remained in place while standards of care and obligation fell short of those in evidence in preceding decades; a period of bruised retreat for radical causes, undoubtedly, as economic circumstances strengthened the hand of those who sought a conservative retrenchment; but a period, too, of restlessness and disillusion in which the sound of the grumbling hive can be heard gathering in intensity.

Taking an episode of infant mortality as its starting point, this chapter will demonstrate how power relations and social structures in the mid-nineteenth century were reflected in the landscape, in the built environment and in the "public space" represented by the parish church. It will examine how the first signs of a new politics of resistance can be detected among the rural poor at this time, and how the sequestered space of the Methodist chapel and the privatised space of enclosed common land contributed in their different ways to a new and more vigorous form of labour politics that, after a few false starts, eventually broke cover in the early decades of the twentieth century. In so doing, the chapter will draw upon evidence from rural East Anglia and industrial North-East England.

In some respects these regions could hardly be more different: the one a lowland agricultural district, the other an upland district that is, in parts, heavily industrialised. By the mid-nineteenth century Norfolk's only substantial non-agricultural industry–textile manufacture–was in terminal decline as the trade migrated northwards into the new textile districts of Yorkshire and Lancashire. Migrating with it was a substantial proportion of Norfolk's population, making the county an area of population decline.[3] Some of those migrating Norfolk workers made it as far north as the coalfields of Co. Durham and Northumberland, an area of phenomenal population growth during the nineteenth century.[4] But despite the profound differences between them, Norfolk and Co. Durham also revealed striking similarities. Politically they were both radical places, their early development of trade unionism often having its roots in

Nonconformist religion, and in particular in the working-class denomination of Primitive Methodism. It will be argued that in the North-East the survival of rural patterns of resistance politics can be detected deep into the twentieth century where they co-existed with some of the most radical forms of conventional party politics yet seen in modern British history, and a link will be attempted in this chapter between the "politics of resistance" becoming visible in the 1860s with that clearly visible in the 1920s.

In both regions hostility to the established Church of England had a sharply secular, political edge. Consequently, a comparative study of the way in which religion operated in these communities may take us a long way towards answering key questions about the interaction between religion, politics and society: how did religious affiliation and/or religious belief affect the social, political and cultural development of local communities? Did religion perform a mainly secular function, reinforcing or challenging existing power structures in a way that informed future political allegiance? How did theology mix with worldly experience and social background to shape the attitudes and actions of ministers of religion? To what extent was the behaviour of congregations influenced by what they heard on a Sunday morning? Did the pulpit encourage or discourage their aspirations? Did the religion they were exposed to promote or retard the cause of social justice?

En passant a case will also be made for comparative regional histories of this kind. Can general lessons can be drawn from a combined study of two very different particularities?

My starting point is a domestic tragedy from 1863. The story of "Death and the Jarvises" broke in the autumn of that year when a newspaper reporter arrived in the North Norfolk village of Corpusty.[5] His brief was to make door-to-door enquiries, to interview the people that lived there, and to find out about their lives. What the reporter found in Corpusty clearly appalled him. His account describes the deplorable overcrowding he found in cottage after cottage, the fact that each toilet was shared by several families, and the fact that raw sewage discharged into the same foul watercourse from which the villagers drew their drinking water. A widow and her son of 23 years occupied a cottage that contained not one stick of furniture, all possessions having been seized by the bailiff in lieu of £2 rent arrears; a family slept under sacking, four generations to the same room; others occupied houses where the roofs were in such poor repair that the rain simply poured through. Landlords either refused to contemplate repairs or threatened rent increases to cover the cost of them. The tales of hardship mounted, but few things prepared the reporter for the story he encountered in one cottage in particular. This is the stark way he wrote it up:

> The cottage is occupied by J.J., his wife and two children, a boy aged four and a girl aged thirteen. The woman told me that she had lost four children from fever recently and three previously. There is no privy.

The Corpusty story appeared in a series that ran for several weeks in the *Norfolk News* entitled "The Cottage Homes of England". The series was intended as an exposé of the harsh living conditions experienced by agricultural workers throughout rural East Anglia and was clearly the product of a relatively new phenomenon, that of the campaigning newspaper with a socio-political agenda. Such newspapers were not content merely to report the news but to go out and find it, and to use stories to bring about change. They were not confined to rural Norfolk, of course. A few years later, in the North-East of England, the *Newcastle Weekly Chronicle* ran a series exhibiting many similarities, entitled "Our Colliery Villages".[6] Here were tales of the jerry-built, overcrowded and insanitary conditions endured by coalminers and their families, the tenants of wealthy coalowners and colliery companies.

As both the *Norfolk News* and the *Newcastle Weekly Chronicle* were Liberal-radical newspapers with a definite political axe to grind, their stories need to be verified. An investigation of the 1861 census for the parish of Corpusty reveals "J.J" to have been a 41 year-old agricultural labourer called Josiah Jarvis and the woman to have been his 36 year-old wife, Anne. The tragic loss of so many of the couple's children can be traced in the Corpusty burial register. This reveals that on 3 May 1863 Anne and Josiah had buried Richard, aged ten, and Charles, aged eight. Three days later they buried six-year old Hannah and two-year old Louisa. All four now lay somewhere close to their brothers, twelve year old John (who had died in 1860), four year old Charles (died December 1850) and an infant, Richard, who had died in March 1850 before reaching his first birthday.[7]

Further inspection of the Corpusty burial records reveals that the Jarvises were by no means alone in their tragedy. Cholera or some other contemporary scourge, periodically sweeping through this insanitary village, left a clear mark on the pages of the parish burial register, accounting in quick succession for members of other families: Thomas and Mary Hill (who died in September and October 1850); Samuel and Francis Goldsmith (January 1851); James and Philip Pegg (March and April 1851); Robert and Samuel Pegg (December 1851 and December 1852); William and John Brown (May and June 1859); Sarah, Mary and

Charles Carr (August to December 1861); Elizabeth and Richard Westney (April and May 1863); Owen and James Roberts (February 1864).

If the newspaper reports were not exaggerated, what (if anything) might they suggest to us about the society in which these harsh and recurrent visitations of child mortality were happening?

The newspaper article goes on to explain that Josiah Jarvis was employed as a labourer on the estate of a landowner named William Bulwer who lived at Heydon Hall. Heydon was the next village to Corpusty, but Jarvis was not allowed to live there. Bulwer had turned the village into a picturesque confection of model cottages at the gates to his park and estate workers like Jarvis had to live in surrounding villages, from where they would walk two or three miles to work every day. This was a common enough feature of the rural landscape in southern England: Heydon was a "closed" parish, by which is usually meant a parish in the hands of one landowner or a very small cartel. "Closed" parishes like Heydon were often surrounded by their alter ego "open" parishes, which were parishes typically in the hands of multiple owners and speculators. Here house building was not governed even by aesthetic considerations and rough cottages were thrown up to accommodate the workers that the "closed" parish would not have. Corpusty was one such "open" parish and there were two or three others associated with the Heydon estate.[8] William Bulwer did not own all the cottages in these open parishes, but the proximity of his estate created the conditions in which speculators could build cheap houses and rent them out to Bulwer's estate workers.

Why did the dichotomy between open and closed parishes arise?[9] At least part of the reason was aesthetic, and at Heydon Bulwer wanted to ensure that the approach to his park was as pleasing to the eye as possible for himself and his visitors. In this respect he certainly succeeded. The village of Heydon is exceptionally attractive and remains much in demand among film and TV crews anxious to capture something of the imagined archetype and idyll of rural life. The open-closed parish division was also heavily paternalistic in origin. For the select few allowed to live in Heydon, the village offered good quality housing, a clean water supply and decent sanitation and Bulwer might expect to be rewarded with a peaceful, deferential atmosphere in the immediate vicinity of his Hall. But the predominant motivation behind the division was economic. The logic ran something like this: limiting the number of houses in a parish like Heydon limited its population; limiting the population minimised the risk of unemployment during periodic (and seasonal) downturns in the agricultural economy; minimising unemployment meant that the ratepayers'–and the landowner's–contribution towards maintaining the unemployed via the parish Poor Rate would also be kept to a minimum. Consequently "closed" parishes like Heydon were usually associated with very low levels of local taxation.

Taken to its fullest extent a combination of the potentially exploitative power relationships offered by the closed parish with the new administrative opportunities afforded by the post-1834 Poor Law could elevate community management onto a whole new plane of social engineering. The Thetford maltster James Fison was one of many who celebrated the change:

> The New Poor Law has had a very excellent effect on the character of the labourers. It has also improved their moral condition. I have a great deal to do with the lower orders; I have interested myself much in promoting emigration, and had very great difficulty in inducing them to stir for some time; they would not leave their parishes. But as soon as this Poor Law began to operate I had no difficulty; I and my brother have succeeded so that we have assisted upwards of 200 to remove from our neighbourhood to Yorkshire. The Poor Law is the very best measure that ever was devised for the effectual relief of the agricultural interest with respect to the farmer in a variety of ways. The obligation to offer employment to the poor, whether needed or not, has been replaced with a system that allows farmers to make much more business-like decisions, including the use of machinery.[10]

In some respects, then, the nineteenth century "closed" parish was the remnant of a paternalistic system of social relations, with all that that could entail to the benefit or detriment of the labouring poor. By the 1860s there are clear indications that the ground beneath this system was beginning to shift. It has already been suggested that the period was one of "paternalistic neglect" in which many of the keystones of paternalistic power appeared to be in place while the necessary levels of mutual comprehension and obligation were increasingly absent, and at least part of the reason for this decline in cross-class understanding lies in the erosion of custom. It requires a rather crude broad brush to illustrate this in a limited space, but it is certainly sustainable to argue that a combination of the Enclosure of common land, the New Poor Law, the triumph of written law over orally-transmitted memory, and the stopping-up of customary rights of way–all of which could be characterised as the privatisation of public space–created a new landscape of social relations.[11]

Authority's assault on custom was ideologically based. As Bushaway has written, "attempts to suppress popular calendar customs and ceremonies, to undermine their validity, to question their morality, to challenge their sources of support, to deny access to customary venues and to break up their continuity were part of a coherent process".[12] Custom stemmed from, and was sustained by, an essentially localist mentality, through which the customary calendar legitimated and explained almost every aspect of work, leisure and social relations. This profoundly local provenance of custom reinforced senses of belonging and identity. It provided the mental map of what might be termed the "moral community"–the parish's complex network of economic and social relationships–and the "physical community", defined by landmarks, field-names and footpaths. Custom thus exercised a potential stranglehold on centralised and nationalised initiatives, one that had to be prised open by the law if new capital-based, time-oriented disciplines of living and working were to prevail. By the mid-1850s the selective, capricious and iniquitous way the law was being applied had stirred the anger of those campaigning journalists on the *Norfolk News*:

> This system of punishing by fine, and in default of payment by imprisonment is manifestly unjust towards the poor. The rich man convicted of a violation of the law, takes out his purse, pays the penalty and walks off with an air of unconcern, if not of insolence. [The poor man is ordered to] prison and the treadmill, and his . . . weeping wife and children [consigned] to the workhouse. Money makes the only difference between the convict at large and the convict at the wheel.[13]

As the old landscape of mental maps and understood boundaries began to disappear, our apocryphal poacher, treading traditional paths across the estate in pursuit of the fourteenth Earl's rabbits and pheasants, now became a multiply subversive figure. His was no straightforward act of criminality, but one that challenged the age-old rights of property, disregarded and held in contempt the new written laws of ownership, and traced in the landscape the ghostly echoes of remembered ways and half-forgotten custom.[14]

Inevitably, perhaps, we have to consider the figure of "Parson Woodforde" in this context. The incumbent of a Norfolk parish between 1776 and 1803, Woodforde's diaries have provided generations of readers with an apparent short-cut to understanding social relations in eighteenth-century rural society.[15] In this version the country parson lives well, with a rich and varied diet supplemented with smuggled brandies, while he takes a genial and avuncular interest in the well-being of the parish poor. They, in their turn, are willing enough to tug their forelocks in appreciation and anticipation of the good things that come their way: the Christmas suppers, the charity doles, the one-off special-needs payments. From the moment of his arrival in Norfolk, James Woodforde not only accepted but actively sponsored the local culture that he found there. His diaries record his participation in a world that was cyclical and, in developmental terms, largely static.

Certainly, for the Jarvises of Corpusty, the mechanism of this kind of paternalistic local government had broken-down by the 1860s. Where, for instance, could they turn for support and guidance after the loss of their children? Might they turn to the Church of England? After all, somebody connected with the Church was compiling those parish registers and seeing at first hand the devastating impact that landlord neglect was having on the families of the poor. Here the Jarvises would have run into just the kind of clergy-landowner nexus that was bringing the Church of England into conflict with the labouring (and radicalising) poor of the mid- to late-nineteenth century, for the hand that compiled at least part of the Corpusty burial register belonged to the Rev Edward Bulwer, brother of the Heydon estate landowner. At Heydon the cosiness of this link becomes visible in a particularly poignant way. In the aftermath of the *Norfolk News* investigation and the mini-scandal that it stirred, Heydon estate accounts reveal that William Bulwer was moved to expend the sum of £13 on the repair of his Corpusty cottages in 1864.[16] In the same year he also commissioned a new burial vault to be constructed for the Bulwer family in Heydon church that was to cost £425.[17]

There were, of course, a host of reasons why the labouring poor drifted away from the Church of England and into the arms of Nonconformity in the middle decades of the nineteenth century and the straightforward one of theological difference should not be overlooked, but social disillusion and political antagonism towards the role of the Church were significant motivating forces. It was at the secondary level–as landowner, farmer, poor relief guardian, magistrate, school manager and charity administrator– that the clergyman had his most frequent interchange with other members of the parish community and it is here, rather than in his primary role as minister of religion, that contemporaries saw his hands on the levers of social control. Clergymen were prevalent on Poor Law Boards of Guardians in Norfolk, even taking an increasing role as the nineteenth century became the twentieth. Equally, the clerical collar was still encountered often enough on the Norfolk magistrates' bench, fining poachers and turnip-stealers, enforcing bastardy orders and committing incendiarists to the jurisdiction of a higher court. These phenomena are not so clearly seen in the North-East of England. In Co. Durham, what little clerical input there had been into Poor Law administration was receding further in the early decades of the twentieth century as Boards fell increasingly into the hands of the miner-guardian, the trade unions and local Labour Party activists.[18] Clerical magistrates were also always less prevalent. Their presence on the bench showed a similar declining trajectory to that of Norfolk, but always at a significantly lower level.[19]

During its decades of pre-eminence, the clerical magistracy was thought by many contemporaries to be symptomatic of the way in which the clergy shared the values of the landed classes. In Norfolk this was given added impetus by the voting record of clergymen in nineteenth-century elections. Before the advent of the secret ballot in 1869 poll books clearly demonstrate how clergy voting patterns bent to the will of the local landowner, strongly suggesting either that clergymen were being appointed on the strength of their political allegiances or that many clergymen regarded political unity with the local landowner to be a matter of over-riding social importance.[20] That unity was most clearly manifested in the issues of magistracy, land enclosure and Poor Law management.

There is a paradox here. If the enclosed, Poor Law landscape *outside* the parish church was increasingly symptomatic of the privatisation of public space, it is fair to say that the pewscape *inside* the church frequently suggested the democratisation of private space. The Victorians' enthusiastic restoration of churches often entailed the removal of old box pews and the labrynthine systems of pew rentals that went with them. Together these had been a powerful force for regimenting congregations into a public representation of parochial social hierarchies. The most prestigious (and most expensive) seats in church tended to be towards the east end, clustered around the pulpit or in the chancel. The poorer people occupied "free seats" which were situated towards the west end or in galleries. Consequently any visitor moving from west to east inside a parish church on a Sunday morning would find themselves making a graphic and clearly-defined journey upwards, through the socio-economic groups of the community.[21]

However, while the new, open rows of pitch pine pews were a clear attempt to eradicate such obvious affronts to the poorest members of the congregation, the new arrangement still fell a long way short of egalitarianism. There remained the whole issue of squire-in-his-pew and the need for congregation and clergy alike to watch and wait for their cue to proceed with divine service. This coincided with the newly-imposed panoply of *spectatorship* that was replacing *participation* in many Church of England establishments, one key component of which was the abolition of parish bands and singers and their replacement with choirs and organists.[22] Certainly there were men who would later become influential trade unionists who traced their radicalisation to an early exposure to the social order in churches like these, where the organisation of space made a clear declaration of their place in the scheme of things, and where the intention was to demonstrate the unalterable permanence of their status. Both Joseph Arch and George Edwards, early pioneers of agricultural trade unionism and among the first working-class men to become Westminster MPs, testified to the resentment they felt when confronted with class-based social segregation in church.[23]

Of course, it was not only in the landscape or in the interior organisation of church buildings that strong political links between the clergy and their powerful landowner/employer neighbours could be detected. Frequently subtle, and often less visible, were the social and kinship ties between them. Together they forged a byzantine network of intermarriage and patronage that brokered power and influence in all corners of society. It was often at the level of the "younger son who went into the church" that many crucial networks and contacts seem to have been consolidated. It is hard to avoid the sense that these junior associates of powerful dynasties were expected to "deliver" a parish politically.

In the North-East of England complex inter-relationships of this kind were given added significance and depth by the fact that the Church was a major land and coalowner and consequently in direct economic and political alignment with the patrons of many of its livings. Between 1829 and 1835, Royal Commission enquiries into the funding of dioceses in England and Wales found that the Bishop of Durham's revenues from land and coal for the period totalled £170,632 while his expenditure totalled £31,936. [24] By 1890 "the annual income from coal-mining royalties accruing to the Church of England [in Durham] exceeded £200,000".[25] At the core of political–and Nonconformist–objections to the Church's material wealth lay the conviction that no institution so clearly advantaged by the *status quo* could be expected to encourage the development of more meritocratic systems of social and economic organisation. A good deal of the wealth circulating in the Durham diocese was directed into church building and church restoration projects, and funding for such programmes often began to resemble a direct assertion of the power of local magnates. Certain coalowning dynasties in the North-East launched themselves whole-heartedly into church building projects, not least the Londonderry family with their construction of SS Hild and Helen, Dawdon, between 1910 and 1912. Between them, Lord and Lady Londonderry gave the land for the church and vicarage, laid the foundation stone, gave £1000 towards the building fund, gave a further £500 to the Diocesan Building Fund with the pledge of an annual subscription for a further 25 years, contributed an annual sum towards the clergyman's stipend, donated the font, gave the bells, gave the organ, and gave the alms bags, markers and altar linen.

Their personal contribution amounted to just less than half the total cost of £10,400.[26] Such a level of input conferred power of an almost medieval kind: the Londonderrys had a private pew with strategically placed screens so that the occupants could only be seen from certain angles,[27] and there was even the suggestion that Lady Londonderry herself might be depicted on the rood screen.[28]

Elsewhere the Durham coalfield witnessed the continued adoption of parish churches as the private memorial space for elite families. Just as Dawdon church was dominated by memorials to the Londonderrys, the east window at Hetton-le-Hole became a memorial to the coalowner Nicholas Wood.[29] In 1829 churchwardens at Chester-le-Street approved a family pew and vault for Lord Durham, to the design of Ignatius Bonomi.[30] The Londonderry mausoleum at Long Newton was even grander, its Minton floor tiles alone costing £2960 in 1856, an amount that might tellingly be contrasted with the amount of time, effort and expenditure being devoted to colliery houses elsewhere in the diocese.[31] Here, as with the proposed Heydon mausoleum in Norfolk, the contrast between working-class housing and elite burial-places seems laden with social and political significance. Everywhere the working-class churchgoer looked, his gaze fell upon unwelcome reminders of his employer's wealth and influence, and in a few places this kind of ostentatious display was not taken lying down. In 1866, for instance, someone crept into the newly-restored church at Little Walsingham in Norfolk, lay a charge of gunpowder under the brand new organ that had been funded by friends, relatives and associates of the Rev Lee Warner, and blew the whole thing to pieces.[32]

By the middle of the nineteenth century the Church of England had made a serious attempt to come to grips with some of the issues that so antagonised its opponents, not least the matter of clerical absenteeism. This was a clear strategy to make clergymen more relevant to the life of their parish by ensuring that they lived there, but it is possible that the initiative may actually have made matters worse in some places. As the policy on residency changed, a new and visible symbol of clergy privilege began to appear: palatial new rectories and vicarages were being constructed in parishes that were otherwise characterised by the poor quality of their working-class housing. Alongside the Gothic schoolroom and the restored parish church a new iconography asserted itself on the rural skyline: the rectory as "country residence", with sweeping, rhododenron-lined drives and lawns shaded by towering Cedars of Lebanon. The new rectory posed as many questions about the relevance of the clergyman in his community as it answered. In Burston, Norfolk, where a famous dispute between the clergyman and his parishioners precipitated one of the longest strikes in British labour history, it was noted by local trade unionists that the Rev. Charles Tucker Eland, his wife and two children, occupied a twelve-bedroomed house "with winding paths and sheltering trees, cricket and croquet lawns, orchards and ornamental gardens" which, together with a salary of £495 per year, were his to enjoy "because he preaches a sermon once a week to three old ladies and the sexton".[33]

Norwich diocesan records house the plans of 619 new rectories and rectory extensions built between 1791 and 1906.[34] Two peaks may be discerned in this activity, each with its own crucial significance. In the 1840s a rush of building activity coincided with attempts by parishioners to come to terms with the impact of the New Poor Law, while between 1860 and 1880 a similar surge took place against the backdrop of a growing awareness of the scandalous living conditions endured by many labourers. In a climate of increased trade union activism, such jarring discrepancies as these were doing irreparable harm to the standing of the Church and to the political system that it favoured. The *Norfolk News* encapsulated the growing sense that the 'moral trickle-down' effect of new rectories and restored churches had come too late to satisfy a rural community that needed immediate solutions and would, in the next ten years, find the voice to demand them:

> It is useless to boast that churches have been improved, that clergymen's residences have been erected, and that new and enlarged farm houses have been built, when the subject under consideration [is] the insufficiency of cottage accommodation for the poor.[35]

Demonstrating a kind of synchronous growth with trade unionism in both regions, the unpretentious simplicity of Nonconformity often stood as a rebuke to the wealth of the Church of England. The Primitive Methodist church in particular began to break down notions of parochial identity and established hinterlands that challenged the influence of political and kinship networks operated by the gentry and clergy. Nonconformity broadened horizons and introduced the concept of a wider brotherhood by virtue of being *circuit* rather than *parish* based. Rejection of the Church of England did not equate to rejection of religion; the labouring poor were simply beginning to seek their religion elsewhere. As the agricultural trade union leader George Edwards put it, "With my study of *theology* I soon began to realise that the social conditions of the people were not as God intended they should be . . . as I preached every Sunday my soul burned with indignation".[36] In the North-East, the miners' leader Thomas Burt traced his own political awakening to his experiences on the Primitive Methodist circuits of the coalfield.[37]

Table 1: Trade Union links with Primitive Methodism (East Dereham branch of the Norfolk Agricultural Labourers' Union, 1872)

Position in NALU branch	Name	Occupation	
Secretary	George Rix	Grocer	PM lay-preacher Sunday School teacher
President	David Reeder	Agric. labourer	PM lay-preacher
Treasurer	William Hubbard	Higgler	PM lay-preacher
Committee	William Lane	Brickmaker	PM lay-preacher
Committee	John Culley	Agric. labourer	PM lay-preacher
Committee	John Harris	Carpenter	PM lay-preacher
Committee	Benjamin Brett	Agric. labourer	PM lay-preacher
Committee	Robert Jude		PM lay-preacher
Committee	Archibald Pearce		PM lay-preacher

[SOURCE: Based on work published in A Howkins, *Poor Labouring Men: Rural Radicalism in Norfolk, 1870 – 1923* (London: Routledge & Kegan Paul, 1985), 11]

The Nonconformist chapel in which these men gathered may, in so many ways, have been the antithesis of the alehouse, but it was a "sequestered social space" all the same,[38] and when the labouring poor arrived there they found themselves exposed to an entirely new set of social contacts and political ideas. This was often expressed architecturally, with the Primitive Methodist chapel of the 1860s making a modest statement in the rural landscape: the extravagant Gothic 'architecture of moral purpose' so enthusiastically embraced by the Church of England was rejected in favour of the homely wayside bethel; the inclusive, simple hand-built structure that reflected the human scale on which Primitive Methodism was organised.[39]

Politically the links between Primitive Methodism and trade unionism were very strong. Table 1 demonstrates the extraordinarily detailed links between Primitive Methodism and trade unionism among the officials of one branch of the Norfolk Amalgamated Labourers' Union in 1872, where it can be seen that every official and member of the committee was closely associated with the Primitive Methodist church. From agricultural trade unionism, fired and inspired by Primitive Methodist religion, strong political links were forged with the Liberal Party and, subsequently, the Labour Party, with the result that the power of landowners like Bulwer at Heydon faced an unprecedented and two-pronged political challenge. The consequences of this began to be visible in the day-to-day running of landed estates. When Lord Walsingham, owner of the Merton estate on the Breckland, arranged for a gang of poachers to be infiltrated by one of his agents in the early 1870s, he very quickly realised that he had also infiltrated the neighbourhood's most active cell of agricultural trade unionism. Local poachers and local trade unionists were the same men.[40] All those decades of chasing pheasants and rabbits seems finally to have translated (as, to do them justice, the aristocracy always seemed to sense that it would) into something with a much harder, political edge: something that was prepared to stand toe-to-toe with any fourteenth Earl and question the right and legitimacy of property.

On the Melton Constable estate in North Norfolk in 1900, a Conservative landowner, Lord Hastings, flexed his muscles by dismissing a tenant and an estate worker who had voted Liberal in the general election.[41] Coming at the very dawn of the twentieth century, both Hastings' action and the outraged reaction that greeted it seem deeply symbolic. The general election had been fought on international and Empire issues, with particular reference to the conduct of the Boer War, and Hastings had clearly tried to use local influence to mobilise a deferential vote. What he found was that old systems of paternalism and patronage no longer fully responded to his call. Instead he experienced at first hand a new stage in the evolution of a politics of resistance: a politics that, from the middle of the nineteenth century, had appeared to eschew party trappings and tribal allegiances but which had nevertheless, on a long fuse, simmered at the margins of power until it re-ignited as something stronger, more determined and self-confident.

Lord Hastings acts as a bridge between the two distinct geographical areas and the two historical periods under scrutiny in this chapter. In the 1840s Jacob Astley of Melton Constable had come (by means so labrynthine that even he would have struggled to explain them to any poacher on his land) into the Hastings title and the ownership of the coal-rich Seaton Delaval estate in Northumberland. For much of the remainder of the nineteenth century successive Lord Hastings made Seaton Delaval Hall their principal residence. Their mark is clearly to be seen in the Northumberland village to this day, including the presence of an Astley School and a Melton Constable Hotel. In Northumberland the Hastings dynasty encountered a very different set of social and industrial relations, for although all the same elements were there–resistance, Primitive Methodism, trade unionism–they were on a developmental cycle roughly thirty years ahead of that in Norfolk. By the mid-nineteenth century Hastings in Norfolk was still waging a full-scale battle to keep these elements at bay; Hastings in Northumberland was having to deal with the fact that they were already firmly entrenched.

While considering this it is nevertheless important to remember that there was no rigid division between the developmental stages of resistance politics. For an intriguingly long time elements of protest, politics and popular culture continued to cross-fertilise, as an example from the North-East of England may demonstrate. On a summer night in 1925 a strange pursuit took place through the churchyard at Chopwell, a pit village on the Durham coalfield. A contemporary account says:

> As soon as we knew that he'd started in the pit as a blackleg we went to the pit and waited for him coming out. We walked him up to the church gates and we sang 'Lead kindly light' and 'Rock of ages' all the way making a big noise. When we got to the church gates he thought we'd take him straight to the vicarage but instead we took him through the churchyard and some of the women as they passed the graves picked up the wreaths and put them round his neck. He had a nervous breakdown after it. So that was one blackleg we finished the day he started. But he really thought in his mind that he wasn't going to be attacked because he was the vicar's son. But we showed him that it didn't matter who he was, if they were against the miners and what we were fighting for, then they were on the other side.[42]

The Chopwell incident, then, starts with the humiliation of the vicar's son in a Co. Durham pit village. It is fair to say that the undercurrent of hostility towards the Church of England in the North-East came to something of a head in the early decades of the twentieth century.[43] During the 1920s the Durham diocese was led by the despised, conservative figures of Bishop Hensley Henson and Dean George Welldon, the latter a man who miners had memorably attempted to push into the River Wear at the 1925 Miners' Gala.[44] Angus MacDonald, the vicar of Chopwell and father of the young man chased through the churchyard, was a Conservative clergyman very much in tune with the Henson/Welldon regime. Only a few weeks earlier he had been voted off the Blaydon Urban District Council and Gateshead Poor Law Union and replaced by radical miners' representatives.[45] His parish was becoming widely-renowned as a "Little Moscow", many of the commanding heights of its local government and administration having been seized by Communists.[46]

But if the context of the Chopwell incident is very much one of twentieth-century politics, the treatment dished out to the vicar's son seems to come from a much earlier time. Taunted, jostled and manhandled through the churchyard, draped in wreaths from the graves, MacDonald junior was being subjected to nothing less than *charivari* or rough music, that old staple of ritual humiliation by which communities since medieval times had regulated the behaviour of delinquent members. Unsurprisingly in this context, perhaps, it is the womenfolk of Chopwell who are draping the wreaths over MacDonald's head. In the decidedly industrial setting of the Durham coalfield, women continued to provide an active backdrop to strikes in a way that echoed their traditional role as guardians of a pre-industrial "moral economy".[47] Furthermore, the Chopwell rough-musickers may well have been influenced by Communism but they were clearly not card-carrying atheists. Young MacDonald was sent on his way to the tune of 'Lead kindly light amid th'encircling gloom' and 'Rock of ages, cleft for me', Methodist standards, both.

The physical space in the landscape occupied by the parish church of St. John, Chopwell, and Angus MacDonald's vicarage is an object lesson in the awkward relationship between the Church of England and militant communities at the turn of the twentieth century, just as the location of the wayside bethel can tell a similar story in the back lanes of rural Norfolk. Not built until 1907, isolated and remote on a hillside to the north-west of the village, Chopwell's church and vicarage are visibly detached from community life, in stark contrast to the Methodist (and Catholic) meeting-places which stand close to the village centre, at the hub of village activity. The "public space" of the religious denominations in Chopwell is a strong indication of their "political space", and a visible depiction of the politics of resistance in action. But this was also a politics of multi-layered cultural complexity. Peel back the layers, and young MacDonald's undignified flight across Chopwell churchyard and his humiliatingly brief career as a strike-breaker seem to reveal how, for a brief and unlikely moment, threads of connection between revolutionary Russia, medieval rural England and the Primitive Methodism of the nineteenth-century working-class were temporarily intertwined.

The pursuit of MacDonald and the attempted dunking of Dean Welldon find their echo in the plight of a Norfolk clergyman, the Rev William Allen.[48] On Christmas Eve 1869, hurrying through the village of Shouldham, Allen was anxious to get to his church and to ring a Christmas peal of bells, as he had in every one of the preceding thirty years of his ministry. When he reached the church, however, Allen found that the door leading up to the bell chamber was securely locked against him. He knew immediately that this was the work of one of his great enemies in the village, the parish clerk. There was another way into the bell chamber, however. Some metres above the vicar's head there was a narrow trapdoor. Showing a determination and physical agility that belied his seventy years, the clergyman fetched some steps, and managed to swing himself up into the belfry through the trapdoor in its floor. Now the traditional Christmas peal could be rung, but not before Allen had descended the tower stairs and bolted the door from the inside, so that the parish clerk was, in his turn, locked out. Between them the Allen and MacDonald incidents–sixty years apart–seem to sit comfortably within a much longer tradition of popular anti-clericalism: the Norfolk clergyman who returned home late one night and knocked his head against an effigy of himself hanging just inside the rectory gateway;[49] or the vicar who couldn't go out after dark without being surrounded by groups of villagers who would jostle and taunt him in the street;[50] or the vicar of Little Walsingham, scarcely recovered from the explosion that wrecked his church and organ, seeing an effigy of himself in a coffin in a shop window on the High Street.[51]

William Allen had a long ministry in Shouldham, during which he became embroiled in years of ill-feeling, litigation and political turmoil. His early arrival at the church on that Christmas Eve in 1869 was due to the fact that he had disbanded the 'parish ringers' and taken upon himself the principal responsibility for bell-ringing. He had been locked out of the bell chamber by James Malby, an unofficial parish clerk who was fighting a civil war with the man that Allen had nominated for the role, John Towler. Malby's appointment had owed much to a kind of vestry coup, during the course of which agricultural labourers had gathered on the village green and had marched *en masse* to the church, demanding the election of an independent churchwarden to scrutinise Allen's management of various financial affairs in the parish. Allen had restored Shouldham church in the Gothic style, and had overseen the development of one of the best parish choirs in west Norfolk. He preached specifically that a ritualistic church service, filled with spectacle and music that was designed to be performed rather than participated in, was intended for the "edification" of the congregation. All that he expected of his parishioners was that they should trust to his good intentions, even if they did not understand what he was doing. A restored church and a ritualist service were, Allen believed, the keys to an appreciation of higher things, and the complementary role of education was to weave the spirituality of Sunday service into the secular atmosphere of the working week. Education was best placed in the hands of clergymen, and it should have the Church of England catechism at the centre of its curriculum. It should be primarily religious and moral in character, and should begin to distance children from the negative influence of their parents. Allen made explicit links between the education of the poor and a new complicity with the social order that was becoming apparent to him in the late 1860s.

In due course Allen came to face a concerted challenge to his authority from leading parishioners, principal among whom were a group of Nonconformist farmers that seemed to have widespread support through all the social classes in the village. Allen had established an agenda that simply trod on too many toes; that challenged too many customs and too many vested interests; that gave too many people cause to put a negative construction on his involvement. He may have been the very antithesis of an uncaring, lazy parson but here, as was the case for dedicated clergymen in many other communities, Allen's huge workload earned him little by way of respect and gratitude but attracted suspicion and resentment that control, management and manipulation were everywhere.

Fifty years later, Dean Welldon offered a sober assessment of the Church's standing in such communities:

> The Church might or might not have lost influence, but beyond all question she had lost authority. She could no longer rely upon an unquestioning submission to popular doctrines or her commands. She had made her appeal to the reason and the conscience of mankind, and by their reason and their conscience she must stand or fall.[52]

Poor Dean Welldon, of course, would come close to taking that fall himself at the Durham Miners' Gala of 1925. Even as he clambered aboard the police launch that had been sent to rescue him from the chilly waters of the River Wear, Welldon was consoling himself with the thought that the miners had got the wrong man and he had been mistaken for Bishop Henson. The distinction was a fine one, however: both men were Conservatives and both had antagonized the miners with recent political pronouncements. The miners who seized Welldon were probably less interested in personal identity than in political identity. Henson was, at around the same time, receiving regular reports from parish clergymen that indicated their profound dissatisfaction with his leadership of the diocese, suggesting that by the mid-1920s the Church of England in North-East England was entering a period of profound political crisis.[53]

This was not a crisis that faced the Durham diocese alone, but one that confronted all religious authorities at the start of a secularising century. Religious belief was coming under the most profound challenge – not just from the usual suspects like Darwinism but from a sudden realisation of Man's new capacity to overturn previously immutable laws of what it meant to be human and to reconstruct his very relationship with nature. In an agricultural context these changes had been wrought by the mechanisation and de-skilling of age-old working practices and the enforced separation of those practices from popular culture and custom. On the East Durham coalfield the capacity to transform nature on a massive scale had been demonstrated and an apparently pre-determined set of human tolerances to smoke and noise and ugliness had now given way to a kind of sensory deprivation that was required of the industrial-worker and the urban-liver. For rural and industrial workers alike the ever-fluctuating condition of a market-based political economy made for working lives and home lives that were unstable, uncertain and at the mercy of remote and incomprehensible forces. Keeping afloat in these aggressively a-spiritual environments required concentration on a rather different set of values and priorities from those espoused by the Church. From the Durham diocese one clergyman acknowledged how 'questions of P[rayer] B[ook] Revision fall in importance before [the] social & industrial iniquity [of unemployment]'.[54]

Sixty years and about two hundred and fifty miles separates the Jarvises of Corpusty and the miners of Chopwell and the churchyards in which their dramas were played out, and extreme caution has to be exercised before any common meaning can be read into the two stories. Comparative regional histories conducted across two such disparate regions as East Anglia and North-East England are also fraught with hazard. The essential problem of inter-regional research is one that should continually be borne in mind. Is like being compared with like? Should widely diverse regions be chosen, like Norfolk and Durham, or ones that ostensibly have more in common? Can a match be found in the records sufficient for meaningful quantitative surveys to be carried out? But, despite their many profound differences, Norfolk and Co. Durham continue to reveal striking similarities. Politically they were both radical places, their early development of trade unionism often having its roots in Nonconformist religion and, in particular, in the working-class denomination of Primitive Methodism. Consequently there is a common pulse that beats under these stories of political development, and it is one that increases in volume the more these apparently very different regions and their societies are researched. The pulse is that of the politics of resistance: the statement of that resistance in expressions of private space and public space, and the endless struggle for the independence that ownership of resources could confer. The Hastings dynasty is there, ticking away under both stories, too: battling Liberalism in Norfolk and facing nascent Communism on the Northern Coalfield and realising–like the apocryphal fourteenth Earl, perhaps–that from now on it was going to have to *fight* to justify its position and its property.

Notes

[1] Alan Plater, "Seriously, though: Old jokes and the zeitgeist", *Northern Review* 6 (Summer, 1992).
[2] See, for instance, Alun Howkins, "Politics or Quietism: The Social History of Nonconformity" in *Religious Dissent in East Anglia,* eds, N. Virgoe and T. Williamson (Norwich: University of East Anglia, 1993), 73-92.
[3] G. Howells, "Emigration and the New Poor Law: The Norfolk Emigration Fever of 1836", *Rural History* 11:2 (2000): 145-64.
[4] Between 1811 and 1921 the population of Co. Durham increased by 795% at the same time as the population of the United Kingdom increased by 273%. See R. Lee, *The Church of England and the Durham Coalfield, 1810 - 1926: Clergymen, Capitalists and Colliers* (Woodbridge: Boydell, 2007), 5.
[5] *Norfolk News,* 31 October, 1863.
[6] "Our Colliery Villages", *Newcastle Weekly Chronicle,* 2 October, 1872 – 25 April, 1874.
[7] Norfolk Record Office (henceforth NRO) MF/RO 559 Corpusty Burial Registers, 1850 – 1865.
[8] The villages of Saxthorpe, Wood Dalling, Reepham and Cawston are all likely candidates here.
[9] It is fair to say that some historians question its existence or significance, but my own view is that there is sufficient contemporary material to indicate *some kind* of disparity between neighbouring parishes, and *some kind* of social unease that was being experienced as a result. S. Banks, "Nineteenth-century scandal or twentieth-century model? A new look at 'open' and 'close' parishes", *Economic History Review* 41 (1988): 51-73 was an early and influential expression of the sceptics' view. Other aspects of the discussion can be found in B. A. Holderness, "Open and Close Parishes in the Eighteenth and Nineteenth centuries", *Agricultural History Review* XX (1972) and D. Spencer, "'Reformulating the "closed" parish thesis: associations, interests and interaction'", *Journal of Historical Geography* 26:1

(2000): 83 – 98. The debate is joined in R. Lee, *Rural Society and the Anglican Clergy, 1815 – 1914: Encountering and Managing the Poor* (Woodbridge: Boydell, 2006).
[10] *Parliamentary Papers VIII* (1836) Report of the Select Committee on Agriculture. Evidence of James Fison (maltster), Norfolk.
[11] Among the influential works covering this area of nineteenth-century social relations are E. P. Thompson, *Customs in Common* (London: The New Press, 1993) and R. Bushaway, *By Rite: Custom, Ceremony and Community in England, 1700 – 1880* (London: Humanities Press, 1982).
[12] R. Bushaway, "Rite, Legitimation and Community in Southern England, 1700 - 1850: the Ideology of Custom", in *Conflict and Community in Southern England*, ed. B. Stapleton, (Stroud: Alan Sutton, 1992), 110-134.
[13] *Norfolk News,* 29 November, 1856.
[14] Alun Howkins, "Economic Crime and Class Law: Poaching and the Game Laws 1840-1880" in *The Imposition of Law,* eds, S. Burman and B. Harrell-Bond (London: Academic Press, 1979), 273-87.
[15] Rev J. Woodforde, *The Diary of a Country Parson,* ed. J. Beresford (Oxford: Oxford University Press, 1978).
[16] NRO BUL 11/31 615 x 7, Heydon Estate Accounts 1864-5.
[17] NRO BUL 11/508 618 x 9, specification of Heydon vault, 1864.
[18] Lee, *The Church of England and the Durham Coalfield,* 146-50.
[19] Ibid., 144-6.
[20] Lee, *Rural Society,* 160-2.
[21] Ibid., 44-55.
[22] See V. Gammon, "Babylonian Performances: The Rise and Suppression of Popular Church Music, 1660-1870" in *Popular Culture and Class Conflict 1590-1914,* eds, E. and S. Yeo, (Brighton: Harvester Press, 1981) for an academic account of this phenomenon and Thomas Hardy's novel *Under The Greenwood Tree* for a fictionalized account of the social disruption that such changes could cause.
[23] Pamela Horn, *Joseph Arch (1826-1919): The Farmworkers' Leader* (Kineton: Roundwood Press, 1971); George Edwards, *From Crow-Scaring to Westminster* (London: The Labour Publishing Company, 1922).
[24] W. Fordyce, *The History and Antiquities of the County Palatine of Durham* (Newcastle: A Fullarton & Co., 1857), 135.
[25] D. Spring, "The English Landed Estate in the Age of Coal and Iron: 1830-1880", *Journal of Economic History* 11 (1951): 5.
[26] Durham County Record Office (henceforth DCRO) D/Lo/F1137: A short sketch of SS Hild and Helen, Dawdon (1912).
[27] DCRO D/Lo/E547 Londonderry correspondence, W. H. Wood to M. Dillon, 30 November, 1911.
[28] Ibid., 23 November, 1911.
[29] *Newcastle Weekly Chronicle,* 18 January and 1 February, 1873.
[30] DCRO EP/CS 4/96.
[31] DCRO D/Lo/C 795/1/64-5 Long Newton church restoration, 1856.

[32] *Norfolk Chronicle,* 10 November, 1866.
[33] NRO MC 31/3 478x1: *The Burston Rebellion* (January 1916).
[34] NRO DN/DPL 1/1/1-17; 1/2/18-75; 2/1/3-547: Norwich Diocese, rectory building and extension plans, 1791 – 1906.
[35] *Norfolk News,* 28 November, 1863.
[36] Edwards, *Crow-Scaring to Westminster,* 29.
[37] Thomas Burt, *Thomas Burt: From Pitman to Privy Counsellor. An Autobiography* (London: T FisherUnwin, 1924).
[38] The notion of "sequestered social space" is explored in Mark Hailwood's chapter, posited on James Scott's theory of a place where subordinate social classes could meet to articulate a shared consciousness of their oppression.
[39] Tom Williamson, "The Nonconformist Chapels Survey: Some Preliminary Results" in *Religious Dissent,* eds, Virgoe and Williamson, 47-58.
[40] NRO WLS/LX/27 429 x 8, Walsingham Papers: Campaign against Poaching and Political Agitation, 1873.
[41] *Eastern Daily Press,* 19 October, 1900.
[42] L. Turnbull, *Chopwell's Story* (Gateshead: Gateshead Metropolitan Borough Council, 1979).
[43] Lee, *The Church of England and the Durham Coalfield,* passim.
[44] N. Emery, *Banners of the Northern Coalfield* (Stroud: Alan Sutton, 1999), 48.
[45] Turnbull, *Chopwell's Story.*
[46] S. MacIntyre, *Little Moscows: Communism and Working-Class Militancy in Inter-War Britain* (London: Croom Helm, 1980), 13–17.
[47] This was as true in 1984 as it had been in 1831. During the 1831 strike the miners' union leader Tommy Hepburn had urged his members to keep their womenfolk under control: C. Jones, "Experiences of a Strike: The North-East Coalowners and the Pitmen, 1831-32" in *Pitmen, Viewers and Coalmasters* ed. R. W. Sturgess, (Newcastle: North East Labour History Society, 1986), 41. In the 1984-5 strike the role of women as supporters of their menfolk, and as independent political activists in their own right is described in J. Spence, "Women, Wives and the Campaign against Pit Closures in Co. Durham", *Feminist Review* 60 (Autumn, 1998).
[48] Allen's experiences were fully detailed by him in a journal and cautionary record for future incumbents, NRO PD 356/125.
[49] M. F. Serpell, *A History of the Lophams* (London: Phillimore, 1980), 160.
[50] *Norfolk News,* 12 October, 1867.
[51] *Norfolk Chronicle,* 15 December, 1866.
[52] *Durham County Advertiser,* 12 December, 1919.
[53] Lee, *The Church of England and the Durham Coalfield,* 174-8.
[54] Durham University Library Palace Green AUC 4/14 Visitation Returns (1928), Rev Alexander Begg, Usworth.

CONTRIBUTORS

Mark Hailwood is a doctoral student at the University of Warwick, where he is also a seminar tutor in early modern English and European history. His research interests are focused on popular politics, popular culture and plebeian identity in early modern England. Mark's thesis looks to explore these themes through a study of alehouses and sociability in the seventeenth century.

Robert Lee is Lecturer in Modern British History at Teesside University. His research interests embrace the political, cultural and social history of modern Britain, with particular reference to the way in which regional, national and international trends could affect the day-to-day experience of life for ordinary people. His published books include 'Rural Society and the Anglican Clergy, 1815 - 1914'; 'The Church of England and the Durham Coalfield 1810 - 1926'; and 'Unquiet Country: Voices of the Rural Poor 1820 - 1880'. His current research examines comparatively aspects of landownership and social relations in agricultural East Anglia and industrial North East England.

George Oppitz-Trotman is a final year PhD student at Corpus Christi College, Cambridge. His research is into the historical origins of the revenge play in England, a project which also attempts to reconstruct a historical theory of genre. He maintains interests in many aspects of late medieval and early modern history and literature, as well as modernist poetics, Marxism and other social theory.

Simon Sandall completed his doctoral research into custom and popular senses of the past in the Forest of Dean (c.1550-1832) under the supervision of Professor Andy Wood at the University of East Anglia. He is currently working at the University of York on the Andrew Mellon funded York church court cause papers project in the Borthwick Institute for Historical Research. His ongoing research regarding collective and individual memory practices is primarily concerned with the intersection of customary litigious senses, more formalised legal processes and the mediation of such through local and popular cultures in early modern England.

Brodie Waddell has recently submitted his PhD at the University of Warwick. His thesis – 'Poverty, Property and Profit in English Popular Culture, 1660-1720' – is a study of the way cultural traditions and beliefs shaped attitudes toward economic and social relations, focusing specifically on the lives of the "poorer sort". He has also published an article in *Culture and Social History* entitled "Economic Immorality and Social Reformation in English Popular Preaching, 1585-1625". For his next project, he plans to examine the series of economic crises that struck Britain in the 1690s.

Fiona Williamson is a Lecturer in Early Modern History at the University of East Anglia. Her primary research area is seventeenth-century social history, with a particular interest in social relations, space, gender, agency and popular politics for the middling sorts and below. She is currently working on several projects, including mapping the social topography of Norwich and a monograph based around seventeenth century urban politics and culture.

Andy Wood is Professor of Social History at the University of East Anglia. His research interests focus on early modern English social history, in particular the history of popular politics, riot and rebellion, memory, and social relations. His latest book is "The 1549 rebellions and the making of early modern England" (Cambridge University Press, 2006). He is currently writing a book dealing with customary law and popular memory in England, c.1500-1800, also to be published by Cambridge University Press.

INDEX

Adorno, Theodor, 20, 44
adultery, *see,* illicit sex
"agency", definition of, 1-6
Aiken, John, 182, 192
alehouse, 2-4, 6, 8-9, 51-76, 87-88,
    99, 205; licensing laws, 8, 52,
    65-9
Allen, William, 209-10, 214
Arch, Joseph, 202, 213
Aristotle, 29, 47
Ashton-under-Lyne, 180-4, 192
assizes, 151, 160
Aubrey, John, 184

Bacon, Sir Francis, 19, 44
ballads, 10, 73, 104, 106, 109-10,
    112, 126, 130
Bamford, Samuel, 183, 192
Barry, Jonathan, 107, 125, 128-9
Bath, 61
Beaver, Dan, 80, 95-96,
beggars, *see* vagrancy
"belonging", 4, 6, 9-10, 15-16, 82,
    90, 94, 99, 103, 107-8, 111-12,
    114, 126-29, 176, 183, 191, 199
Benjamin, Walter, 24, 45
Black Knight, *see* Black Lad
Black Lad, Riding of the, 13, 181-
    5, 192
Blomefield, Francis, 97-9, 163,
    174, 186, 190
Bodin, Jean, 29-30, 47
Boer War, 206
Bourdieu, Pierre, 3-4, 16
bourgeois: 24, 34, 60, 74, 150, 182;
    "bourgeois collectivism", 107,
    123, 125, 128-9
Bower, Fredson, 23, 45

Braddick, Michael, 1, 15, 73, 75,
    94, 130
Braudel, Fernand, 157, 160
Brecht, Bertolt, 20, 42, 44
British Empire, 206
Brown, James, 8, 58, 62, 70, 72-3,
    75
Bulwer, William, 197, 200, 206
Burston, 203-4, 214
Burt, Thomas, 204-5, 214
Bury St Edmund, 78
Bushaway, Bob, 151-2, 160, 198,
    213
Butterworth, Edwin, 182-3, 192

Cade, Jack, 50, 163
calendar customs, 107-8
Cambridge, 34, 115
Cambridgeshire, 176, 190
Camden, William, 170, 189
"camping", 179; "camping tyme",
    178-9
    see also, football
Capp, Bernard, 127, 143-4, 159
Carter, William, 134
Catholic, 90, 95, 208
Chapman, John, Pedlar of
    Swaffham, 12-13, 161-4
charity, 76, 104-5, 107-9, 111-114,
    117, 126, 199-200, 202
charivari, 139, 140-5, 158-9, 208
    see also rough music or
    "skymington"
Charles I, 77, 90, 152, 158
Charles II, 60, 74, 78, 110-11, 116-
    7, 119, 123, 130, 152, 155
Chartism, 14, 181, 192, 194
    see also, strike, Labour
    Movement

218 Index

Cheke, Sir John, 34-5, 49
Chopwell, 207-8, 211, 214
Christmas, 33, 40-1, 108, 199, 209
Church Court, *see* Diocesan Court
church building, patronage, 202-4
churchwarden, 68, 91, 108, 152, 203, 209
citizenship, *see,* "freedom"
Clare, John, 171-2, 175, 190
Clark, Peter, 8, 51, 53-7, 59, 65, 68-9, 72, 74-6, 125, 128, 130
cleric: clerical absenteeism, 79, 88-90, 95, 203-4; clerical privilege, 83-4, 200-1, 202-4
   see also, pluralism, rectory
"closed" parish, 14, 197-8, 212
   see also, "open parish"
coal: coalfields, coal-pits, 139, 150-1, 194, 202-3, 205, 207-8, 211-14
   see also, mines
coffee house, 59-60, 74
Coke, Sir Edward, 30, 47
Collinson, Patrick, 1, 15
common land, 107, 119, 128, 180, 194, 198
Common Pleas, Court of, 26
common rights, 11, 13-14, 114, 128-9, 143, 152, 171, 177, 180
commonwealth, commonweal, 7, 15, 17, 29-32, 35, 42, 47-8, 103, 106, 120, 122-5, 128-9, 137
Communist, 208-9
Connerton, Paul, 134, 158
constable, 68-9, 74, 77, 79, 86, 118, 121, 137
Corpusty, 14, 195-7, 200, 211-212
County Durham, 14, 194, 200, 202-3, 207-8, 211-14
Court of Wards, 88
Crab, Roger, 57
Cromwell, Oliver, 111
custom: customary rights or practice, "politics of", 2, 6, 10, 11-13, 15, 25, 67-8, 71, 76, 106-8, 110-12, 114, 119, 125-6, 128-9, 131, 133-60, 165, 170, 175-8, 180-1, 184, 187-8, 190-2, 194, 198-9, 210-11, 21

Darnton, Robert, 162, 186
De Assheton, Sir Ralph, 181-3
De Certeau, Michel, 3, 16, 124
"deserving" poor, 10, 112
"dialectical materialism", *theory of,* 166
Diocesan Court, 8, 78-83, 85, 87, 89, 93, 94-7, 204
domestic: domestic ideals, 20, 29-32, 143; domestic economy, 30, 144
Dorchester, 144-145
drunkenness, 53, 55, 60, 62-3, 65-69, 79, 86-89, 182, 190
Dugdale, Sir William, 161-2, 171, 189, 191
Durkheim, Emile, 164, 166, 186

Edward I, 25
Edwards, George, 202, 204, 213, 214
elections, 59, 62, 77, 105, 125, 201, 206, 209
Elizabeth I, 135, 158
Elyot, Sir Thomas, 35, 42, 49-50
enclosure, 11, 24, 76, 111, 114, 120, 128-9, 131, 139, 140-1, 150, 152, 154-6, 198, 201
English Civil War, 59, 78, 85-6, 98, 130, 184
Essex, 6, 35, 40, 62, 91, 144
equity courts, 24, 134, 136, 145, 148-50
estate management, Elizabethan, 134-6
"exclusion" *see* "marginalisation"

family authority, 29-31, 146
   see also, householder
family networks, 82, 84-5, 91-2, 200-3

fens, 11, 119, 131, 159, 170-85, 189-92
Fisher, Chris, 155, 160
Flather, Amanda, 6, 17
Fletcher, Anthony, 24, 46, 55-6, 69, 72-3, 76
folklore, 6, 12-14, 161-192
football, 74, 109, 174, 179
  see also, camping
"foreigners", 109, 115, 131, 151-3, 180
  see also "strangers"
Forest of Dean, 11, 15, 120, 131, 133-160
Fox, Adam, 15, 56, 73, 75, 129, 148, 159, 189
"freedom", freemen, 17, 77, 103, 106, 114-6, 123, 124-6, 128

gambling, 40, 87
Geertz, Clifford, 166, 187
gender, 4-6, 63, 97, 99, 123, 143-5
  see also, women
gentry, 13, 25, 94, 114, 131, 138, 140, 163-4, 170, 179, 183, 204
Giddens, Anthony, 149, 159
Gloucester Journal, 155
gossip, 57, 77, 143, 175
Gough, Richard, 115, 129
Gowing, Laura, 5, 17, 94, 99, 124, 143, 159
Gramsci, Antonio, 11, 13, 16, 54, 133, 161, 166-9, 178, 187-9
Graves, Pamela, 6, 16-17, 100
Griffith, F. H., 182-3, 192
Griffiths, Paul, 5, 15, 17, 75, 129, 146, 158-9
Grose, Francis, 184, 192
guilds, 48, 115, 121, 125, 129, 130, 146
guild day, 107, 111
  see also, "popular culture"
Gurr, 41, 45, 50
Gyes, John, 145-6

"habit memory", *theory of,* 134
Halbwachs, Maurice, 13, 164, 166, 174, 186-7
Hall, David, 175, 191
Hamlet, 19, 27, 36
Hastings, Lord, 206-7, 212
hegemony, *theory of,* 11, 13, 16, 52, 54, 56, 58, 64, 71, 133, 140, 148-50, 152, 156-7, 166-9, 188-9
Henry VII, 26, 163
Herbert, William, Earl of Pembroke, 136, 138, 149
Heydon, 197-8, 200, 203, 206, 213
Heydon, John, 163-4
Hickafhrifte: Hikifricke, Hickifric, Tom, legends of, 170-80, 189-90
"hidden transcript", 8, 15, 48, 52, 56-8, 62, 64, 69, 70, 73-4, 96
Hillen, H. J., 172-4
Hindle, Steve, 1, 15-17, 24, 46, 48, 72-3, 75-6, 94, 97, 99, 115, 123, 126-9, 131, 146-7, 159, 187, 191
Hobsbawm, Eric, 165, 186-7
Holinshed, Raphael: Holinshed's Chronicles, 33
Home Office, 155-7, 160
Hone, William, 182
household: *theory of,* 25, 29-30, 32, 46-7; "household economy", 29-30; householder: legal definitions, 110, 114, 128, 152, 162, 177
  see also, family authority
Howard, Henry, Earl of Northampton, 138
Howard, Jean, 33, 48
Hoyle, Richard, 134-5
Hurt of Sedition, The, 34, 49
Hutson, Lorna, 25, 36, 38, 39, 43, 49
Hutton, Ronald, 107, 125-7

illegitimacy, 127
illicit sex, 36, 65, 87-88, 99, 111
impropriation, 88
"inclusion" *see* "belonging"
incontinency, *see*, illicit sex
industrialisation, 14, 76, 138, 145, 150, 152, 154, 181, 184, 194, 207-8, 211
Ingram, Martin, 94, 140, 158, 159
infant mortality, 194, 196-7
inhabitants, 8, 67-8, 81-5, 89, 93-4, 97, 103-10, 114, 131, 134, 139-40, 147, 152, 155-6, 162, 170, 177-82
inheritance, 30
Ipswich, 78

James I, 30, 65, 75, 88, 134, 136, 152
James II, 63
Jarvis, Josiah, 14, 193, 195-7, 200, 211
Jews, 105, 124
Justice of the Peace, 24, 51, 55, 60-2, 65, 138

Kett's Rebellion, 178-9
Kett, Robert, 24, 34-5, 50
King James Bible, 105
King's Bench, 25-6
King's Lynn, 90, 171, 175
Knight Marshal, 25-6, 34, 39, 41, 46
Knight of the Shire, 62
Kümin, Beat, 59-60, 71-6
Kyd, Thomas, 7, 19, 21, 30, 39, 41, 43, 45, 47

Labour Movement, 14, 194, 201, 204-6, 214
   see also, strike, Chartism
Labour Party, 201, 206
Lancashire, 180-4, 192, 194
land disputes, 25, 105, 134-158, 165, 173-4, 179-80, 194, 199
Laud, William, 95

Lefèbvre, Henri, 3, 16, 21, 38, 45, 47, 49, 100
Le Gros, Thomas, 85-6, 98
Liberal Party, 196, 206, 212
literacy, 98, 175, 184-5
   see also print
Littledean, 150-1
Little Walsingham, 203, 209
livery companies, 34
"localism", 10, 103-4, 111, 117, 169, 185, 191
London, 5, 34-6, 40-1, 49, 98, 105-9, 112, 114-5, 118, 121, 124, 128-30, 144, 146, 161, 164
Londonderry, Lord and Lady, 202-3, 213
Lukács, György, 20, 44, 49

MacCulloch, Diarmaid, 24, 46
MacDonald, Angus, 208
Machen, Edward, 154-7
Mailescott Woods, 139
Maine, Henry, 150
Malcolmson, Robert, 107, 125, 127
Maldon, 144-5, 159
Maltby, Judith, 81, 95, 100
Manning, Brian, 34, 48, 96
"marginalisation", 3, 7, 9, 14, 46, 53, 108-9, 111-12, 115-16, 129
Marlowe, Christopher, 21
Marsh, Christopher, 6, 17, 100
Marshalsea Court, 25-6, 46-7
Marxism, Marxist, 20, 167-8, 189
Mary I, 178
Mary II, 62
May Day Riots, 34
   see also, riots
Melton Constable, 206-7
memory: collective and social, 11-12-14, 67, 133-4, 140-5, 150, 153, 157-9, 164-166, 170, 172, 177-9, 184, 186-7, 198; and place, 2, 13, 126, 140-5, 169, 198
"memory palace", 12, 140-1
Mendips, 65-6

Methodist, Methodism, 2, 14-15, 194-5, 204-6, 208-9, 212
"middling sorts", 1, 5, 7-8, 12-13, 39, 53-55, 77-8, 81, 83, 93-4, 96-7, 125, 146
Midland Rising, 33, 48
mines: mining, miners, 11, 76, 114, 121, 129, 133, 137, 139-40, 142, 144-5 149-58, 160, 196, 200, 202, 204, 207-8, 210-11, 214; Mine Law Court, 11, 133-60
see also coal
Mint, The, Minters, 118-19, 121, 123, 131
Mompesson, Sir Giles, 139
Monmouth, Duke of, 60
Monmouthshire Merlin, 154-5, 160
Monteyne, Joseph, 6, 17

Naunton, Sir Robert, 88-9, 93, 99
neighbour: neighbourhood, neighbourliness, 93, 96, 103, 104-6, 108, 110-114, 118, 121, 123-4, 127, 138, 144, 157, 159, 169, 170, 176, 178, 198, 202, 206, 212
Newcastle Weekly Chronicle, 196, 212-3
New Poor Law, 14, 150, 159, 194, 198, 204, 208, 212
Nidderdale, 58
non-conformism, 14-15, 79, 90, 95-6, 100, 195, 200, 204
Norfolk, 12, 14, 58, 70, 77-101, 122, 162-4, 170-180, 186, 190-1, 193-202, 205-214
Norfolk Agricultural Labourers' Union, 205-6
Norfolk News, 195-6, 199-200, 204, 212-4
Northamptonshire, 114, 158
Northbrooke, John, 34, 49
Norwich, 34, 78, 85-7, 90, 94-100, 107, 111, 115-6, 128, 179, 204, 214

"open" parish, 14, 197-8, 212
see also, "closed parish"
oral culture, 11, 174, 184-5

Palace Court, 26
pamphlets, pamphleteering, 34, 109-10, 171-2, 190
Paston, Sir William, 85-86, 98
Paul, Sir George Onesiphorus, 150
petition, petitioning, 8, 33, 43, 55, 60, 65-8, 77, 80, 90, 163
pews, 6, 91-2, 201-3
place: sense of, 4, 10, 16-17, 37, 43, 59-61, 65, 106, 109-10, 115, 124, 130, 132, 164-5, 169, 175, 178-9, 182-4, 187, 189, 191, 214; social, 13, 27, 41, 82-4, 90-3, 100, 202
see also status, rank
plague, 35, 41
"plebeian": protest, culture, agency, identity, 8, 12-13, 24, 33, 37, 52, 54-73, 79, 94, 96-7, 138, 163-4, 187
Plug Riots, 183
see also, riots
pluralism, 79, 88-9, 95
see also, cleric
poaching, 193-4, 199-200, 206-7, 213-4
"politics of resistance", 14, 195, 206-8, 212
"politics of the parish", 64, 68-9, 71, 76, 159
poor relief: parochial, 10, 16-17, 99, 104, 113-4, 116, 123, 128, 146, 159, 200
"popular culture", 2, 53-7, 62, 71, 104, 106, 168, 172, 185, 207, 211
see also, guild day
popular politics, 1, 15, 46, 51-76, 94, 169
Porter, Enid, 173, 175, 180, 190
Postles, Dave, 6, 17

print, 6, 105-6, 143, 171-2, 174, 184, 189
  see also, literacy
Privy Council, 35, 40, 49
"public sphere", 52, 59-60, 54, 70, 74
Puritan, Puritanism, 53, 55-6, 72, 76, 89-91, 100, 130
Puttenham, George, 42, 50

Randall, Arthur, 174-5, 180, 190-1
Ranger, Terence, 165, 187
rank, 2, 13, 78, 82-3, 93, 97, 111, 114
  see also, social hierarchy, status, place
rebellions, 1, 7, 13, 24, 33-5, 37, 39, 46, 48-9, 58, 73-4, 94, 163, 178-9, 191, 214
rectory, 203-4
  see also, cleric
Reformation, The, 54, 80, 109
"reformation of manners", 56, 59, 96
Restoration, The, 59-60, 78, 108, 110, 116-7, 119, 127, 130
revelry: civic, rural, 10, 104, 107-111, 122-3, 132, 140
riots, 14, 24, 34, 74, 104, 119-21, 130-1, 139-40, 143-45, 151, 153, 159-60, 183, 191, 194
  see also, May Day Riots, Midland Rising, Plug Riots, Swing Riots and Warren James Riots
rogation: Rogationtide, 10, 100, 108, 123, 125-6.
Rollison, David, 6, 12, 17, 125-6, 140, 158, 161, 175, 191
"rough music", *see* charivari
Royalist, 85-6, 98

Sackville, Thomas, Baron Buckhurst, 134
Said, Edward, 32, 48

St Briavels, 133, 137, 139, 151-2
Sayer, Derek, 24, 46
Scott, James C., 1, 8, 15-16, 35, 48, 56-8, 64, 69, 73-75, 96-7, 149, 159, 188, 214
Scott, Joan, 64
sedition, seditious speech, 8, 20, 33-6, 44, 48, 52, 59-65, 73, 75, 97
Seneca, 21-2, 33
Shakespeare, William, 33, 45-50, 167
Shoemaker, Robert, 5-6, 17
Shropshire, 115, 130
"skymington", "skimmington", *see* charivari
Smeeth, The, legends of, 170-80
Smith, Thomas, husbandman, 165
Smith, Sir Thomas, 29, 47
social conflict, 9, 97, 124-5, 181, 184, 189
social description, 53, 81, 96, 114, 138
social hierarchy, 6, 13, 107, 140
  see also, rank, status
Somerset, 52, 65-70, 76, 112, 130
Southampton, 58, 63, 70, 72, 73, 144-5
Spanish Tragedy, The, 7-8, 19-50
"spatial turn", 3, 6, 8, 14, 51
  see also, place
Sports, Book of, 54
Spufford, Margaret, 101, 162, 186
Star Chamber, Court of, 24, 137, 140
status, 1, 3, 9, 62, 69, 78, 81, 83-4, 91-4, 97, 99, 100, 103, 107, 155, 202
  see also, rank, social hierarchy
Staunton, 140-1
Steinberg, Marc, 182, 192
Stow, John, 17, 33, 35, 48-9
"strangers", 10, 99, 103, 105-6, 108, 121, 129, 182
  see also "foreigners"

strike, strike breaking, 181, 204, 207-9, 214
  see also, Chartism, Labour Movement
Strohm, Paul, 33, 48
"subaltern politics", "subalternity", 13, 167-9, 178, 185, 188-9
Suffolk, 78, 83, 90, 129
surveillance culture, 8, 52, 56-71, 73-75
Swaffham, 12, 92, 161-4, 169, 185-6
Swallowfield, 97, 147, 159
Swing Riots, 14, 194
  see also, riots

Tadmor, Naomi, 105, 124, 127
Tarleton, Richard, 40-1, 50
Tasso, Torquato, 30, 47
Terling, 70, 72, 91, 100
Thetford, 78, 198
Thirsk, Joan, 136, 158
Thompson, Edward, 37, 54, 67, 72, 75-6, 128-9, 167, 188, 213
Tilney, 170-180
  see also Smeeth, The
tithes, tithe disputes, 80-1, 83, 86, 95, 97, 142
Tittler, Robert, 5, 6, 16-17, 100
Tönnies, Ferdinand, 11, 122, 124, 132
trade union, trade unionism, 14, 181, 194, 200-8, 212, 214
Tuddenham, Sir Thomas, 163-4

"undeserving" poor, 10, 112

vagabond, see, vagrancy
vagrancy, 10, 34, 40-1, 50, 96, 104, 109-10, 115, 126, 129
vestry, vestrymen, 77, 82, 97, 129, 146-7, 209
Villiers, Lady Barbara, 139,
vote, voting, 77, 118, 206, 208

Walpole St Peter, 174

Walsingham, Lord, 206
Walter, John, 1, 15, 56, 64, 73, 75-6, 131, 144, 159
Warminster, 60, 74
Warren James Riots, 151, 153-8, 160
  see also, riots
"weapons of the weak", 15, 64, 71, 75, 96, 188
Weever, John, 170, 174, 178-9, 189
Weil, Rachel, 63, 74-5
Welldon, Dean, 210-11
Whigs, 111
William III, 62, 111
Williams, Raymond, 165, 168-9, 172, 185, 187-90
Wilson, Luke, 36, 49
Wiltshire, 51, 61, 63, 70, 74, 130, 147
Winter, Sir Edward, 12, 137-8, 140, 142, 146
Wisbech, 173, 175
Withington, Phil, 15, 17, 107, 124-5, 128-9, 132
women, 5-6, 79, 87-8, 99, 112, 148, 155, 182-3, 185; women's agency, 11, 62, 93, 120-3, 142-5, 207-8, 214
  see also, gender
Wood, Nicholas, 203
Woodforde, Parson James, 199-200, 213
work-house, 109
working class, 14, 169, 171, 180-1, 183-4, 192, 195, 202-3, 212, 214
Wrightson, Keith, 1, 9, 15-16, 51, 54-8, 64, 67, 69, 72-3, 75-6, 100, 111-12, 123-4, 127-8, 130, 132, 143-4, 159

xenophobia, 109, 122, 191
Xenophon, 29, 47

Yarmouth, 78, 87
Yeovil, 68

York, 115-6, 128
Yorkshire, 58, 119, 194, 198
youth, 35, 97, 165

Žižek, Slavoj, 21, 23, 45